What Critics and Professionals Say About the "Impact Guides"

"*THE DEFINITIVE GUIDE to shopping in Asia.*"—**Arthur Frommer**, The Arthur Frommer Almanac of Travel

"*THE BEST travel book I've ever read.*"—Kathy Osiro, **TravelAge West**

"*AN EXCELLENT, EXHAUSTIVE, AND FASCINATING look at shopping in the East . . . it's difficult to imagine a shopping tour without this pocket-size book in hand.*"—**Travel & Leisure**

"*BOOKS IN THE SERIES help travelers recognize quality and gain insight to local customs.*"—**Travel-Holiday**

"*THE BEST GUIDE I've seen on shopping in Asia. If you enjoy the sport, you'll find it hard to put down . . . They tell you not only the where and what of shopping but the important how, and all in enormous but easy-to-read detail.*"—**Seattle Post-Intelligencer**

"*ONE OF THE BEST GUIDEBOOKS of the season—not just shopping strategies, but a Baedeker to getting around . . . definitely a quality work. Highly recommended.*"—**Arkansas Democrat**

"*WILL WANT TO LOOK INTO . . . has shopping strategies and travel tips about making the most of a visit to those areas. The book covers Asia's shopping centers, department stores, emporiums, factory outlets, markets and hotel shopping arcades where visitors can find jewelry, leather goods, woodcarvings, textiles, antiques, cameras, and primitive artifacts.*"
—**Chicago Tribune**

"*FULL OF SUGGESTIONS. The art of bartering, including everyday shopping basics are clearly defined, along with places to hang your hat or lift a fork.*"—**The Washington Post**

"*A WONDERFUL GUIDE . . . filled with essential tips as well as a lot of background information . . . a welcome addition on your trip.*"—
Travel Book Tips

"*WELL ORGANIZED AND COMPREHENSIVE BOOK. A useful companion for anyone planning a shopping spree in Asia.*"—
International Living

"*OFFERS SOME EXTREMELY VALUABLE INFORMATION and advice about what is all too often a spur-of-the-moment aspect of your overseas travel.*"—**Trip & Tour**

"*A MORE UNUSUAL, PRACTICAL GUIDE than most and is no mere listing of convenience stores abroad . . . contains unusual tips on bargaining in Asia . . . country-specific tips are some of the most valuable chapters of the guidebook, setting it apart from others which may generalized upon Asia as a whole, or focus upon the well-known Hong Kong shopping pleasures.*"—**The Midwest Book Review**

*"**I LOVED THE BOOK!** Why didn't I have this book two months ago! . . . a valuable guide . . . very helpful for the first time traveler in Asia . . . worth packing in the suitcase for a return visit."*—Editor, **Unique & Exotic Travel Reporter**

*"**VERY USEFUL, PERFECTLY ORGANIZED.** Finally a guide that combines Asian shopping opportunities with the tips and know-how to really get the best buys."*—**National Motorist**

*"**INFORMATION-PACKED PAGES** point out where the best shops are located, how to save time when shopping, and where and when to deal . . . You'll be a smarter travel shopper if you follow the advice of this new book."*—**AAA World**

*"**DETAILED, AND RELEVANT, EVEN ABSORBING** in places . . . The authors know their subject thoroughly, and the reader can benefit greatly from their advice and tips. They go a long way to removing any mystery or uneasiness about shopping in Asia by the neophyte."*—**The Small Press Book Review**

What Seasoned Travelers Say

*"**IMMENSELY USEFUL** . . . thanks for sharing the fruits of your incredibly thorough research. You saved me hours of time and put me in touch with the best."*—C.N., DeKalb, Illinois

*"**FABULOUS!** I've just returned from my third shopping trip to Southeast Asia in three years. This book, which is now wrinkled, torn, and looking much abused, has been my bible for the past three years. All your suggestions (pre-trip) and information was so great . . . When I get ready to go again, my 'bible,' even though tattered and torn, will accompany me again! Thanks again for all your wonderful knowledge, and for sharing it!"*—D.P., Havertown, Pennsylvania

*"**I LOVE IT** . . . I've read a lot of travel books, and of all the books of this nature, this is the best I've ever read. Especially for first timers, the how-to information is invaluable."*—A.K., Portland, Oregon.

*"**THE BEST TRAVEL BOOK I'VE EVER READ.** Believe me, I know my travel books!"*—S.T., Washington, DC

*"**MANY MANY THANKS** for your wonderful, useful travel guide! You have done a tremendous job. It is so complete and precise and full of neat info."*—K.H., Seattle, Washington

*"**FABULOUS BOOK!** I just came back from Hong Kong, Thailand, and Singapore and found your book invaluable. Every place you recommended I found wonderful quality shopping. Send me another copy for my friend in Singapore who was fascinated with it."*—M.G., Escondido, California

The Treasures and Pleasures of Italy

Books & CD-ROMs by Drs. Ron and Caryl Krannich

101 Dynamite Answers to Interview Questions
201 Dynamite Job Search Letters
The Almanac of International Jobs and Careers
Best Jobs for the 1990s and Into the 21st Century
Change Your Job, Change Your Life
The Complete Guide to International Jobs and Careers
The Complete Guide to Public Employment
The Directory of Federal Jobs and Employers
Discover the Best Jobs for You!
Dynamite Cover Letters
Dynamite Networking for Dynamite Jobs
Dynamite Resumes
Dynamite Salary Negotiations
Dynamite Tele-Search
The Educator's Guide to Alternative Jobs and Careers
Find a Federal Job Fast!
From Air Force Blue to Corporate Gray
From Army Green to Corporate Gray
From Navy Blue to Corporate Gray
High Impact Resumes and Letters
Interview for Success
Job-Power Source CD-ROM
Jobs and Careers With Nonprofit Organizations
Jobs for People Who Love Travel
Mayors and Managers
Moving Out of Education
Moving Out of Government
The Politics of Family Planning Policy
Re-Careering in Turbulent Times
Resumes and Cover Letters for Transitioning Military Personnel
Shopping and Traveling in Exotic Asia
Shopping in Exotic Places
Shopping the Exotic South Pacific
Treasures and Pleasures of Australia
Treasures and Pleasures of China
Treasures and Pleasures of Hong Kong
Treasures and Pleasures of India
Treasures and Pleasures of Indonesia
Treasures and Pleasures of Italy
Treasures and Pleasures of Morocco
Treasures and Pleasures of Paris and the French Riviera
Treasures and Pleasures of Singapore and Malaysia
Treasures and Pleasures of Thailand
Treasures and Pleasures of the Philippines
Ultimate Job Source CD-ROM

IMPACT GUIDES

THE TREASURES AND PLEASURES OF

Italy

BEST OF THE BEST

RON AND CARYL KRANNICH, PH.DS

IMPACT PUBLICATIONS
MANASSAS PARK, VA

The Treasures and Pleasures of Italy: Best of the Best

Library of Congress Cataloging-in-Publication Data

Krannich, Ronald L.
The treasures and pleasures of Italy: best of the best / Ron and Caryl Krannich.
p. cm. — (Impact guides)
Includes bibliographical references and index.
ISBN 1-57023-058-7 (alk. paper)
1. Shopping—Italy—Guidebooks. 2. Italy—Guidebooks. I. Krannich, Caryl Rae. II. Title. III. Series.
TX337.I8K73 1997
380.1'45'0002545—dc20 96-44838
CIP

For information on distribution or quantity discounts, call (703/361-7300), fax (703/335-9486), e-mail (impactp@impactpublications.com), or write: Sales Department, IMPACT PUBLICATIONS, 9104-N Manassas Drive, Manassas Park, VA 20111-2366. Distributed to the trade by National Book Network, 4720 Boston Way, Suite A, Lanham, MD 20706, Tel. 301/459-8696.

Contents

Liabilities and Warranties

While the authors have attempted to provide accurate and up-to-date information in this book, please be advised that names, addresses, and phone numbers do change and shops, restaurants, and hotels do move, go out of business, or change ownership and management. Such changes are a constant fact of life. We regret any inconvenience such changes may cause to your travel plans.

Inclusion of shops, restaurants, hotels, and other hospitality providers in this book in no way implies guarantees nor endorsements by either the authors or publisher. The information and recommendations appearing in this book are provided solely for your reference. The honesty and reliability of shops is best ensured by **you**—always ask the right questions and request proper receipts and documents.

The Treasures and Pleasures of Italy provides numerous tips on how you can best experience a trouble-free adventure. As in any unfamiliar place or situation, or regardless of how trusting strangers may appear, the watch-words are always the same—watch your wallet! If it's too good to be true, it probably is.

The Treasures and Pleasures of Italy

1

Welcome to Fabulous Italy

Welcome to the wonderful treasures and pleasures of Italy. You'll in for a real treat, probably one of the best trips you will ever make. While nearly 30 million visitors (5.15 percent of all tourists in the world) descend on this country each year, capturing some cities in toto, most eventually find their way to Italy's four major mecca's for shopping, sightseeing, and dining—Florence, Milan, Rome, and Venice. And they come to love these cities. Although they may not represent the "real" Italy, like much of the rest of Italy, they constitute unique places that make up the checkerboard landscape of this intriguing and diverse country. Not surprising, they may quickly become your favorite Italy.

Each of our four cities offers its own distinctive "Italian" character and lifestyle. They are, in a sense, four Italys standing in the midst of several hundred other Italys.

A Top Quality Adventure

Italy seems to be everyone's favorite country, and for good reason. It has all the major elements of an exciting and satisfying adventure—beautiful cities and countrysides, numerous historical sites, wonderful food, interesting people, fabulous shopping, and convenient tourist infrastructure. It's simply a delightful place to visit. There's a certain passion or drama to life in Italy, as clearly expressed in its art, architecture, and food, and in the personalities of its people, places, and products. Add to these positives a falling lira, and you also get a relatively inexpensive European destination to visit.

While things may not always work in Italy like back home, and tourist crowds in Florence and Venice may at times feel oppressive, overall Italy remains one of the world's most fabulous travel destinations. If you are like many other visitors to this unique country, you'll fall in love with the place and want to return soon to explore its many additional treasures and pleasures found within close proximity to these delightful cities.

- **Florence, Milan, Rome, and Venice are four Italys standing in the midst of several hundred other Italys.**
- **Italy yields some of the world's finest quality shopping, restaurants, hotels, and sightseeing.**
- **Italian quality is so high that you may be forever disappointed with your shopping choices back home!**

Above all, our four Italian cities are top quality destinations. Indeed, Italians are world renowned for offering outstanding quality products. Their long, passionate, and often contentious love affair with art, design, architecture, and artisan traditions is clearly reflected in contemporary Italian products, especially the fine textiles that have made Italian clothes unequalled for quality. Indeed, "Made in Italy" usually means made to exacting standards. In Italy "quality" has real substantive meaning as a code word summarizing exquisite design, attention to detail, fine products, expert skills, and expensive prices. As you will quickly discover, in Italy you immediately know quality when you see, feel, taste, and buy it.

Not surprising, Italy yields some of the world's finest quality shopping, restaurants, hotels, and sightseeing. Here you'll discover quality Italian design incorporated in top name-brand clothing and accessory shops such as Gucci, Versace, Armani, Missoni, Trussardi, Moschino, and Valentino. You may become captivated by the jewelry designs of one of the world's greatest family of jewelers—the Buccellatis. You'll marvel at the outstanding products offered along the major shopping streets of Milan, Florence, Rome, and Venice. Just make a quick shopping foray into the Montenapoleone/Spiga area of Milan, along Via dei Tornabuoni in Florence, or along the streets adjacent to the Spanish Steps in Rome and you'll quickly discover what Italian quality is all about. The quality is so high that you may become disappointed with your shopping choices back home! And it's quality you'll find in abundance as you explore Italy's many restaurants, hotels, and sights.

SHOPPING TREASURES

While Italy offers many treasures and pleasures to discerning travelers, its shopping treasures especially intrigue us. In fact, throughout this book, we give disproportionate attention to Italy's many treasures as found in the numerous shops of Milan, Florence, Rome, and Venice. We love our Italian sights, restaurants, and hotels, but we're especially partial to Italy's many quality shops and markets. As you will quickly discover throughout Italy, each city has its own particular mix of treasures that distinguishes it from other cities.

MILAN

Milan is Italy's leading commercial city and Europe's unquestioned shopping capital for fashion and accessories. Even Paris defers to Milan when it comes to fashion and design. Here you will find some of the world's top design talent working in major fashion houses that set the tone for the international fashion world. Top designers, such as Armani, Prada, Gucci, Missoni, Krizia, Prada, Trussardi, and Versace, showcase their latest creations in Milan's many boutiques, showrooms, and factories. Just head for Via Montenapoleone and Via Spiga and you'll quickly discover a treasure-trove of top quality Milanese products. In addition to fashion and accessories, you'll find terrific jewelry, home furnishings, and art to challenge your budget in this incredible Italian and European shopping capital.

- ❑ **Milan is Italy's leading commercial city and Europe's unquestioned shopping capital for fashion and accessories.**
- ❑ **Florence is considered by many seasoned travelers to be the most beautiful city in the world.**
- ❑ **Rome is truly one of the world's magnificent sensory experiences, a big city with a larger than life history.**
- ❑ **Venice is one of those unique tourist traps you'll probably love being trapped in!**

FLORENCE

Florence, one of the world's most important art and culture centers, also used to be Italy's fashion capital until Milan displaced it nearly two decades ago. However, no other major city in Italy, with the exception of perhaps Venice, can match the charm and beauty, as well as the tourist crowds, of Florence. Many seasoned travelers consider this to be the most beautiful city in the world with its fabulous wealth of Renaissance art and architecture delightfully situated along the banks of the lovely Arno river. It's also one of the most visited cities in the world, hosting over 20 million visitors each year. At certain times of the year Florence is literally wall-to-wall tourists in search of this city's many treasures and pleasures. Especially famous for its art and architecture, Florence also is well noted for its shopping treasures. The city offers excellent quality fashion, accessories, art, ceramics, marbled paper, carvings, and jewelry. Stroll down its exclusive Via Tornabuoni lined with the famous boutiques of Ferragamo, Gucci, House of Florence, and Pucci, or visit the popular San Lorenzo street market, and you'll discover that Florence offers a wide range of varying quality products for its diverse set of visitors—from five-star travelers to the ubiquitous budget back-packers.

ROME

You can try to by-pass it, but all roads indeed lead to Rome. Known as the Eternal City, this is a great city exuding a grand history, haunting monuments, and a treasure-trove of art. Truly one of the world's magnificent sensory experiences, from the fabled Colosseum to the Vatican's inspiring Sistine Chapel, Rome dazzles visitors with its numerous treasures and pleasures spanning more than 2,500 years. It's a big city with a larger than life history. It's also a great city for shopping and dining. Head for the Spanish Steps and you'll find yourself in the midst of some of Italy's finest shops offering outstanding fashion, accessories, jewelry, ceramics, and art. There's more to see and do in Rome than you will probably have time, so you might as well plan to come back even before you visit Rome!

VENICE

Venice is one of those unique tourist traps you'll probably love being trapped in. All indicators, especially its heavy concentration of tourists (79,000 local residents hosting over 20 million visitors each year, or 90 percent of the total population each day), tell you this is a place you probably should avoid. But you become seduced by its setting and ambience. There is something very magical about Venice, despite its Disneyland-on-the-water setting, that continues to enthrall even the most jaded travelers. Perhaps its the fabled canals, charming gondoliers, beautiful Piazza San Marco, remarkable palaces and churches, or romantic setting. Or maybe it's the fun of getting lost in its labyrinth of narrow walkways and canals and discovering a way out. Crammed with delightful small shops, restaurants, and hotels, Venice seems to be everyone's favorite city, despite its high prices and touristy nature. If you're like many other travelers to this city, you'll probably leave with some type of souvenir of your Venetian experience, most likely the famous Murano glass, Venetian lace, Carnival masks, or marbleized paper products. Best of all, you'll leave with some wonderful memories of a truly unique city unlike any other in the world.

Unique Pleasures

What makes Italy such a delightful travel destination is the sheer variety of travel treasures and pleasures that appeal to so many different types of travelers. If you're into scenic beauty, Italy seems to have it all, from beautiful snow-capped mountains and lakeside resorts to charming seaside resorts and quaint villages. If you love grand hotels, Italy offers some of the world's very best. If you judge a country by its cuisine, you'll find no finer country in the world than Italy; you're likely to leave Italy five to ten pounds heavier! And if you love to shop, Italy offers some of the world's best quality shopping, from fashion and accessories to arts and crafts. For both seasoned and neophyte travelers, it simply doesn't get better than Italy.

Anticipated Costs

Italy offers one of the best quality travel experiences you will find anywhere in the world. It's not particularly cheap, but it need not be excessively expensive—if you know what you're doing. While the lira remains weak against the U.S. dollar, and thus Italy may seem a bargain compared to prices three years ago, our four cities in Italy still remain expensive destinations. You can easily spend US$500 a night on a hotel and US$200 per person at a restaurant if you insist on staying and dining in top places. At the same time, you can spend much less by joining a tour to Italy. Indeed, many first-time visitors to Italy prefer all-inclusive packaged tours that can cost as little as US$120 per day, including international transportation to and from Italy. Many of these tours, such as the 13-day "The Italian Mosaic" sponsored by Globus, offer excellent value for one of the most popular tours of Italy. Contact your travel agent for information on this and other reputable packaged tours to Italy.

Trips For Treasures

So where are we going and what will we be doing? We're going to explore the many treasures and pleasures of Milan, Florence,

Rome, and Venice. While our primarily focus is on acquiring the treasures (shopping), we're into much more than just procurement and acquisitions. There are a lot of great things to see and do in Italy. We're going into the heart of these cities, highlight their many wonderful sights (piazzas, churches, museums, monuments), restaurants, and hotels. In Rome, for example, we'll shop the Spanish Steps as well as visit the Colosseum, St. Peter's, and the Vatican and discover some terrific restaurants. In Florence we'll shop the exclusive shops along Via Tornabuoni and go bargain shopping in the markets as well as tour its famous piazzas, museums, and churches and visit its landmark Duomo. In Milan we'll visit the shops that have made Milan the world's leading fashion center, discover some wonderful art, enjoy its many fine restaurants, and marvel at the city's incredible Duomo and opera house. In Venice we'll make the obligatory visit to the glass factories, window-shop its many streets, and enjoy the many pleasures, from canals to churches, that make this city such a memorable experience. What we outline here are numerous treasures and pleasures you can experience within an intense two to three week period.

- ❑ **If you judge a country by its cuisine, you'll find no finer country in the world than Italy.**
- ❑ **Italy is not particularly cheap but it need not be excessively expensive.**
- ❑ **Many first-time visitors to Italy prefer all-inclusive packed tours that can cost as little as US$120 per day, including international airfare.**
- ❑ **You may find Italy's famous markets for cheap goods disappointing and a waste of precious travel time.**

THE TREASURES AND PLEASURES

The Treasures and Pleasures of Italy is a different kind of travel book for a very special type of traveler. Like other books in this series, this is not another smorgesboard of names, addresses, popular sites, sightseeing tours, or pretty pictures nor does it promote cheap travel or the latest travel fads. You'll find plenty of excellent travel guides—most of which are ostensibly revised annually—that already cover such travel experiences. We, on the other hand, primarily focus on quality shopping, dining, and accommodations as well as special tours for people who wish to experience the best of the best of what Italy has to offer discriminating travelers.

The book is designed to provide you with the necessary information to enjoy this country's many treasures and pleasures. Going beyond popular sites, including major museums, churches, and monuments, we focus on the where, what, and how of acquiring Italy's many treasures. We especially organized the book with three major considerations in mind:

- Learn a great deal about Italy by meeting its many talented artists, craftspeople, and shopkeepers and exploring its many cities.

- Do quality shopping for items having good value.

- Discover unique items that can be integrated into your home and/or wardrobe.

As you will quickly discover, this and other books in the *"Treasures and Pleasures . . . Best of the Best"* series are not guides on how to find great shopping bargains, although whenever possible we share with you our discoveries on where and how to find bargains on quality items. Nor are we preoccupied with shopping in Italy's famous markets for cheap goods—places that may initially seem fun but which you may quickly find disappointing and, with a few exceptions, a waste of precious travel time. And we are not particularly interested in shopping for items imported from neighboring countries, such as France, Switzerland, or Germany, which tend to be very expensive. Given such close proximity to these countries, we prefer visiting them on our own and thus buying directly at the source.

Our primary focus is on "Made in Italy" products. Unlike neighboring France, which experienced a recent colonial period (17th to 20th centuries), Italy's colonial period is really ancient history (pre-4th century). In France you'll find a rich selection of antiques, arts, crafts, and home decorative items from former French colonies in Africa, Asia, and the South Pacific; in Italy you tend to find primarily "Made in Italy" products. In fact, you'll quickly discover the rather insular nature of Italy is reflected in its shopping: most everything is literally made in Italy. Italy's major shopping strengths—fashion and accessories —set the standards for the industry worldwide and thus are exported to other countries. In this sense, Italy's shopping is both insular and international; it represents the best of the best.

While you will find bargains in Italy, and goods and services in Italy are generally less expensive than in neighboring France Switzerland, and Germany, this book focuses on quality shopping for unique items that will retain their value. As such, we are less concerned with shopping to save money and to get great bargains than with shopping for unique products that can be taken home, integrated into one's wardrobe and home decor, and appreciated for years to come. We prefer finding the best of what there is available and selectively choose those items we both enjoy and can afford. Rather than purchase several pieces of fake jewelry, we prefer purchasing a single piece of exquisite jewelry that will last longer and be appreciated for many years to come. We learned long ago that while purchasing cheap items and tourist kitsch may seem appropriate at the time, such items quickly loose their value as well as our interest.

Our general shopping rule is this: A "good buy" is one that results in acquiring something that has good value; when in doubt, go for quality because quality items will hold their value and you will enjoy them much more in the long run.

Many Italians are good at practicing this rule especially when it comes to buying clothes. Rather than having a closet full of suits and coats—most of which are seldom worn—many Italians buy one or two good quality suits and coats that will last a long time in terms of fabrics, colors, and styling. While they may wear the same suit or coat over and over again, these people tend to remain stylish by accessorizing themselves and their clothes with attractive belts, scarves, hats, shoes, and jewelry. Many Italians do not spend a lot money on a lot of clothes. Rather, they buy a few very good quality garments that will give them repeated good use. For example, instead of buying five $200 coats that you may only wear five times each and which may appear dated quickly, why not invest in one $800 coat that you will get repeated use from and which will last for years? In this sense, the high-quality and much used $800 coat becomes relatively inexpensive when compared to the inexpensive alternatives.

We also include many of the best hotels and restaurants in our four Italian cities. By "best" we mean places that offer excellent value, service, and product. Make no mistake about it, hotels and restaurants tend to be expensive in Italy compared to similar places back home. While many of the best hotels and restaurants also are extremely expensive (US$600+ per night for a hotel room or US$200 per person for dinner), we identify many other outstanding hotels and restaurants that are relatively inexpensive or moderately priced. In this sense, we've tried to provide a good range of hotels and restaurants that meet our criteria of "the best" and respond to the varied preferences of our readers. After all, you may be the type of traveler who seeks out the finest hotels and restaurants because you want to pamper yourself when traveling in Italy—you want everything to be as good or better than back home! On the other hand, you might be the type of traveler who would rather spend your money on shopping and sightseeing; you only need a comfortable place to sleep and prefer finding inexpensive places to eat. We've attempted throughout this book to respond to the needs of these two types of travelers. For both groups, we outline some of the best of the best hotels and restaurants.

Our selections for sightseeing tend to follow a similar pattern. While we survey many of the standard sights in Milan, Florence, Rome, and Venice, especially museums and monuments, we're also aware that many of our readers are not great museum-goers, monument-climbers, or art-lovers. Although some may be embarrassed to admit it (*"Others may think I'm uncultured!"*), many of these people get bored after an hour at an ostensibly great yet highly redundant museum. The same people also may get bored visiting more than two Duomos or feel trapped in the Sistene Chapel! On the other hand, many of these people prefer walking the streets, observing people, or exploring villages and neighborhoods to "doing" museums, churches, and monuments. We understand these varied preferences. Accordingly, we include things to do, especially shopping, in addition to the standard museums, churches, and monuments that our four cities are so famous for.

- **We primarily focus on quality shopping, dining, and accommodations as well as special tours for people who wish to experience the best of the best of what Italy has to offer discriminating travelers.**
- **A "good buy" is one that results in acquiring something that has good value; when in doubt, go for quality because quality items will hold their value and you will enjoy them much more in the long run.**
- **By "best" we mean places that offer excellent value, service, and product.**

BEWARE OF RECOMMENDED SHOPS

Throughout this book we concentrate on providing you with information on the best of the best of Italy's treasures and pleasures. We prefer not recommending and listing specific shops and services—even though we have favorite places when visiting Italy. We know the pitfalls of doing so. Shops that offered excellent products and service during one of our visits, for example, may change ownership, personnel, and policies from one year to another. In addition, our shopping preferences may not be the same as your's.

Our major concern is to outline your shopping options in Milan, Florence, Rome, and Venice, show you where to locate the best shopping areas, and share some useful shopping strategies that you can use anywhere in Italy. Armed with this knowledge and some basic shopping skills, you will be better prepared to locate your own shops and determine which ones offer the best products and service in relation to your own shopping and travel goals.

However, we also recognize the "need to know" when

shopping in Italy. Therefore, throughout this book, we list the names and locations of various shops we have found to offer good quality products. In many cases we have purchased items in these shops and can also recommend them for service and reliability. But in most cases we surveyed shops to determine the type and quality of products offered without making purchases. To buy in every shop would be beyond our budget, as well as our home storage capabilities! When we do list specific shops, we do so only as reference points from which to start your shopping. We do not guarantee the quality of products or service. In many cases we have found our recommendations to be shops of exceptional quality, honesty, and service. We believe you should have the advantage of this information, but we also caution you to again evaluate the business by asking the necessary questions.

If you rely solely on our listings, you will miss out on one of the great adventures of shopping in Italy—discovering your own special shops that offer unique items, exceptional value, and excellent service.

Should you encounter problems with these recommendations, we would appreciate hearing about your experiences. We can be contacted through our publisher:

Ron and Caryl Krannich
IMPACT PUBLICATIONS
9104-N Manassas Drive
Manassas Park, VA 20111-2366
Fax 703/335-9486
E-mail: impactp@impactpublications.com

While we cannot solve your problems, future editions of this book will reflect the experiences—both positive and negative—of our readers. We appreciate your thoughtful observations and comments.

Expect a Rewarding Adventure

Whatever you do, enjoy Italy's many treasures and pleasures as found in Milan, Florence, Rome, and Venice. This is a very special country that offers a very unique travel adventure.

So arrange your flights and accommodations, pack your credit cards and traveler's checks, take your sense of humor, and head for four of Italy's, if not the world's, great destinations. You should return home with much more than a set of photos and travel brochures and a weight gain attendant with new eating habits. You will acquire some wonderful products and accumulate many interesting travel tales that can be enjoyed and relived for a lifetime.

Experiencing the treasures and pleasures of Italy only takes time, money, and a sense of adventure. Take the time, be willing to part with some of your money, and open yourself to a whole new world of treasures and pleasures. If you are like us, your adventure will introduce you to an exciting world of quality products, friendly people, and interesting places that you might have otherwise missed had you passed through these places only to eat, sleep, sightsee, and take pictures. When you travel and shop in Italy, you learn about some exciting places by way of the people, products, and places that define this country's many treasures and pleasures.

PART I

Traveling Smart

2

Know Before You Go

The more you know about Italy before you depart on your adventure, the better prepared you should be to enjoy its many treasures and pleasures. Indeed, you should be aware of several myths as well as numerous practical realities, such as weather, documents, transportation, duties, customs, and recommended resources, as you prepare for your trip to Italy.

Myths and Realities

The following myths prevent some travelers from truly enjoying Italy:

MYTH #1: **The Italians are often unfriendly and uncooperative.**

REALITY: Like the French, many Italians have a reputation for being less than helpful and often contentious in their relationships. Some restaurant service can be surly, and many people in official positions tend to be extremely bureaucratic—expounding mindless rules and regulations rather than genuinely attempt to solve problems. Given the nature of their jobs, we understand why these may be the least friendly people you may encounter! However, we have seldom encountered such difficulties, especially once we go beyond the jaded tourist areas. Indeed, you may find less than friendly people in many of the highly touristed areas which often become overwhelmed with demanding tourists. But that is probably the exception rather than the general rule. If you don't speak Italian and since many locals do not speak English, you may not have an opportunity to really experience genuine Italian hospitality and warmth. Most people will try to be helpful and accommodating if you approach them right and if you are not demanding and unreasonable. Even in Venice, with a local population of only 79,000 hosting over 20 million visitors a year, the locals are still noted for their willingness to help tourists who invariably get lost trying to find their way along narrow pathways. And some locals have to give the same directions 20 times a day, and graciously do so with a smile. Part of the problem is that you may not have an opportunity to meet many Italians because everywhere you go it seems like everyone is a foreign tourist!

MYTH #2: **It's difficult to get around in Italy because of the language barrier. You need to speak some Italian or you're likely to get lost.**

REALITY: More and more Italians speak English and are willing do so when approached by non-Italian speaking visitors. However, this is still a rather insular European destination despite the millions of tourists who visit this country each year. While you can expect many people will not speak English, especially outside the major cities, this so-called language barrier posses few if any serious problems. In the major tourist destinations, signs, maps, menus, and literature are often in English. Many restaurants offer menus in English, and waiters and waitresses often speak some English; if not, they will usually find someone who does speak English to assist you.

You will seldom have difficulty getting around because of your lack of local language skills. The major problem with language is found outside the large cities where few people may speak or understand English. In these places you may need to use a combination of a phrase book and sign language to communicate your needs. Try to learn a few basic Italian words or phrases for approaching people. We have yet to hear of anyone who got lost or went hungry in Italy for more than a few minutes because they did not speak Italian!

MYTH #3: Everything in Italy is expensive; I can't afford to go.

REALITY: Cost is always a relative concept. Compared to the rest of Europe, Italy appears to be a bargain destination these days. The lira remains weak against most major currencies, and many repeat visitors report prices are 30 percent less than they were five years ago. However, Italy is not a cheap destination compared to what you may be use to back home, especially when it comes to accommodations, restaurants, and shopping. Like in other parts of Europe, the cost of living in major Italian cities is very high. In addition, the US dollar is weak against many major world currencies. Rome and Milan, for example, are major international cities on par with Tokyo, London, Hong Kong, and New York. When was the last time you visited these places and didn't complain about costs? Don't expect to get a great deal of value for your money given the state of the Italian economy and the weak US dollar. Hotels can be very expensive, with many places charging more than US$250 a night for what are rather mediocre accommodations; Venice will be the most costly. Lunch can easily become a US$30-60 per person affair. But you also can find many inexpensive alternatives, as many a young backpacker to Italy will testify to. Shopping is very expensive, as it well should be given Italy's reputation as the world's leader for quality fashion and accessories. It all depends on how you like to travel. One of the least expensive ways to visit Italy is to join an all-inclusive tour, many of which include our four Italys. Check with your travel agent. One of the best value package tours, which includes our four cities, is the "Italian Mosiac" available through Globus (5301 S. Federal Circle, Littleton, CO 80123, Tel. 800/221-0090 or 303/797-2800). A 14-day guided tour, including roundtrip air transportation from New York City and first-class hotels, costs only $1969.00. In fact, this is the company's most popular tour of Italy.

MYTH #4: **Italy is a safe place to travel.**

REALITY: It depends on where you come from and how you handle yourself in Italy. While Italy is relatively safe to travel, you need to watch yourself carefully in Italy. Italian drivers are notorious for their unsafe driving habits. If you decide to drive, only do so defensively; it's always best to defer to more aggressive drivers. Crime against tourists is a growing and disturbing reality. Expect to encounter pickpockets and other assorted thieves in Italy's major tourist destinations, including the Vatican. And these people are expert at what they do. Be particularly careful in Florence and Rome and wherever you see bands of gypsy children who approach you. They are expert at distracting tourists while picking their pockets. Whatever you do, try not to look like a vulnerable tourist. Our point is that you should expect the unexpected in Italy. Watch your valuables. Take normal sensible precautions. And just be careful for your personal safety.

MYTH #5: **Rome, Florence, Milan, and Venice are too crowded with tourists to truly enjoy these places.**

REALITY: If you insist on traveling during the peak tourist season, which normally runs from mid-May through mid-September, you will experience a tremendous crush of tourists, especially in Florence, Rome, and Venice. Avoid August when Europeans take their traditional annual holiday and when may shops and restaurants close for two to three weeks. However, this old rule of thumb for "avoiding the tourist crowds" is not always reliable these days. The tourist season seems to be extending into October and parts of November, especially for Florence and Venice. Milan tends to be a crowded business city during much of the year because of its heavily attended international conventions and trade shows. Travelers are well advised to make hotel reservations at least two months before arrival. If you're visiting during peak season and have a particular place you wish to stay, try to book a room six to eight months in advance. If you want to avoid the crowds, consider traveling to Italy in November or early spring. The weather is often beautiful, and the crowds have disappeared! Furthermore, prices on everything seem to be cheaper during this delightful off-season period.

MYTH #6: The best food and the greatest restaurants in the world are found in Italy.

REALITY: Everything is relative, depending on where you come from and where you have traveled before. Like the French, the Italians tend to be very chauvinistic about their cuisine, and for good reason. Italian food is one of the world's great cuisines. But restaurants in Italy, especially in the heavily touristed areas, are often overrated and overpriced for what you get. Service is often slow, portions small, rooms smoke-filled and noisy, and the check shocking. Make no mistake about it; you can find some great restaurants in Rome, Florence, Milan, and Venice, and we identify these accordingly. Indeed, some of the best restaurants and dining experiences in the world can be found in Italy. But most restaurants are simply average and many are very disappointing. If you arrive with very high expectations for food and restaurants, you may be disappointed. We come from the Washington, DC area where we are used to great restaurants and good service—every coup d'etat worldwide gives us four new international restaurants—and we have some terrific Italian restaurants at half the price of our Italian experiences. Consequently, we've not been overly-impressed with many of our Italian dining experiences.

MYTH#6: **The traffic in Rome is the worst in the world; it's not much better elsewhere in Italy! It's best to take a train or public transportation.**

REALITY: The traffic in Rome looks and feels like traffic in most other large busy cities of the world. If you think it's the worst, then you haven't traveled much! In fact, the traffic in Rome is relatively orderly and sane compared to other places we've visited, including Los Angeles and Washington, DC. Even driving in Rome is not too bad, except for finding a parking place and the long traffic jams one inevitably encounters during rush hour. If you plan to drive, do so between the major cities. Parking a car in Florence and Rome is nearly impossible and also very expensive. Parking in Venice takes place outside the city since Venice has no roads for cars. Plan to walk and use public transportation within cities. Driving between cities, especially in the northern lake region and along the Amalfi Coast and the Italian Riviera, can be very delightful experiences as you have the flexibility to stop along the way to see Italy's many sites and charming towns. You can easily rent a car in Italy, but for the best rates, be sure to make reservations and negotiate a daily rate before you arrive in Italy. If you decide not to drive, plan to take trains between cities. Italian trains are very clean and efficient.

MYTH#7: **It's best to skip Milan since there's not much to see and do there.**

REALITY: Milan may not be one of Italy's most beautiful cities in the architecture department, and it lacks the heady profusion of art found in Florence or the ancient ruins of Rome. But Milan offers the *"best of the best"* shopping treasures that Italy has to offer the world. Go there for its great shopping, restaurants, hotels, art, and culture. This is where Italy's reputation for quality design and craftsmanship gets its name.

MYTH#8: **Florence is the most beautiful city in the world.**

REALITY: It's pretty and it's romantic. But there are lots of other candidates for this honor, including Venice, Paris, Sydney, Hong Kong, and San Francisco. It does rank somewhere on the list of 10 most beautiful cities in the world. It's also one of the most heavily touristed cities in the world with 19 million visitors crowding its narrow streets and piazzas each year.

MYTH#9: **Venice is one big expensive tourist trip and it's sinking!**

REALITY: It's not sinking any longer, but it continues to crumble from a combination of age, pollution, and lapping sea water. And, yes, it is a big tourist trap organized primarily to process tourists through its expensive hotels, restaurants, and shops. But unlike most tourist traps, Venice is the one tourists come to love. Don't miss it in spite of its high prices and wall to wall tourists.

MYTH#10: **The real Italy is found outside the major cities.**

REALITY: There's no such thing as a "real Italy." This is a very diverse country consisting of different regions with their own distinct characteristics. We refer to our four cities as our "Four Italys" amongst many other Italys. Each has its own distinct character that makes Italy such an exciting place to visit.

CLIMATE, SEASONS, WHEN TO GO

Being a Mediterranean country, Italy boasts a delightful Mediterranean climate characterized by dry, warm summers and relatively mild winters. Except in the northern Alps, with its continental climate, you won't find much snow in Italy. October to December can be very rainy months.

The best time to visit Italy is the shoulder seasons—late September to mid-October and April to mid-May. During this period the weather usually is very nice and you'll encounter fewer tourists which translates into shorter lines and more hotel rooms and restaurant tables. However, the so-called shoulder season seems to be becoming more and more a part of the peak season for Florence and Venice.

We generally avoid the peak season which normally runs from mid-May to mid-September. Dedicated shoppers should avoid August when many shops are closed as shopkeepers take their traditional annual holidays as well as the week before and after Christmas when many shops also close for the holidays. Many restaurants also close for two to three weeks during August.

- **Venice is the one tourist trap most tourists come to love.**
- **Italy boasts a delightful Mediterranean climate of dry, warm summers and relatively mild winters.**
- **Dedicated shoppers should avoid visiting Italy in August when many shops are closed.**
- **Prices tend to be cheaper during the off season which runs between November and March.**
- **Some of the best travel deals on Italy are package tours.**

If you visit Italy during the off season, which runs from November through much of March, you'll find prices cheaper, crowds smaller, and weather often delightful. Venice in the winter, for example, can be a wonderful experience as you feel you have the city to yourself!

REQUIRED DOCUMENTS

There are no visas required for entry to Italy by citizens of the United States, Canada, Great Britain, Australia, New Zealand, and South Africa for visits of less than three months. A valid passport is all that is required, and it is usually good for a stay of up to 90 days. You can extend your stay for another 90 days by applying at any police station (*questura*). However, such extensions are not automatic.

All travelers must register with the local police within three days of arrival in country as well as every time you move from one location to another. This registration procedure is done automatically for you at hotels. Hotels will ask for your passport: most will return it after they have taken care of the registration formalities whereas some will keep it until you leave to both register you and hold it as collateral until you pay your bill in full. Both U.S. and Canadian drivers' licenses are valid in Italy.

The following items are allowed into Italy duty-free: 400 cigarettes and 1.1 pounds of cigars or tobacco; 2 bottles of wine and 1 bottle of hard liquor; 2 regular cameras and 10 rolls of film per camera; and 1 movie camera or camcorder and 10 films or cartridges for either.

GETTING THERE

AIR

Italy is served by most international airlines. United Airlines, TWA, Delta, and Alitalia fly directly between the U.S. and Italy's two major gateway cities—Milan and Rome. A direct flight from New York City to Rome will take about 8½ hours. Several other airlines connect to Rome and Milan via major cities in Europe and Asia. Airfares to Italy from the United States vary considerably, depending on how well you shop around for special fares. A regular roundtrip economy fare from New York City to Rome can run over $1500. However, if you watch for specials or work with a consolidator, you can fly the same route, and often with the same airline, for under $600.00. It pays to shop around and work with a travel agent who, in turn, works with consolidators.

If you initially fly into Rome or Milan, plan to either drive or take a train to get around Italy. While domestic air links are readily available to Florence and Venice, you may find it's much cheaper and more convenient to drive or take a train to these destinations. Keep in mind that Italy is a relatively small country in which distances between major cities are not great.

Given the highly competitive nature of the tourist industry in Italy, you are likely to find several special package deals on airfare and hotels to Rome, Florence, and Venice. Again, check with your travel agent for the latest "deal" on Italy. You may be surprised to discover how affordable Italy is when in comes to international airfare.

TRAIN

Our four cities are well serviced by Italy's infamous trains that Mussolini literally got to "run on time." They've stayed that way ever since his demise. If you're arriving in Italy from other European destinations, chances are you will want to do so by train. Inter-European airfares are prohibitively expensive—it may cost you more to fly from Paris to Rome than it does from New York City to Rome. In addition, they are relatively inexpensive compared to train travel in other European countries. Eurailpasses can be used to get into Italy from other European destination and they are valid for travel within the country. Trains run frequently and they are clean, efficient, and pleasant to ride, although pickpockets also tend to travel by train and are known to relieve sleeping passengers of their valuables. Since train stations tend to be centrally located within each city, taking the train often means avoiding an expensive and time consuming airport to city taxi ride. It also means you will probably be within walking distance, or a short taxi ride, of your hotel.

Since trains are very popular in Italy, it's a good idea to make reservations at least 24 hours before your planned departure. If you don't, you're likely to encounter long lines as well as be disappointed in not getting a seat.

CAR

If you plan to travel to several places and have more luggage than you care to haul on and off trains or just wish to have maximum flexibility, you may decide to rent a car. Car rentals in Italy seem expensive compared to prices in the United States. You can get the best prices on a car rental by booking the car and prepaying the fees before you leave home. Call the major car rental firms and compare prices; the company that gave us the best deal when we called (Hertz) may not be offering the best prices when/where you want to travel.

- Hertz 800/654-3131
- Avis 800/331-1084
- National 800/477-6285
- Kenwel 800/678-0678

Given the highly competitive nature of the European car rental business, several rental firms are willing to bargain over the telephone—they'll beat the best rate you can find amongst their competition. If you call around and bargain hard, you should be able to get a car for about US$35 a day. Otherwise, you may end up paying nearly US$100 a day for the same car.

During our last trip we initially flew into Milan, took a train from Milan to Florence, and then picked up our prepaid car in Florence on the day we were leaving the city for our next destinations—Pisa, Portofino, Monaco, the French Riviera, and Paris. With a car we had flexibility to alternate our time between the seaside towns and villages in the hills. The train was nice, but having a car is a real treat in Italy since there are so many things you may want to see and do at your own pace.

If you travel by car, do keep all your luggage as well as other valuables locked in the trunk out of sight of would-be thieves. Do not leave maps or other things that indicate you are a tourist in sight either.

VAT

Like other European Union countries, Italy has the infamous Value Added Tax (VAT). In Italy this tax is called the IVA or *imposto sul valore aggiunta*. It differs from the sales tax levied in the United States in that it is already added onto the price quoted for goods rather than added at the point of sale. Italy impose two VAT rates: an IVA of 16% (actually 13.8% of the sale price) on fashion, textiles, and shoes and an IVA of 19% (16% of sale price) on all other goods and services. Non-residents of EU countries can request a VAT refund if their purchases meet the following conditions:

1. Purchases in a single store must total at least 300,000 lira (before the VAT is added).

2. The store must issue you an official store invoice, which includes your passport number, showing where you purchased your items and for how much. If the store does not volunteer this invoice, be sure to ask. Indeed, many small shops may not be used to issuing these special VAT refund invoices. You may even need to help them complete the invoice! You must remember to ask about the VAT refund every time you are contemplating a large purchase. If the store doesn't volunteer or you don't ask—you'll walk away without the proper documents which means you will not be eligible for a refund.

3. You claim your VAT refund when you leave your last EU country. You fill out a form and present your passport, invoice, and goods to a Customs official who stamps it accordingly. You then mail the form and invoices in a special envelope provided at Customs or already given to you by the store where you made your purchases. The envelope goes to the proper authorities who then have the store issue the refund.

At some airports you can get an instant cash refund for your VAT, but expect these operations to charge accordingly for this convenience—nearly 30% of your refund. If you can be patient, you'll normally get a refund check in the mail within 90 days. However, don't expect to get a full refund. Processing fees are normally subtracted; you'll probably end up with 80% of what was initially due to you. For more information on how the VAT refund works in Italy, contact Italy Tax-Free Shopping, Via C.

Battisti 3, 21045 Gazzada (Varese), Tel. (0332) 870770 or fax (0332) 870171.

SAFETY AND SECURITY

Italy, especially big city Italy, has a growing reputation for crimes against tourists. Pickpockets are the main culprits, although more and more tourists have reported assaults and robberies. Whatever you do, be careful with your valuables. Consider wearing a money belt, use hotel safe deposit boxes, and avoid situations that could lead to trouble. If you rent a car, make sure you never leave valuables in sight when the car is unattended; and unpack the car at night. If you travel by train, stay awake during the day and secure your compartment at night. Be especially alert in crowds or if approached by bands of gypsy kids who are most likely intent upon distracting you while one or two of them pick your pockets. It's good to be a little paranoid in Italy since crime against tourists appears to be widespread.

CUSTOMS: RETURNING HOME

It's always good to know U.S. Customs regulations before leaving home. If you are a U.S. citizen planning to travel abroad, the United States Customs Service provides several helpful publications which are available free of charge from your nearest U.S. Customs Office, or write P.O. Box 7407, Washington, D.C. 20044.

- ***Know Before You Go*** (Publication #512): outlines facts about exemptions, mailing gifts, duty-free articles, as well as prohibited and restricted articles.

- ***Trademark Information For Travelers*** (Publication #508): deals with unauthorized importation of trademarked goods. Since you will find copies of trademarked items in markets—ubiquitous "knock-offs"—this publication will alert you to potential problems with Custom inspectors prior to returning home.

- ***International Mail Imports:*** answers many travelers' questions regarding mailing items back to the U.S. The U.S. Postal Service sends all packages to Customs for examination and assessment of duty before they are delivered to the addressee. Some items are free of duty and some are dutiable. Do check on this before you leave the U.S. so you won't be surprised after you make your purchases in Italy.

U.S. citizens may bring in U.S. $400 worth of goods free of U.S. taxes every 30 days; the next $1000 is subject to a flat 10% tax. Goods beyond $1400 are dutied at varying rates applied to different classes of goods. If you are in Rome and uncertain about U.S. duties on particular items, contact the U.S. Embassy and ask for local U.S. Customs assistance.

CURRENCY AND EXCHANGE RATES

The Italian monetary unit is the lira (L). The value of the lira relative to the dollar fluctuates; at the time this book went to press US$1 was equal to 1520 lira or L1520; CDN$1 was equal to L1199. The small coin is a L10 coin; the smallest bill is a L1000 note.

You can easily change your currency into lira at exchange offices (look for the *"cambio"* sign) in airports, train stations, hotels, and banks. While banks give the best exchange rates, they also charge 1-2% commissions for such transactions. In the end, you may want to exchange your money wherever it is most convenient, which means where you find the shortest lines. You may save a few cents at the bank, but you also may be working for those paultry savings by spending more time in line!

ELECTRICITY

Electricity in Italy, as well as most of Europe, is 220 volts AC. You will need a converter to change the foreign voltage to the lower voltage required by the appliances you normally use in the U.S. if your appliance is not dual voltage. You will also need an adapter plug so that you can plug into the different wall plugs—most are two pin (round) plugs—found in Italy.

You can readily find both adapter plugs and voltage converters in most Radio Shack stores, or if you have difficulty finding them locally you may wish to contact either of two mail order firms:

Magellan's
Box 5485
Santa Barbara, CA 93150
Phone 1-800-962-4943
Fax 1-805-568-5406

Franzus Company
P.O. Box 142
Beacon Falls, CT 06403
Phone 1-203-723-6664
Fax 1-203-723-6666

If you forget to bring the proper plug adapter with you, your hotel may be able to loan you one, or you can purchase an inexpensive one (US$1.00) at a local electrical shop.

ANTICIPATED COSTS

While Italy is not as expensive as some other European destinations, especially Germany, France, and Switzerland, it still can be an expensive place to visit if you are traveling on your own and if you are used to getting good value for your travel dollar. Prices are especially high in our four cities for such basics as hotels and restaurants. Top hotels can easily cost US$400 to $600 per night for a double; inexpensive hotels will run from US120 to $180 per night. If you drive, expect to pay US$5 or more per gallon for gasoline. Restaurant meals can easily run US$40 or more for lunch and US$100 or more per person for dinner. You can easily spend US$1000 a day on hotels, meals, and entertainment, not to mention a few thousand dollars more a day on shopping! If money is no object, go ahead and enjoy the many pricey treasures and pleasures Milan, Florence, Rome, and Venice readily offer.

The cost of travel in Italy is relatively high for several reasons. First, the US dollar remains weak, although it is doing better against the Italian lira than most other European currencies. Second, the cost of Italian labor tends to be high and thus reflected in your cost of travel. Third, Italian taxes are high, especially the ubiquitous Value Added Tax which is hidden in most prices. Indeed, one-fourth of a price could very well be taxes. Overall, Italy is not a bargain destination. Like most visitors, you'll probably have to pay a lot for your Italian adventure.

However, given the highly competitive nature of the Italian tourist industry, you can always find a bargain on travel to Italy if you shop around. Your best travel deal will be a group tour. A seven to ten-day tour for under US$1,700, including round-trip transportation, is a real steal compared to what the same trip might cost you if you attempted to do it on your own. Given the cost of independent travel in Italy, group tours can dramatically save you money on hotels, restaurants, and transportation. In the United States, companies such a Globus (800/221-0090), Perillo Tours (800/431-1515), and Trafalgar Tours (800/854-0103) offer excellent value package tours. However, if you prefer doing this trip on your own and you wish to watch your costs, we strongly recommend that you do a great deal of pre-trip planning. With sufficient planning, you can significantly cut the costs of travel to our four Italian cities. We recommend doing the following:

- **Transportation:** Use the public transportation system whenever possible. Trains in Italy are less expensive than elsewhere in Europe and they are relatively convenient for travel between cities. The buses and subway systems in Milan and Rome also are relatively inexpensive and convenient for getting around the cities; each city offers specially priced public transportation passes for short-term visitors. Plan to do a lot of walking in both Florence and Venice.

  Alternatively, you may want to rent a car for exploring Italy. While the cost of gasoline may be high, most cars get good gas mileage, and renting a car is one of the most convenient and inexpensive way of seeing Italy. However, avoid taking a car into our four cities where parking is nearly impossible as well as extremely expensive. Do your driving between the cities. But be careful how you go about arranging for your car rental. If you wait until you arrive in Italy to arrange a car rental, you could pay over US$100 a day for a car. You can rent a car for under US$35 a day if you reserve it before you arrive in Italy. Comparative shop for your car rental by calling several of the car rental firms identified on page 24. You may be surprised what you learn. A firm that offered the best price three months ago may now be the most expensive. You literally need to shop around for the best deal every time you plan to visit Italy. Hertz, Avis, Budget, and Kenwel offer competitive prices—but be sure to compare prices and ask about special deals and discounts. We normally do such planning at least eight weeks before we arrive in Italy. If you plan to visit Italy during the high season, arrange your car at least three months in advance. Within the cities, plan to do a lot of walking as well as use the relatively inexpensive public transportation systems—buses, trams, subways, and taxis.

- **Accommodations:** While hotel rooms tend to be expensive, you can cut costs by making reservations directly with the hotel (call or fax directly to the property) and asking for any special rates. Many hotels, especially in Venice, offer special off-season rates. If you reserve a room by calling a toll-free 800 number, you will most likely be quoted the full rack rate. Most prices quoted will include breakfast which could be US$25-30 of the daily rate; it's not much of a breakfast considering what you are paying.

Ask for the room rate without breakfast. The same, if not better, breakfast is probably available at a nearby coffee bar for one-third the hotel price. For a good survey of inexpensive accommodations in Florence, Rome, and Venice, see Sandra Gustafson's always popular, reliable, and thoroughly researched ***Cheap Sleeps in Italy*** (Chronicle Books). Her latest edition should be available in most bookstores with a large travel section on Italy.

- **Restaurants:** If you want to experience the best of the best restaurants available in our four cities, expect to pay a high price for such an experience. Dinner at a top restaurant can easily cost US$150 per person. Every time you sit down at a restaurant table, you will be charged a table fee, regardless of what you order. Standing up at a counter or purchasing take-out food is always less expensive than sitting at a table; in fact, it can be very cheap. Assuming you may not be budgeted to dine at such rates on a daily basis, you should plan to seek less expensive alternatives. Our general rule of thumb is that most restaurants, including very basic ones, cost at least two to three times more than back home. If, for example, you are used to paying US$25 per person for dinner back home, expect to pay US$50 for a comparable dinner. However, comparables may be difficult to find since portions tend to be smaller and meals tend to be served in courses. If you really want to cut the costs of dining in Milan, Florence, Rome, and Paris, consider doing the following:

    - **Consult several books on inexpensive restaurants:** One of our favorite and most reliable guides to reasonably priced restaurants in Florence, Rome, and Venice is Sandra Gustafson's popular ***Cheap Eats in Italy*** (Chronicle Books). Pick up her latest edition which is available in bookstores with travel sections on Italy.

    - **Seek alternatives to restaurants:** In addition to restaurants, eateries in Italy come in several different forms and cost levels: cafés, trattoria, snack bars, pizzeria, wine bars, cafeterias, bars, and self-service snack counters. We also find pastry shops, take out shops, and the usual assortment of fast-food restaurants, such as Burghy, Wendys, and Quick. One of the least expensive ways to eat is to frequent the many take-out shops that offer a wide variety of food, from pizza and pasta to roasted chicken and ribs.

- **Economize your dining style:** Look for the daily specials and the set-price meals (*menù turisto*). Keep in mind that Italian restaurant meals tend to come in many different, and extremely filling, courses. If you order all of the courses, your dining tab will probably be high and you're likely to experience a weight gain. You may find two courses to be plenty, especially a pasta and main course. Indeed, many people skip the *antipasti* and desserts altogether.

- **Organize a picnic in a piazza or in your hotel room:** Small grocery stores, supermarkets, and take-out shops are well stocked with wine, soft drinks, fruit juices, cheeses, meats, fruits, vegetables, and prepared deli foods. You can easily put together a wonderful and relatively inexpensive picnic by organizing a meal in this manner. You also may want to purchase drinks here rather than use your hotel mini-bar. Take, for example, the relative costs of your basic can of Coca Cola. It may cost you US$8 in your hotel mini-bar, US$5 in a restaurant, US$3 from a street vendor, US$2 at a tiny market, or US$1 at a supermarket. We usually try to locate a supermarket near our hotel which results in saving a great deal of money on the high cost of soft drinks. Wine is surprising cheap if purchased at the right place. Given the over-production of European wines, the prices are relatively inexpensive. You can get a good bottle of wine in a supermarket for under US$7. However, a similar bottle of wine may cost more than US$40 when ordered at a restaurant.

- **Entertainment:** Some of the cheapest and most satisfying entertainment in Italy is either free or almost free—just walking the streets (free), strolling around a piazza (free), sitting at a sidewalk café (US$3-4 coffee), or visiting museums and monuments. Other forms of organized entertainment can get very expensive.

- **Shopping:** This is a tough one to estimate. Shopping in Milan, Florence, Rome, and Venice can quickly deplete any semblance of a budget! First time visitors often become overwhelmed with the numerous shopping choices and the high prices of everything. However, you also quickly discover that shopping in Italy falls into a different category from shopping elsewhere, except perhaps France. The emphasis here is on quality, quality, and quality. Everything from art, antiques, and jewelry to clothes and accessories seems to scream quality. Add to this high rents, high taxes, and the high cost of labor and you have the perfect formula for high priced shopping. At the same time, you can find "bargains" and "deals" on sale items, and you may have fun exploring some of Italy's major markets which are filled with unique, and at times inexpensive, items.

ITALIAN TOURIST OFFICES

Most cities have tourist offices located at the airports, train stations, and central part of the city. These offices provide information on accommodations, transportation, and local sightseeing. If you arrive without hotel reservations, you may want to visit one of these offices for assistance.

3

Prepare For a Unique Adventure

Preparation is the key to experiencing a successful and enjoyable adventure to our four Italys. But it involves much more than just examining maps, reading travel literature, and making airline and hotel reservations. Preparation, at the very least, is a process of minimizing uncertainty by learning how to develop a shopping plan, manage your money, determine the value of products, handle Customs, and pack for the occasion. It involves knowing what products are good deals to buy in Italy in comparison to similar items back home. Preparation helps organize all the aspects of your trip.

Develop an Action Plan

Time is money when traveling abroad. This is especially true in the cases of Milan, Florence, Rome, and Venice where the cost of unnecessary travel, especially an extra night or two in a hotel, can be very expensive. The better you plan and use your time, the more time you will have to enjoy your trip.

If you want to use your time wisely and literally hit the ground running, you should plan a detailed, yet tentative, schedule for each day. Most people visiting Rome, for example, want to visit many of the ancient Roman ruins and the Vatican as well as have time for shopping and other sightseeing. In Florence it's museum after museum after museum along with lots of excellent shopping. If you don't plan properly, you can easily experience museum burn out which will leave little time for shopping and sightseeing. You can get started with your planning by doing the following: for each city **list** in order of priority the 10 things you most hope to accomplish in the time you have. At the end of each day **summarize** what you actually accomplished in relation to your 10 priorities and set your priorities for the following day.

Planning is fine but it will not ensure a successful trip. People who engage in excessive planning often overdo it and thus ruin their trip by accumulating a list of unfulfilled expectations. Planning needs to be adapted to good luck. You also should be open to unexpected events which may well become the major highlights of your travel and shopping experiences.

CONDUCT RESEARCH AND NETWORK

Do as much research as possible before you depart. A good starting place is the periodical section of your local library. Here you will find numerous magazine and newspaper articles on travel and shopping in Italy with special emphasis on our four cities. Indeed, these destinations are some of the most popular subjects for travel writers. When you find references to shops, add these names to your growing list of places to visit.

You should also **network for information and advice**. You'll find many people, including relatives, friends, and acquaintances, who have traveled to Italy. Many of these people are eager to talk about their trip as well as share their particular travel secrets with you. They may direct you to some great shops where they found arts, crafts, jewelry, clothes, and accessories of good quality or at exceptional prices. Everyone seems to have their favorite restaurant recommendations and tips on what to see and how long to stay in any one place. When organizing your shopping plan, ask basic who, what, where, why, and how questions:

- **What** shops did you particularly like?
- **What** do they sell?
- **Whom** should I talk to?
- **Where** is the shop located?
- **How** did you pack and ship large items?
- **When** were you last there?

This final question is particularly significant. Not only do shops change ownership or go out of business, but prices constantly change. Information gleaned from people's experiences over the past 2-3 years will be most relevant.

Be sure to record all the information that you receive in an orderly manner. Use, for example, an ordinary address book to list the names, addresses, telephone numbers, and products of shops; list them alphabetically by types of merchandise.

Don't neglect to contact the Italian tourist office nearest you. Ask for a map and any information on travel and shopping in Italy that would assist you in planning your trip. In the United States and Canada, the Italian Government Travel Office can be contacted as follows:

New York: ENIT, 630 5th Avenue, Suite 1565, New York, NY 10111, Tel. 212/245-4822 or Fax 212/586-9249.

Los Angeles: 12400 Wilshire Blvd., Suite 550, Los Angeles, CA 90025, Tel. 310/820-0098 or Fax 310/820-6357.

Montréal: 1 Place Ville Marie, Montréal, Québec, Canada H3B 3M9, Tel. 514/866-7667 or Fax 514/392-1429.

MANAGE YOUR MONEY WELL

It's best to carry traveler's checks, two or more major credit cards with sufficient credit limits, U.S. dollars, and a few personal checks. If you use ATMs, you might want to take your ATM card with you. Our basic money rule is to take enough money and sufficient credit limits so you don't run short. How much you take is entirely up to you, but it's better to have too much than not enough when you're shopping in Italy.

Credit cards are the most convenient means for managing your money in Italy. We prefer using credit cards to pay for major purchases as well as for those unanticipated expenses incurred when shopping. Most major hotels and stores honor MasterCard, Visa, American Express, and Diner's cards. It's a good idea to take one or two bank cards and an American Express card.

Take plenty of **traveler's checks** in U.S. denominations of $50 and $100. Smaller denominations are often more trouble than they are worth. In Italy you will usually receive a better exchange rate with traveler's checks than with cash. Most major banks, hotels, restaurants, and shops will also take traveler's checks, although some do add a small service charge for accepting them. Banks and money changers will give you the best exchange rates, but at times you'll find hotels to be more convenient because of their close proximity and better hours.

Personal checks can be used to obtain traveler's checks with an American Express card or to pay for goods to be shipped later—after your check has cleared your bank. Some shops will also accept personal checks. Remember to keep one personal check aside to pay Customs should you have dutiable goods when you return home, although Customs also accepts credit cards.

Use your own judgment concerning how much **cash** you should carry with you. Contrary to some fearful ads, cash is awfully nice to have in moderate amounts to supplement your traveler's checks and credit cards. Several US$1 bills are handy for tips when you first arrive. Consider carrying an "emergency cash reserve" primarily in $50 and $100 denominations, but also a few $20's. Cash can be used instead of your larger denomination traveler's checks when you want to change a small amount of money to local currency.

- ❑ **Use credit cards to pay for hotels and restaurants and for major purchases.**
- ❑ **Carry one or two bank cards and an American Express card.**
- ❑ **Consider requesting a higher credit limit on your bank cards.**
- ❑ **Take plenty of $50 and $100 traveler's checks.**
- ❑ **Keep one personal check aside to pay Customs should you have dutiable goods when you return home.**
- ❑ **Carry an "emergency cash reserve" primarily in $50 and $100 denominations.**
- ❑ **Keep a good record of all charges in local currency—and at official exchange rates.**

Use Credit Cards Wisely

Credit cards can be a shopper's blessing if used in the right manner. They are your tickets to serendipity, convenience, good exchange rates, and a useful form of insurance. Widely accepted in our four Italian cities, they enable you to draw on credit reserves for purchasing many wonderful items you did not anticipate finding when you initially planned your adventure. In addition to being convenient, you usually will get good exchange rates once the local currency amount appearing on your credit slip is converted by the bank at the official rate into your home currency. Credit cards also allow you to float your expenses into the following month or two without paying interest charges and may even add miles to your frequent flyer account. Most important, should you have a problem with a purchase, your credit card company may assist you in recovering your money and returning the goods. Once you discover your problem, contact the credit card company with your complaint and refuse to pay the amount while the matter is in dispute. Although your credit card company is not obligated to do so, many times they will assist you in resolving a problem. Businesses accepting these cards must maintain a certain standard of honesty and integrity. In this sense, credit cards may be an excellent and inexpensive form of insurance against possible fraud and damaged goods when shopping abroad. If you rely only on cash or traveler's checks, you have no such institutional recourse for recovering your money.

A few other tips on the use and abuse of credit cards may be useful in planning your trip. Use your credit cards for the things that will cost you the same amount no matter how you pay, such as lodging and meals in the better hotels and restaurants or purchases in most department stores. Consider requesting a higher credit limit on your bank cards if you think you will be charging more than your current limit allows. Indeed, many visitors to Italy quickly max out their credit cards on the many quality shopping treasures they find!

Be extremely careful with your credit cards. Keep a good record of all charges in Italian lira—and at official exchange rates—so you don't have any surprises once you return home!

SECURE YOUR VALUABLES

Be sure to keep your traveler's checks, credit cards, and cash in a safe place along with your travel documents and other valuables. Consider wearing a money belt or a similar safety cache. While the money belt may be the safest approach, the typical 4" x 8" nylon belts can be uncomfortable in hot and humid weather. Women may want to make a money pouch which can fasten inside their clothing. Another approach for women is to carry money and documents in a leather shoulder bag which should be kept with you at all times, however inconvenient, even when passing through buffet lines. Choose a purse with a strap long enough to sling around your neck bandolier style. Secure the purse with a strong grip and always keep it between you and the person accompanying you. Purse snatchers, who are readily found at Italy's more popular tourist sites, can quickly ruin your vacation if you are not careful.

Men should carry their wallet in a front pocket. If you keep it in a rear pocket, as you may do at home, you invite pickpockets to demonstrate their varied talents in relieving you of your money, and possibly venting your trousers in the process. If your front pocket is an uncomfortable location, you probably need to clean out your wallet so it will fit better.

You may also want to use the free hotel safety deposit boxes for your cash and other valuables. If one is not provided in your room, ask the cashier to assign you a private box in their vault. Under no circumstances should you leave your money and valuables unattended in your hotel room, at restaurant tables, or in dressing rooms. Remember, there are many talented and highly motivated thieves who prey upon what they see as unsuspecting rich tourists. You may want to leave your expensive jewelry at home so as not to be as likely a target of theft. If you get robbed, chances are it will be in part your own fault, because you invited someone to take advantage of your weaknesses by not being more cautious in securing your valuables. In our many years of traveling we have not been robbed. But we try to be careful not to encourage someone to take advantage of us. We know people who have had problems, but invariably they were easy and predictable targets, because they failed to take elementary precautions against thieves.

TAKE KEY SHOPPING INFORMATION

Depending on what you plan to buy, you should take all the necessary information you need to make informed shopping decisions. After all, you don't want to end up purchasing a Gucci watch in Florence for US$500 and then discover you can get the same item back home for US$280, or even purchase it on your flight back home for only US$250! Put this information in a separate envelope. If you are looking for home furnishings, include with your "wish list" room measurements to help you determine if particular items will fit into your home. You might take photographs with you of particular rooms you hope to furnish. Be sure to include measurements of dining tables and beds just in case you find some wonderful table linens and bedspreads in Italy.

- ❑ **Take with you measurements and photographs of rooms that could become candidates for home decorative items.**
- ❑ **Be sure to take information on any particular clothes, accessories, or jewelry (sizes, colors, comparative prices) with you to look for or have made when in Italy.**
- ❑ **Do comparative shopping before arriving in Italy.**

If you plan to shop for clothes, your homework should include taking an inventory of your closets and identifying particular colors, fabrics, and designs you wish to acquire to complement and enlarge your present wardrobe. Keep in mind that good quality clothes and accessories in Italy can be very expensive. But you will most likely be buying top quality designer-label clothes, purses, and belts which are also very expensive back home. If you are from the U.S., you should look at comparable selections found at the top department stores, such as Saks Fifth Avenue, Neiman Marcus, Macy's, and Nordstrom. This means visiting their designer-label and couture sections for comparable quality and prices. When doing comparative pricing, keep in mind that you may be eligible for a VAT refund which could mean reducing the price by 10-13 percent (that's what you may end up with after processing fees are deducted from your refund).

DO COMPARATIVE SHOPPING

You should do comparison shopping before you leave home. Once you arrive in Italy, the only comparisons you can make are between various shops you encounter in Milan, Florence, Rome, and Venice. You'll never know if you are getting a good deal unless you have done your homework beforehand.

Unless you know the comparable value of goods back home, you won't recognize a bargain when it stares you in the face. Since few things are bargains in Italy, chances are you will be looking for unique items that are not readily available elsewhere. This is especially true in the cases of clothes, accessories, jewelry, and crafts, such as marbleized papers and inlaid mosaic art. Italian design and styling is unique, and you will quickly recognize it once you begin surveying shops in our four cities. Take, for example, leather goods. The Italians are especially talented at designing stylish leather coats, bags, shoes, belts, and gloves. Chances are you won't find the large variety of quality leather goods because many of these products are produced by small factories and shops they do not export abroad. They also are very expensive. Leather gloves can range from US$25 to US$500 a pair. But you may quickly fall in love with a $300 pair and decide to spend the money on something you simply can't get back home and for something you decided you really can't live without. So much for comparative shopping! At least you know you can't find such items back home at any price.

The first step in doing comparative shopping is determining exactly what you want and need. Make lists. As you compile your list, spend some time "window" shopping in the local stores, examining catalogs, and telephoning for information.

Keep Track of Receipts

It's important to keep track of all of your purchases for making an accurate Customs declaration. Since it's so easy to misplace receipts, you might want to organize your receipts using a form similar to the following example. Staple a sheet or two of notebook or accountant's paper to the front of a large manila envelope and number down the left side of the page. Draw one or two vertical columns down the right side. Each evening sort through that day's purchases, write a description including style and color of the purchase on the accompanying receipt, and enter that item on your receipt record. Record the receipt so later you'll know exactly which item belongs to the receipt.

Customs Declaration Record Form

	RECEIPT #	ITEM	PRICE (Lira)	PRICE (US$)
1.	241158	Prada bag	551,760	$363.00
2.				
3.				
4.				

Put the receipts in the manila envelope and pack the purchases away. If you're missing a receipt, make a note of it beside the appropriate entry.

Pack Right For Italy

Packing is one of the great travel challenges for many people. Trying to get everything you think you need into one or two bags can be frustrating, especially if you are visiting two or more countries which have different climates. You'll either take too much, and carry more than is necessary, or you'll take too little, thinking you'll buy what you need there, only to find that just the right items are ever so elusive.

We've learned over the years to err on the side of taking too little. If we start with less, we'll have room for more. Our ultimate goal is to make do with three changes of very versatile outfits, loosely packed into the lightest and largest bag the airlines will allow. We fill the extra space with bubble wrap for protecting delicate purchases on the way home. Good hotels provide efficient laundry and dry-cleaning services, and you can always hand wash your "undies" yourself if you choose. Since inexpensive luggage is readily available in department stores and markets, there's really no need to take extra luggage for purchases you may make along the way. However, if you know you're going to buy a lot, you might decide to take a second empty suitcase with you. We have done this by nesting one inside the other with our trip clothing packed in the inside piece of luggage as well as by stuffing a second piece of luggage with bubble wrap and other packing materials we will need to protect our purchases. While softsided luggage is lighter weight, it may not provide as much protection as a good hardsided piece for either your clothing or your shopping treasures.

Your goal should be to avoid lugging extensive wardrobe, cosmetics, library, and household goods around the world! Why not adopt our guiding principle for packing: *"When in doubt, leave it out."*

Above all, you want to return home loaded down with wonderful new purchases without paying extra weight charges. Hence, pack for the future rather than load yourself down with the past.

TAKE COMFORTABLE SHOES

All four of our Italian cities are walking cities which require good walking shoes to navigate many miles of very hard concrete and cobblestone walkways. Please don't buy new shoes for your trip unless you have several weeks to break them in. We prefer to clean up and polish two very comfortable pair of shoes which we've worn for a year or more.

We recommend taking at least one pair of comfortable walking shoes and one pair of dress shoes. Several major manufacturers of sport shoes make attractive shoes designed just for walking. Take only essential shoes which will coordinate with all of your outfits.

SHOP BY THE RULES

One of the great pleasures of visiting Milan, Florence, Rome, and Venice is shopping. It's likely to be shopping like you've never encountered before. The Italians are rightly known for their artisan traditions which stress exacting standards of quality and design and the attention to detail. Such standards translate into Italian style, taste, and class. If you regularly shop for designer label clothes and accessories as well as top jewelry, you know what this quality is all about. It looks and feels rich. Accordingly, you know it also comes with a rather hefty price tag.

So the deal in Italy is basically no deal. This is not a shopper's paradise for bargains. It's a shopper's paradise for some of the most heavenly quality products you'll find anywhere in the world. Fabulous window displays showcase fabulous products that entice visitors to do something they might not do back home—spend more on clothes, accessories, jewelry, ceramics, glassware, and art than you had ever dreamed you might be capable of doing. That's seductive Italy. It's okay. Chances are you'll love your purchase and enjoy it for many years to come. After all, that's what often happens when you buy quality.

Once you get into the shopping culture, here are a few basic rules you'll want to follow:

1. **Don't expect to bargain much or receive major discounts.** Very little bargaining takes place in Italian shops or even in open-air market stalls. Most shops have fixed prices and expect customers to pay accordingly. The best deals are during semi-annual sales periods which take place just after Christmas or New Years and in July, just before the traditional August store closings. However, should you be purchasing a large ticket item, it doesn't hurt to ask for a discount; you might be pleasantly surprised to discover that violating this rule indeed gets you a discount! But do so in a very subtle manner: *"Is it possible to do any better on this price?"* After all, anything is possible, right? And one possibility might be for you to offer cash rather than to use your credit card which costs the merchant a percentage processing fee. We have been able to get 5-10 percent discounts by asking in such a manner.

2. **Travel with your check book:** Some shops will accept a personal check, especially if you are having them ship your goods. Others accept personal checks without asking many questions or requesting much identification. Perhaps you will have to pass a "personal trust" test before they will accept such a check.

3. **Ask for assistance if you want to see something.** Shopkeepers don't appreciate customers who come into their shop and proceed to paw through their goods and pick up items. They prefer you to "ask for help" which means they will pick up an item and show it to you. Merchants in Venice can sometimes become irate with customers who pick up glassware without asking for assistance. Americans, who are used to a self-service and "pick-me-up now" shopping culture are most likely to get into trouble with Italian shopkeepers.

4. **Remember the VAT!** Before making a purchase, ask yourself if you qualify for a VAT refund. Some merchants may volunteer this information, especially if you ask for a discount—they consider the VAT refund a form of discount. Remember, you need to spend at least 300,000 lire (US$197.37) in one shop before you can qualify for a VAT refund from that particular shop. If you qualify, remind the merchant that you need a special receipt in order to claim the refund. The merchant should have a large book of these receipts which need to be completed by hand and taken with you. You, in turn, have it validated by Customs and mail it to the proper authorities at your last Immigration point when departing from your final EU country.

5. **Shops can arrange packing and shipping.** Don't be afraid to purchase large or delicate items that you may not want to take with you. Most shops in our four cities have experience in packing and shipping. However, if you decide to have items shipped, it's always a good idea to get a receipt stating who is doing what and take a picture of the items being shipped. We always take photos just in case we might have a problem with a shipment, which is rare.

6. **Avoid anyone who wants to take you to a recommended shop.** Chances are you will be "taken" at the shop if you follow such an individual. It's always best to shop at reputable shops. These places are well known by hotel concierges and identified in several guidebooks on the various cities.

7. **Hold on to everything.** Thievery is a fact of life in Italy and it seems to be growing. If you are carrying lots of bags from your shopping sojourns, chances are you may quickly become a target of thieves who may try to distract you (their tricks and scams are legend) while others steal your packages.

THE PERFECT TRIP

Whatever you do, enjoy the many treasures and pleasures of Italy. You're in for a real treat of quality shopping, sightseeing, and dining. As you explore this beautiful and appealing place, you'll quickly discover why one out of every twenty world travelers each year are found in Italy. It's a wonderfully seductive place that will beckon you to return again and again to explore Italy's many additional treasures and pleasures. But for now, let's indulge ourselves in the treasures and pleasures of Milan, Florence, Rome, and Venice. These are four great and grand cities that will surely whet your appetite for more of Italy. Let's take this trip and then come back soon.

PART 2

The Four Italys

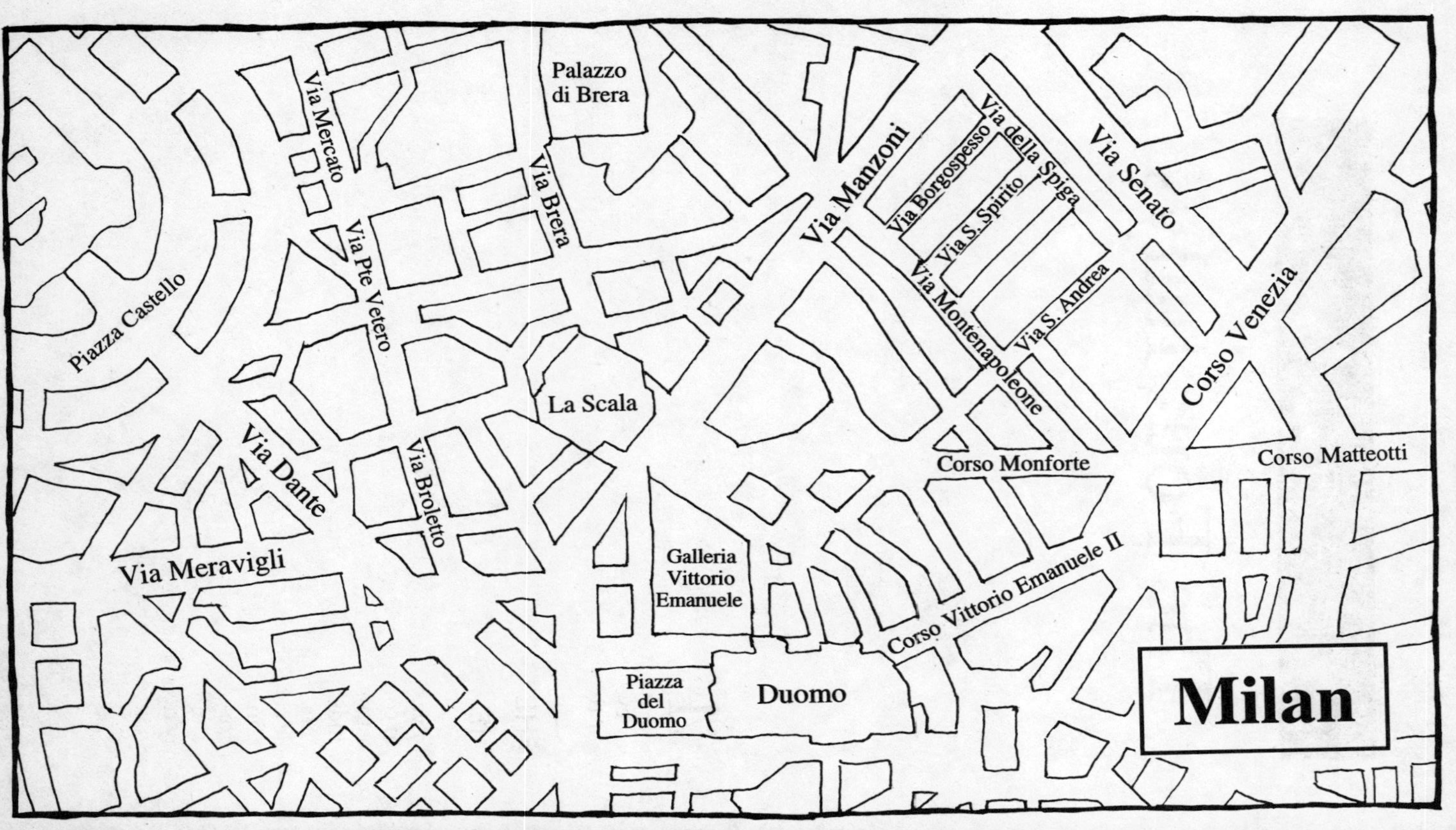
Milan
Palazzo di Brera
Via Mercato
Via Brera
Via Manzoni
Via Borgospesso
Via della Spiga
Via Senato
Via S. Spirito
Via Montenapoleone
Via S. Andrea
Corso Venezia
Piazza Castello
Via Pte Vetero
La Scala
Via Dante
Via Broletto
Corso Monforte
Corso Matteotti
Via Meravigli
Galleria Vittorio Emanuele
Corso Vittorio Emanuele II
Piazza del Duomo
Duomo

4

Milan

Maybe you've heard the negatives about Milan: a drab and ugly urban center; the least Italian of Italian cities; chaotic; very expensive; not much to see and do. You may even become the recipient of this sage advice: don't waste your time visiting Milan or at best spend a few hours there.

Where Have All The Tourists Gone?

We've heard the stories over and over again from individuals who come here for all the wrong reasons. Out of place in Italy's most important city, they're here to once again relive the past or indulge in typical European tourist pursuits: visit old monuments, churches, and museums, or soak up an easy-going lifestyle centered around lounging in sidewalk cafés and patronizing fine restaurants. Many are obsessed with experiencing more history, peeking into another Duomo, or standing in line for one more *"must see"* museum. If they can't satisfy such needs, they're off to another ostensibly more satisfying tourist destination.

Milan has all of these typical tourist attractions plus much much more for discriminating travelers in pursuit of unique Italian experiences. For typical tourism is not what Milan is all about. If you're bored with engaging is such tourist pursuits or tired of only encountering fellow tourists rather than real Italians, this city may just be what you've been waiting for. This is a real city engaged in productive commerce. While it welcomes tourists, it's not dependent on tourist dollars. It's a city of great talent, creativity, and vibrance, one that makes history today rather than preserves it for tourist crowds.

We especially like Milan and only hope you have enough time to experience its many unique treasures and pleasures.

EUROPE'S SHOPPING MECCA

Okay, Milan is an ugly city compared to Florence, Rome, or Venice. But perhaps such comparisons are unfair. After all, our three other Italian cities are exceptionally beautiful compared to most other cities in the world. And Milan can be a very expensive city, especially when it comes to hotels, restaurants, and upscale shopping. In fact, next to Venice, it's our most expensive city. Unfortunately, tourists come here in pursuit of typical tourist activities found in Florence, Venice, and Rome. Looking for more history and art, they judge Milan by what they experienced in these other cities. Most of these tourists are day-trippers who arrive in tour buses from which they may spend no more than three hours introducing themselves to the Milan's historical highlights. Few have time to experience Milan's major strength—shopping for fashion, accessories, jewelry, home decorative items, art, and antiques. While the list of Milanese delights goes on and on, most tourists miss it all by getting back on their buses and heading elsewhere—maybe north to Lake Como, east to Venice, or south to Florence, Pisa, or Rome. What a shame to have come all this way looking for the wrong type of history in all the wrong places.

- ❑ **Typical tourism is not what Milan is all about.**
- ❑ **Milan is a city of great talent, creativity, and vibrance, one that makes history today rather than preserves it for the tourist crowds.**
- ❑ **Banking and commerce reign supreme here.**
- ❑ **Milan is all about shopping for the best of the best that Italy has to offer the world. It is the world's undisputed leader in fashion and design.**
- ❑ **Milan is Italy's premier shopping city for serious shoppers rather than souvenir collectors.**

Primarily concerned with the present and future, Milan is a hard working and bustling city noted for its elegance, class, and creativity. Banking and commerce reign supreme here. But the city also offers some terrific art, culture, museums, monuments, and history. After all, this is a city with a 2,500 year history. Above all, Milan is Italy's and Europe's shopping mecca. If this city is about anything, it's all about shopping for the best of the best that Italy has to offer the world.

Don't let anyone convince you to skip this city or only spend a few hours here. Milan may not have the heady profusion of art, architecture, history, museums, churches, and monuments of Florence and Rome, the unique beauty of Venice, nor the easy-going lifestyle of its southern brethern, but it has much more to offer when it comes to contemporary design, clothing, and accessories. Milan simply is the world's undisputed leader in fashion and design. Paris, London, and New York may have an impact on the fashion world, but Milan is where the action is. If you are interested in shopping for top quality clothes and accessories designed by the world's leading designers (Armani, Versace, Gucci, Prada), put Milan at the top of your list of *"must visit"* places in Italy; it doesn't get any better for quality shopping. Plan to spend a few days in Milan exploring the beauty of contemporary Italy. While you will also have an opportunity to explore major historical sites, such as the Duomo (second largest after St. Peter's in Rome), La Scala (world's most famous opera house), and Santa Maria delle Grazie (home for Leonardo da Vinci's *The Last Supper*), plan to acquaint yourself with ancient and 16th and 17th century Italian history and culture in those other cities where you can spend hours visiting museums, churches, monuments, and ruins representing a once glorious Roman, Venetian, and Florentine history.

Milan's history is in the making, from 1975 to the present, a period in which Milan emerged as the world's fashion and design leader. This is Italy's premier shopping city for serious shoppers rather than souvenir collectors.

GETTING THERE

You can get to Milan by road, rail, and air. Indeed, all major roads connect to Milan, and all major cities in European are linked to the city by rail.

International air connections to Milan are the most convenient for any city in Italy. If you're flying from abroad, you may want to start your Italian adventure in Milan since numerous international flights go directly into Milan. United Airlines, for example, flies directly from the United States into Rome and then proceeds on to Milan after a one hour stopover. We prefer starting in Milan and then proceeding on to Florence, Venice, and Rome by rail or road.

AIRPORT ARRIVAL

Milan has a very well organized and efficient international airport, moreso than in Rome. The baggage retrieval and Immigration lines are so efficient that we are usually in and out of the airport within 20 minutes.

AIRPORT EXCHANGE

You may want to change just enough money at the airport to get into town. The airport exchange office gives a lower rate than many banks plus it charges a 5,000 lira commission per transaction. The exchange rate for cash and traveler's checks is the same—1578 lira per dollar (official exchange rate at the time was 1610; shopkeepers use 1600 when converting from lira to dollars). Some banks in Milan, near the Duomo and Galleria, should give better rates and do not charge commissions. However, many banks give similar rates and charge the same commissions as the airport exchange office. Thus, you may find it most convenient to exchange more money at the airport.

AIRPORT SERVICES

Just after leaving Customs you will enter the arrival hall that includes several convenient services. Here you will find the major car rental companies with offices for arranging a rental car: Hertz, Avis, Budget, Dollar, and Europcar. The Exchange office is also here but located at the end of the corridor. The bus office also is located here. You will need to go to this office to purchase bus tickets into Milan or for other locations.

AIRPORT TO CITY TRANSPORTATION

From the airport, you have three choices for getting into the city: take a taxi, rent a car, or board the bus. The taxi is most convenient as well as most expensive. Expect to pay about US$100 for the ride. You may not want to rent a car, unless you are very familiar with the city. The bus is the least expensive—12,000 lira (US$7.50) per person. The bus departs every 30 to 45 minutes and is located just outside the terminal door, to your right. You will see the sign saying "Milano." Wait in the queue until the bus arrives. This is an air-conditioned bus similar to the tour buses. You load your own luggage underneath where there is plenty of room for all your luggage. The bus takes you to the central train station where you then get a taxi to your hotel. The bus normally stops at the taxi stand. Depending on where your hotel is located, the taxi (Mercedes Benz station wagon) costs between 8,000 and 20,000 lira, with additional charges for luggage). The trip from the airport to the central station takes about 45 minutes, depending on the traffic situation. The problem is that at least half the trip is through congested narrow city streets.

GETTING TO KNOW YOU

An immensely creative and purposeful city, Milan is all about business, commerce, banking, industry, and exporting contemporary Italian culture to other cities and countries. It's Italy's economic powerhouse, where deals are cut and where enormous amounts of money exhange hands.

Situated in the Lombardy region of northern Italy, Milan is located by rail or road just three hours north of Florence and 40 minutes south of Lake Como, Milan's textile center and a popular resort area. Italy's second largest city of over 2 million people, Milan looks and feels unlike any other city in Italy. An old city dating from 600 B.C., it was severely bombed during World War II. While some old buildings remain, especially the impressive Duomo and La Scala opera house, Milan was essentially rebuilt in the aftermath of World War II as Italy's major commercial and industrial city.

If you're looking for beautiful and impressive old architecture, as found in many other Italian cities, you won't find much of it in Milan. Ironically, Milan's steller reputation for being the world's leading fashion and design center, with architects playing a major role, is not well reflected in the city's exterior architecture. Milan is a relatively drab looking city of dark stone buildings and trams that are not particularly charming.

The beauty of Milan is found elsewhere, at the Duomo, inside La Scala and the Galleria Vittorio Emmanuele, and especially in its numerous shops, boutiques, and art galleries where interior architecture tends to triumph. This is a working city that attracts thousands of foreign business people with their hefty expense accounts to the city's numerous upscale hotels, restaurants, and shops. It's a city where major international trade fairs and fashion shows constantly take place. It's where leading designers showcase their latest fashions on the catwalks and in exclusive boutiques that attract worldwide attention, from Tokyo to New York, and set the trends for billion dollar industries. It's also a highly cultured city committed to achieving the best of the best in the arts. Many of its successful business people also are major supporters of the arts, with the La Scala opera house leading the way. Indeed, when La Scala opens its season every December 7th, it becomes an important national cultural event that gets covered in all Italian newspapers as well as in the major foreign media. It's as if Milan becomes Europe's cultural center for one day. And Milan is even where public scandals touch some of Milan's major business leaders, patrons of the arts, and houses of fashion.

Unlike many other Italian cities, you'll find fewer tourists in Milan, and those that do come are often day-trippers stopping for only a few hours to visit the Duomo and do some quick shopping. Best of all, in Milan you actually encounter Italians!

Make no mistake about it, Milan can be an expensive city. This is in large part due to the heavy emphasis on international business and trade and the resulting disproportionate number of quality hotels, restaurants, and shops found in this city. Don't expect to find many bargains in Milan, although you will find a few factory outlets and good sales during the month of January. Remember, the emphasis in Milan is on quality, and top quality goods and services do indeed cost more than those of average or mediocre quality. This is literally the city where you can *"shop 'til you drop"* as long as you have lots of money to afford its many high class treasures.

- ❑ **Don't expect to find many bargains in Milan. The emphasis here is on quality.**
- ❑ **Milan grows on you after a day or two. It may well become one of your favorite Italian cities.**
- ❑ **You can easily get to the major sites and shopping areas on foot if you choose a centrally located hotel.**
- ❑ **Start your Milan adventure at the Piazza del Duomo. Most major shopping areas are within a 10-15 minute walk from here.**

Milan has its own unique mix of treasures and pleasures. Unfortunately, many travelers avoid Milan altogether or spend only one or two days. That's unfortunate. Unlike Florence, Rome, and Venice which immediately speak to you as inviting cities to spend a few days exploring, the treasures and pleasures of Milan are less immediately apparent. As many travelers quickly discover, Milan grows on you after a day or two. It may well become one of your favorite Italian cities. If you enjoy shopping as well as seeing the sights, we recommend spending at least three days in Milan—preferably five. You'll need at least three days to do basic shopping and sightseeing within the city. Another day or two can be well spent by driving or taking a train north to Lake Como which functions as both a resort and a textile production center for the clothing factories in Milan. There you will discover some wonderful silk products and leather goods to complement your wardrobe as well as purchase as gifts items. If you drive, you'll be able to stop at a few factory outlets along the way.

The Streets of Milan

Milan is Italy's second largest city with over 2 million people, but it is a relatively easy city to navigate. While it has an efficient subway and tram system, and taxis are plentiful, you can easily get to the major sites and shopping areas on foot if you choose a centrally located hotel. Most places you'll want to visit are within a 15 to 30 minute walk or a short taxi, tram, or subway ride away.

The city is laid out into three concentric circles. The circle at the center will be of most interest to you since this is where most of the major restaurants, hotels, shops, and attractions are found. At the center of this circle is the Piazza del Duomo, Milan's largest piazza and Italy's second largest Duomo after St. Peter's at the Vatican in Rome. It's the central city landmark from which to locate most other areas of the city.

We highly recommend starting your Milan adventure at the **Piazza del Duomo**. From there you can walk to most major shopping areas and sites which are within a 10-15 minute walk.

Shopping Times

Shopping hours in Milan tend to more liberal than in other parts of Italy. Most shops are closed on Sundays, Monday mornings, and bank holidays. Most shops are open during weekdays from 9-12:30 and from 4pm-7:30pm, although times may vary. Many shops in the upscale shopping areas stay open during lunch. Department stores in the old part of the city do not close for lunch. Since Sunday is usually dead, you may want to visit Como (40 minutes north of Milan) much of which tends to stay open on Sunday.

What to Buy

Milan offers numerous shopping choices. A city noted for high fashion, shop after shop offer exquisite **designer clothes and accessories**. All the big names are either headquartered or maintain major boutiques here: Armani, Celine, Etro, Fendi, Ferragamo, Gianfranco Ferré, Gucci, Krizia, Max Mara, Moschino, Prada, Trussardi, Ungano, Valentino, Gianni Versace, Ermenegildo Zegna. And they all tend to congregate along three adjacant upscale shopping streets: Via della Spiga, Via Montenapoleone, and Via Sant' Andrea, Milan's famous "Golden Triangle."

Milan also is well noted for its fine **jewelry**. Milan's famous jewelers, Mario Buccellati (Via Montenapoleone 4) and Federico Buccellati (Via della Spiga 22), produce some of the world's finest jewelry designs. Other shops, such as Maria Grazia Baldan (Via Tivoli 6) and Rosana Rossi (Via della Spiga 2), produce chic and trendy one-of-a-kind jewelry. A few shops even offer ethnic jewelry (Il Discanto, Via Turati 7). You'll find numerous jewelry shops along Milan's major shopping streets, especially Via Turati. For a wide selection of jewelry at reasonable prices, try Noello at Via Mazzini 10. Be forewarned that many of Milan's jewelry shops may seem intimidating because of the electronic security systems you'll need to pass through to gain entrance. Once you're in, you should get special attention.

Be sure to look for **arts and antiques**. Milan abounds with fine art galleries representing some of Italy's top artists as well as antique shops. Most are found along the major streets in the Brera area, such as Galleria Ponte Rosso (Milano Via Brera 2) and Sil Segno Galleria d'Arte (Via Dell 'Orso 1).

Milan is especially noted as Italy's **furniture** capital. Some of the most innovative and trendy furniture designs, expressive of Milan's strong architectural design tradition, come from numerous studios in Milan. However, be forewarned that the designs have a decided Italian and European look which may not fit well into non-European home decors. Many of these studios also are found in the Brera area.

Milan also is famous for its exquisite **textiles and fabrics**. Most of the fabrics are produced in the Lake Como area (2 hours north of Milan) but available in several fabric shops in Milan. Stop by Al Biano e Nero (Corso Venezia 7/1) or Galtrucco (Piazza Duomo 2), for example, and you'll be introduced to a fabulous world of quality Italian fabrics.

You'll also find several unique shops offering **candles** (Candele Mum Milano, Via Fiori Chiari 16), **tableware** (Point à la Ligne, Via Monazoni 41/a), **Asian imports** (Oltrefrontiera, Via San Carpoforo 6, and Oro Incenso e Mirra, Via San Fermo 15), **linens** (Pratesi, Via Montenapoleone 21), **Venetian glass** (I Lirice, Via Montenapoleone 9), and a wide assortment of unusual **home decorative items**, both Italian and imported (10 Corso Como, Corso Como 10).

WHERE TO SHOP

While Milan is a relatively large city, its major shopping areas are well defined and within close proximity to one another. For shoppers, this is a relatively small city. You can easily cover the major shopping areas on foot within a two to three day period.

Most of the major shops will be found along the streets adjacent to as well as north and northeast of the Piazza del Duomo. These areas are known as Montenapoleone/Spiga, Brera, and Duomo/Vittorio Emanuele.

MONTENAPOLEONE/SPIGA AREA

Milan's premier shopping area lies directly northeast of the Piazza del Duomo. Sometimes referred to as Milan's "Golden Triangle," but actually forming almost a perfect rectangle, this area is noted for three major streets which are lined with Europe's most upscale shops: Via Montenapoleone, Via della Spiga, and Via Sant' Andrea. Additional streets in this area also yield numerous fine shops: Via Borgospesso, Via Verri, and Corso Venezia. This is where you will find Italy's major designer boutiques and jewelers. Shop after shop display the latest fashions and exquisite jewelry designs. This area is to Milan what Rodeo Drive is to Hollywood and Rue du Faubourg-St.-Honoré and Avenue Montaigne are to Paris. Yes, you can *"shop 'til you drop"* here as long as you have enough money to survive the area. Come here in the early evening and the streets are packed with upscale shoppers and Japanese tourists in search of Italy's name brand products.

- **Shopping hours in Milan tend to more liberal than in other parts of Italy.**
- **Milan's "Golden Triangle" for shopping consists of three adjacent streets lined with upscale shops—Via della Spiga, Via Montenapoleone, and Via Sant'Andrea.**
- **Via Montenapoleone is Italy's premier shopping street. It's elegant, it's expensive, and it's literally in-your-face with gorgeous fashion, accessories, jewelry, and home decorative items.**
- **The Lake Como area,two hours by train from Milan, is the center for textile production. Plan to visit there on Sunday when most shops in Milan are closed.**

We prefer starting our shopping adventure in this area along Via della Spiga, a narrow pedestrian walkway which you can enter from the main street, Via Manzoni. From here, walk southeast along Via della Spiga until you come to the intersection with Corso Venezia, turn right and walk one block until you come to Via Montenapoleone (this area is a little confusing; you actually need to go one short block beyond Via Bagutta; Via Montenapoleone actually intersects with Corso Matteotti which is connected to Corso Venezia). If you walk northwest along Via Montenapoleone and explore a few side streets on your right (Sant' Andrea, Gesu, Spirito, Borgospesso) and one to your left (Verri), you will have covered most of the shops in this highly concentrated shopping area. You'll recognize some of the big names, such as Gucci, Missoni, Louis Vuitton, Valentino, and Ungano, but you'll discover numerous relatively unknown but high quality boutiques offering attractive fashions and accessories. This whole area screams "Italian style" which Milan is so well noted for, although you'll find a few French boutiques, especially along Via Sant' Andrea. Expect to spend at least two to three hours just surveying this area. You'll probably want to return to do more serious shopping which may take hours to complete. Be forewarned that this little shopping foray may forever change your view of quality shopping! Moreover, this area may be dangerous to your financial health.

Let's start with Via della Spiga, entering from Via Manzoni which is just south of Piazza Cavour. This is a rather tame entrance into what will become a glittering shopping experience as you get closer to Via Montenapoleone. Several small boutiques line this narrow walkway. You'll immediately see **Letichetta Boutique** (Via della Spiga 50, Tel. 782078) on your left which offers attractive women's jackets and sweaters in wonderful styles and colors. Nearby is our favorite Italian shop for leathergoods, **Ruffo** (Via della Spiga 48, Tel. 76015523). Produced in their factory in Pisa, the styling and quality of leather jackets, coats, shoes, and accessories here are outstanding. While Ruffo has a showroom in Pisa and exports many of their products throughout Europe and North America, this shop is the only Ruffo retail outlet in the world. Be sure to visit the lower level as well as their women's shop next door. You may find something here you can't live without to the tune of US$1500 to $2500.

Several other nice shops line both sides of Via della Spiga. Especially noteworthy are **Byblos** (#42), **Kirzia** (#23), **Gianfranco Ferré** (#11/13), **Fendi** (#9), **Bottega Venta** (#5), **Gianni Versace** (#4), and **Prada** (#1/5).

Via Spiga also is home to two nice jewelry shops. **Frederico Buccellati** (Via Spiga 22) is one of Italy's premier jewelers. You'll see a few showcases in the tall vertical windows downstairs, but you'll need to go to the second floor to visit the showroom. While the shop has very little inventory on display, you will see a few exquisite gold and silver necklaces, bracelets, and rings that have made the Buccellati name so world famous. The small and intricate designs and attention to detail is remarkable—the hallmark of the Buccellati name. Prices are very high but the quality and craftsmanship is simply unequalled except perhaps in another Buccellati shop operated by other members of this family. You'll encounter Buccellati shops in Rome, Paris, Monaco, London, New York, Tokyo, Hong Kong, and other major cities. At the very end of Via della Spiga, near the corner with Corso Venezia, is a relatively new jewelry shop called **Rossana Rossi** (Via della Spiga 2). Located in a small shopping arcade and entered through a vault door, this shop offers unique one-of-a-kind jewelry pieces (earrings, necklaces, bracelets, rings) which mix old—some of them excavated pieces—and new pieces of different materials. These are truly contemporary fashionable works of art. If you're looking for something unusual, be sure to stop by Rossana Rossi.

Now that you are at the end of Via della Spiga, turn right onto Corso Venezia. You'll want to walk south for a block until you reach Via Montenapoleone. Along the way you'll see a few nice shops worth visiting. The first is **Al Bianco e Nero** (also under the name **Valli**, Corso Venezia, 7/1, Tel. 76001986) which is filled from floor to ceiling with some of the most gorgeous fabrics you'll ever see! This is the shop that can quickly educate you about quality Italian fabrics. They have everything here: silk, wool, velvets, beaded laces, and Boucle wools. The designs and colors are simply outstanding. Just a few doors away is **Sorelle Negri** (Corso Venezia 5, San Babila, Tel. 76001786), a small shop offering beautiful women's robes and lingerie. Next door is a small jewelry shop offering some very nice designs, **Grimoldi** (Corso Venezia 5, San Babila, Tel. 76005673).

The entrance into Via Montenapoleone from Corso Venezia is a bit confusing because of two intersecting streets. If you're not careful, you can get lost here. As soon as you come to the corner, which is the intersection of Piazza San Babila, you'll see Via Bagutta on your right. If you turn right onto this street, you'll go to Via Sant' Andrea, another major shopping street in this area. At this point you'll need to take a left which takes you directly to Via Montenapoleone. Most of the shopping is found to your right. However, it's best to turn right at Piazza San Babilo onto Corso Matteotti. Within a minute you'll come to the southeast entrance of Via Montenapoleone. Now you can cover the whole dazzling street.

Via Montenapoleone is Italy's premier shopping street. It's elegant, it's expensive, and it's literally in-your-face from the moment you step into this street until you leave it at the other end. Shop after shop line both sides of this classy street offering the latest in high fashions, accessories, jewelry, and home decorative items. But it's fashions and accessories that dominate this street. Here you'll find the exclusive boutiques of **Salvatore Ferragamo** (#3), **Gucci** (#2-5—be sure to go to the basement level where the action is and which encompasses three full shops), **Benetton** (#13), **Etro** (#5), **Genny** (#8), **Mila Schön** (#2), **Louis Vuitton** (#14), **Gerano, A. Testoni, Valentino** (#10), **Beltrami** (#16), **Nazareno Gabrielli** (#23), **Celine, Ungano** (#27), **Mortarotti** (#24), and **Gianni Versace** (#11).

For jewelry, be sure to stop at **Mario Buccellati, Tiffany and Co., Rolex**, and **Cartier**. But it's Mario Buccellati, at the corner of Via Sant' Andrea and Via Montenapoleone, that stands out along this street with its unique jewelry designs and silver animal figures. This store has the most gorgeous window displays we have ever seen—anywhere. The beauty of the window as a whole, as well as the individual items in it, literally stopped us in our tracks. The Buccellatis are truly goldsmiths who do the most beautiful things we've encountered with precious metals. The mounted stones become an elegant accompaniment to the incredible work in gold.

Other fine shops to look for along this street are **Pratesi** (#27) for beautiful linens, **I Lirice** (#27E) for fine quality Venetian glass, **Giorgetti** (at Santo Spirito) for furniture, and **Pontremoli** for antiques.

Via Sant' Andrea, a small street which connects Via Spiga to Via Montenapoleone, is another major shopping street in this area. Here you'll find lots of big name Italian and French boutiques: **Missoni** (#2), **Trussardi** (#5), **Giorgio Armani** (#9), **Chanel** (#10), **Kenzo** (#11), **Moschina** (#12), **Prada** (#21), and **Hermès** (#21).

BRERA AREA

The Brera area lies immediately to the west of the famous La Scala Opera House, which is a few minutes walk northwest of the Piazza del Duomo. This older section of the city, with its narrow meandering cobblestone streets and aging buildings, has numerous art, antique, furniture, jewelry, home decorative shops, boutiques, and quaint restaurants. Often referred to as Milan's Greenwich Village, the whole area has an artistic and bohemian feel to it. It's the type of area you may want to just enter and aimlessly walk around for a few hours discovering various shops, cafés, restaurants, and music clubs. Much of this action centers around the Brera Art Gallery (Pinacoteca di Brera) at Via Brera 28. It's a very different shopping experience from the upscale and high fashion Montenapoleone/Spiga area.

It also tends to be somewhat overrated and at times a disappointing shopping experience. Nonetheless, let's take a quick tour that primarily focuses on three major shopping streets in Brera.

The main street in the Brera area is **Via Brera** which is reached by entering Via G. Verdi, just to the right of La Scala Opera House. As you walk north along this street, you'll cross Via Dell'Oroso and pass by several art galleries showcasing the works of Italian artists. If you turn left onto Via Dell'Oroso, you'll soon come to one of Milan's fine art galleries, **Sil Segno Galleria d'Arte** (Via Dell'Orso 1, Tel. 877231) which showcases the oil paintings and sculptures of two major Milanese artists, Domenico Colanzi and Giorgia Guarini. The works here are expensive but the quality is superb, especially Colanzi's bronze sculptures. Next door is **La Galleria del Tempo** for large architectural pieces (columns, fireplaces, mantles, tables, light fixtures, marble tops). **Blackout** (Via Dell'Orso 7) offers a large assortment of lamps and lighting fixtures from Milan's major designers. We're not particularly drawn to such modern designs, although others may find something attractive here.

If you return to Via Brera and turn left, you'll immediately come to several art galleries. One of the largest and most comprehensive is **Galleria Ponte Rosso** at Via Brera 2 (Tel. 86461053). Encompassing two shops and displaying paintings and sculptures on two levels, this gallery includes the works of nearly 50 artists who mostly work in oils. Look for two other smaller art galleries in the same block: **Galleria Brera 3** (across the street; very modern art deco paintings and prints) and **Gallera d'Arte Il Castello** (Via Brera 16).

Walking just a few minutes north you'll come to Via Fiori Chiari, a narrow cobblestone pedestrian walkway. If you turn left onto this street, you'll enter a street lined with several nice art, antique, and home decorative shops. Our favorite here is **Candele Mum Milana** (Via Fiori Chiari 16, Tel. 878906). This small shop is literally a candle boutique. The owner produces some of the most attractive sculptured (column tops) one-of-a-kind candles we have ever encountered. The small and medium-sized candles, which burn from 300 to 600 hours, make terrific center pieces for tables. The large multi-wicked candles are perfect for gardens. Prices start at 85,000 lira and go up. The shop currently offers 21 different models to choose from. Unfortunately, most of the candles are too big to put in your suitcase. But the shop is experienced in packing and shipping abroad.

At the end of Via Fiori Chiari you either turn left or right. Most shops are located to the left along Via Madonnina. Here you will find several trendy clothing and accessory shops and a few jewelry shops. Nearby is **Maria Grazia Baldan** (Via Tivoli 6, Tel. 86463559) who is famous for her unique and innovative jewelry designs which incorporate the old and new, precious and semiprecious stones, coral, enamel, gold, and silver. The shop just moved from its previous location along Via Fiori Chiari. Another unique shop in this area is **Oltrefrontiera** (Via San Carpoforo 6, Tel. 89010554) which offers imported furniture and home decorative items from India and Southeast Asia. The selections are excellent and provide affordable alternatives to Italian antiques which are outside most people's budget. Using the store's computer, you can even view what's available in their warehouse!

DUOMO/VITTORIO EMANUELE AREA

This is the most heavily touristed area of Milan, the area where the tour buses stop, where young people congregate, and where Milan's major sightseeing attraction is located—the Duomo, the multi-spiraled cathedral. Centered around the Piazzo del Duomo, this area encompasses the Galleria Vittorio Emanuele, the landmark glass cupola shopping arcade and several streets adjacent to the Piazza. Shopping here is a mixture of upscale shops, department stores, medium-priced street shops, and souvenir stores. The area abounds with restaurants, bars, and banks. It's also where you will find the popular La Scala Opera House and city's tourist office (Milan and District Tourist Board, Via Marconi 1, Tel. 809662).

- **The Brera area is Milan's Greenwich Village. It has an artistic and bohemian feel to it with quaint restaurants, shops, art galleries, cafés, and music clubs.**
- **The Duomo and Galleria Vittorio Emanuele area is the most heavily touristed area of Milan. It's a mixed shopping area.**
- **You actually can find a few bargains in Milan, but they're mainly found in the markets and shops located along the canals and in factory outlet shops outside Milan.**

Shoppers normally head directly for the **Galleria Vittorio Emanuele**, the grand shopping arcade located just north of the Piazza del Duomo. This four-storey arcade with its colorful mosaic floor is a popular shopping, dining, and people-watching center. However, the shopping is somewhat disappointing. It includes a mixture of bookstores, jewelry shops, boutiques, and several shops primarily catering to tourists. The most famous shop here is **Prada** which offers a wide selection of women's leather goods, from handbags to luggage, sweaters, and coats. It also has a small men's section. Be sure to visit the basement level where most of the Prada line is found. The first floor only displays a few handbags and walking sticks. You'll also find

Rizzoli, Italy's premier bookstore, here in the arcade. This particular branch is their flagship store. The shopping arcade also has a fine silver shop, **Bernasconi**, located in the middle of the arcade, directly across from Burghy and directly in front of the famous mosaic bull figure on the floor (a daily parade of visitors step on its testicles to give them good luck). This large shop offers an excellent selection of silver items in traditional designs—serving trays, figures, and picture frames—as well as gold, silver, and pearl jewelry. Prices are displayed on everything in the window. For a delightful food shop brimming with all types of goodies, stop at **Motta** which is located just outside the entrance and facing the Duomo. The best restaurant with the best view of the shopping arcade, **La Galleria Restaurant**, is located upstairs. Go through the food shop to get there.

The streets adjacent to the Piazzo del Duomo are lined with shops, many of which primarily cater to tourists. Just to the north of the Duomo is **Rocco**, a large and very nice jewelry shop offering a wide selection of jewelry, watches, and decorative pieces. Be sure to visit the lower level where you will find several quality decorative pieces. In the next block you'll find **La Rinascenter**, Milan's oldest department store. Its six floors are jammed-packed with typical department store products, few of which may appeal to you. The café on the top floor, **Cento Guglie**, puts you in front of the Duomo.

On the other side of the Piazzo is one of Milan's oldest yard goods stores, **Galtrucco** (Piazza del Duomo 2, Tel. 876256). For more than 120 years Galtrucco has supplied some of the finest quality fabrics to Milan's tailors and seamtresses. You'll find cottons, silks, and wools in a large variety of colors, patterns, and designs. The shop also does tailoring work as well as offers ready-to-wear clothes for both men and women. Be sure to go to the basement level where you'll find the ready-to-wear sections.

Just around the corner from Galtrucco, along Via Mazzini, are two shops worth visiting. **Noello** (Via Mazzini 10, Tel. 861330) is one of the most unique jewelry shops in Italy with its wide selection of jewelry in a variety of price ranges. Their attractive window displays with prices clearly labeled on each item tend to draw curious crowds. Based in Torino, the shop seems to have something for everyone: jewelry, silver tableware and serving pieces, watches, beaded necklaces, loose stones, diamonds, Japanese coral, Indian neckpieces, and cultured and natural pearls. The prices appear reasonable. Further down the street is Milan's oldest glove shop, **El Guanto Perfector** (18 Mazzini, Tel. 875894), established more than 100 years ago. And it looks it. This is literally a hole in the wall shop, extremely worn and tired after 100 years. While they don't have much on display and the personnel are not particularly helpful, you can get good buys here on leather gloves if you know what you're doing. However, you need to know what you're doing—know what gloves you want and ask the right questions. The shop is well stocked once you ask for specific items. It is definitely not for browsing.

The rest of this area has numerous shops lining the streets. Our recommendation: cruise the streets like the rest of the crowd; stop for a gelato or cappuccino; do some people watching; and enjoy the festive atmosphere of this area. If you don't shop much here, you'll at least have a cultural experience.

OTHER AREAS

Milan abounds with shopping opportunities nearby these three shopping areas as well as in other sections of the city. If you walk between these areas by way of **Via Manzoni**, which connects the Brera area with the Montenapoleone/Spiga area (between La Scala Opera House and Piazza Covour), you'll pass several nice jewelry and home decorative shops. Further north of Piazza Covour is **Via Turati** which also includes jewelry and clothing stores. One of our favorite shops along this street is a very small ethnic jewelry store, **Il Discanto** (Via Turati 7, Tel. 29003557), which offers beautiful neckpieces. The same owner, Mrs. Frossi Giovanna, has a newer and much larger and more attractive shop, **Oro Incenso e Mirra** (Via San Fermo 15, Tel. 6554492). It offers ethnic jewelry, textiles, and decorative items and is located within 15 minutes walking distance of her first shop.

Another unique and popular shop located outside the major shopping areas is **10 Corso Como** (Corso Como 10, Tel. 29002674). Basically an eclectic lifestyle shop offering unusual items, from garden candles to designer jewelry and black clothes, this expansive shop is designed to unfold like a fashion magazine. If you're interested in an unusual shopping experience, complete with whimsical products and retailing concepts, and you have extra time, this place may be worth visiting.

If time permits, you may want to explore a few of these shopping streets :

- ❑ **Via Durini:** Located within a 10 minute walk directly east of the Piazza del Duomo, this north-south street connects with Via Borgogna and Via Cavali which, in turn, connects to Largo Augusto. Only one block in length, this street includes several upscale fashion and accessory shops such as Giorgio Armani's **Emporio Armani** (#24), **Nimus Museumshop** (#23), and **Mh Way** for fashions and accessories; **Cassina** (#18) for international design goods; and **Joaquin Berao** (#5) for unique jewelry.

- ❑ **Corso Buenosaires:** Located northwest of the Duomo, between Piazzale Oberdan and Piazzale Loreto, this one mile stretch of road is lined with numerous neighborhood shops primarily appealing to local residents. You'll find better prices in this area, but you may be more interested in the cultural experience than to do serious shopping amongst the locals.

- ❑ **Navigli:** Located southwest of the Duomo and situated along a canal, this colorful working class neighborhood in the process of regentrification offers numerous small boutiques, art shops, studios, secondhand shops, bars, cafés, and restaurants. Two key streets here line both sides of the canal: Alzaia Naviglio Grande on the north bank and Ripa di Porta Ticinese on the south bank. This area also hosts several outdoor markets.

- ❑ **Vercelli/Magenta:** Located just a short walk directly west of the Duomo, this upper class neighborhood boasts numerous upscale boutiques, cafés, restaurants, and popular tourist sites, such as Leonardo da Vinci's "Last Supper" and several churches, monuments, and gardens. Most shopping is found along Corso Vercelli.

Markets and Bargain Shopping

Despite Milan's reputation for being expensive and offering upscale shopping, you can still find a few bargains here. Some of the best bargains are found in the markets and shops located along the canals as well as in factory outlets located outside Milan, especially in the Lake Como area.

Milan has several markets that offer interesting shopping experiences, from fruits, vegetables, and flowers to clothes, fabrics, antiques, collectibles, and lots of junk. Most of these markets are held on different days and in different parts of the city. The best such markets include:

- ❑ **Viale Papiniano:** Tuesday and Saturday mornings.

- ❑ **Largo Quinto Alpini:** Friday mornings.

- **Piazza Mirabello:** Mondays and Thursdays.

- **Fierra di Sinigallia:** In Viale Gabriele D'Annunzio along the Darsena canal harbour. A Saturday flea market with second-hand goods.

- **Brera area:** An upscale flea market held every third Saturday of the month between piazza Formentini and Via Fiori Oscuri.

- **Navigli ("canals") area:** A popular flea market held the last Sunday of each month (8am to 2pm). Located from Porta Ticinese to Porta Génova and the Viale Papiniano.

- **Mercatone dell'Antiquariato:** An antiques fair held the last Sunday of every month except July and August at the Alzaia Naviglio Grande. Includes curios and some valuable antiques

- **Bollate area:** This Sunday antiques market is located in the northern section of the city. Dealers offer lots of furniture, collectibles, and junk.

MAJOR ATTRACTIONS

There's lots to see and do in Milan besides shopping, people watching, eating, and sleeping. Given Milan's long and rich history, it offers numerous sightseeing and cultural opportunities. In fact, Milan prides itself on being one of Italy's leading cultural and artistic centers, boasting excellent churches, museums, and palaces.

THE CATHEDRAL (DUOMO)

For many visitors to Milan, the Duomo is the city's major attraction and its main historical symbol. Standing majestically in vertical exaggeration at the center of the city, the towering Duomo dominates the Piazzo del Duomo and is the historic symbol of the city. The world's second largest cathedral (after St. Peters in Rome), the Duomo is one of the most radical (some might say "outrageous," "gaudy," or "tasteless") Gothic cathedrals ever constructed. The construction statistics alone tell an impressive story: 157 meters long and 92 meters wide; covers an area of 11,700 square meters; includes 2245 white marble statues; 135 marble spires, 96 gargoyles, miles of traceryl; and crowned with a statue of the Virgin Mary, also known as the "Madonnina," which reaches the height of 108.5 meters and is covered with 3,900 leaves of gold. Begun in 1386 and completed in 1809, today the Duomo draws hundreds of visitors each day who stand in awe of such a gingerbread construction feat. The inside boasts 52 columns that stretch nearly to the top of the 48 meter ceiling. The cathedral has the capacity to seat 40,000 worshipers and claims to have the tallest stained glass windows in the world. Inside you'll pass the imposing marble tomb of **Gian Giacomo de Medici**, a 16th century notable. For a great roof-top view of the piazza and the white marble pinnacles of the Duomo, take the elevator (7,000 lira) or staircase (5,000 lira) to the top. The entrance to the top is on the north (left) side of the Duomo. You also may want to visit the 4th century ruins of the **Baptistry of San Giovanni alle Fonti** (also known as the Baptistry of Sant'Ambrogio), an underground area which is entered through the door on the left of the main entrance. The **Duomo Museum** is located just across the piazza in the Royal Palace.

Galleria Vittorio Emanuele II

If you've been shopping, you've already been to the "Galleria." Like the Duomo, you simply can't miss this imposing and opulent four-storey structure. Located immediately to the north of the Piazza del Duomo, this 19th century (built between 1865 and 1877) structure, complete with an attractive glass cupola, literally connects the Duomo with the La Scala Theater. Laid out as a cross with an octagon of iron and glass in the middle, the Galleria is 196 meters long, 105 meters wide, and 47 meters tall at its highest point. You'll find numerous shops and restaurants here as well as lots of people traversing this relatively open structure. Great place for people watching.

La Scala

Located just southwest of the Galleria at the Piazza della Scala, **Teatro alla Scala**, or simply **La Scala**, is the world-renowned opera house. It has hosted all the greats, from Verdi and Maria Callas to today's finest opera singers and orchestra directors. Opera season begins December 7 and runs for six months. If you're planning to attend a performance during that time, be sure to get tickets well in advance and don't expect to get the best seats in the house (they're already gone). Gallery seats can be purchased for as little as 30,000 lira, but you may need binoculars to see the stage! The box office is open daily from noon to 7pm: Tel. 72003744. If you can't get a ticket in advance, go to the museum entrance where you may get lucky and purchase one of the 200 standing-room tickets that are made available 30 minutes before the performance. During the day you may want to visit the theater's small museum, **Museo Theatrale alla Scala** (open Monday through Saturday, 9am-noon and 2-6pm; May through October, Sundays from 9:30am-noon and 2:30-6pm).

CHURCHES

Milan has several churches in addition to the imposing Duomo. If you're into visiting churches, Milan will not disappoint you:

- ❑ **Sant'Ambrogio:** *Piazza Sant'Ambrogio 15.* Originally constructed in AD386, the basilica was reconstructed between the 9th and 11th centuries in its current Romanesque style which is typically found in Lombardy. Houses some of the city's most valuable religious art. Includes the crypt of St. Ambrose. Be sure to visit the Basilica Museum.

- ❑ **Santa Maria Delle Grazies:** *Piazza Santa Maria delle Grazie.* Constructed between 1463 and 1492, this impressive Gothic and Renaissance style church houses Leonardo da Vinci's *The Last Supper* and Donato Montorfano's *Crucifixion.* Undergoing restoration.

- ❑ **San Lorenzo:** *Corso di Porta Ticinese 39.* Originally constructed in the 4th and 5th centuries, and subsequently restored several times in different styles, this church includes numerous interesting architectural details: grand cupola, women's gallery, frescos, mosaics, and exterior columns from a 2nd century Roman temple.

- ❑ **San Simpliciano:** *Piazza delle Crociate 7.* Originially built in the late 4th century and subsequently reconstructed in Romanesque style in the 12th century, this basilica houses Ambrogio da Fossano's famous *Coronation of the Virgin.*

- ❑ **San Satiro:** *Via Speronari 3.* Located almost adjacent to the Piazza del Duomo, this church is famous for its Renaissance architecture and 11th century Lombard Romanesque bell tower.

MUSEUMS

You will find numerous art, historical and church museums throughout Milan. Most museums are open from 9am to 5:30pm, Tuesday through Saturday, and from 9am to 12:30pm on Sunday; most are closed on Monday. Museums usually charge an admissions fee which costs from 6,000 to 12,000 lira. If you are planning to visit several museums, you should consider purchasing a special discounted museum pass that costs 28,000 lira and allows you to visit eighteen museums over a six month period. The pass can be purchased at the Tourist Office (Azienda di Opromozione Turistica, or APT) adjacent to the Piazza del Duomo: 1 Via Marconi.

Some of Milan's major museums include:

ART MUSEUMS

- ❑ **Leonardo da Vinci's "The Last Supper":** *Piazza Santa Maria della Grazie, 4987588.* One of the most sought-after tourist sites in Milan. Leonardo da Vinci's fresco painting of *The Last Supper* on a wall of the refectory of Santa Maria delle Grazie monastery in 1495 has been sadly deteriorating ever since. Unfortunately for visitors, it is often closed because of on-going, and often controversial, reconstruction work.

- ❑ **The Ambrosiana Art Gallery (Pinacoteca Ambrosiana):** *Piazza Pio XI 2, Tel. 8645146.* Displays paintings from the 13th to the early 19th centuries. Includes works by Botticelli, Raphael, Tiepolo, Caravaggio, and Leonardo da Vinci.

- ❑ **Brera Art Gallery (Pinacoteca di Brera):** *Via Brera 28, Tel. 722631.* Includes numerous religious paintings acquired by the state at the end of the 18th century with the dissolution and closure of several religious orders and their churches. Also includes masterpieces by Italian artists painted between the 14th and 19th centuries. Highlights are Raphael's *Betrothal of the Virgin* (Room 22), Piero della Francesca's *Madonna With Saints and Angels* (Room 22), Mantegna's *Dead Christ* (Room 18), and Carrà's *Metaphysical Muse*.

- ❑ **The Poldi-Pezzoli Museum (Museo Poldi-Pezzoli):** *Via Monzoni 12, Tel. 794889.* Houses a large private art collection given to the city in 1879. Includes famous paintings (Pollaiolo's *Portrait of a Young Woman*), Persian carpets, terracottas, gold pieces, Murano glass, bronzes, and antique lace.

- **Modern Art Gallery (Civica Galleria d'Arte Moderna):** *Via Palestro 16, Tel. 76002819.* Exhibits important 19th century paintings by such noted artists as Marino Marini, Pelizza da Volpedo, Gino Rossi, Martini, Carrà, Marino, Morandi, Renoir, Matisse, Vuillard, Roualt, and Picasso. May still be closed for restoration.

- **Museum of Contemporary Art (Museo d'Arte Contemporanea):** *Piazza Duomo 12, Tel. 62361, ext. 3219.* Located on the second floor of the Royal Palace, this museum includes the works of several famous artists of the 1950's and 1960's: Boccioni, De Chirico, Sironi, Carrà, Martini, De Pisis, Morandi, Melotti, and Fontana. Also includes 40 works by 19th century European artists Kandisky, Picasso, and Klee.

- **The Fine Arts Society and Permanent Exhibition Center:** *Via Turati 34, Tel. 6551445.* Includes nearly 100 paintings, sculptures, and graphics from the early 1990s representing noted artists, such as Felice Casorati, Carlo Carrà, and Raffaele De Grada, and sculptors Umberto Milani, Pietro Cascella, and Floriano Bodini.

- **Francesco Messina Studio Museum** (Museo-Studio Francesco Messina): *Via Sisto 4A, Tel. 8690648.* Showcases the works of sculptor Francesco Messina.

- **Treccani Studio Museum (Museo-Studio Francesco Messina):** *Via Carlo Porta 5 (with the Corrente Foundation), Tel. 6572627.* Showcases Treccani's paintings, sculptures, and graphic works.

- **Castle Museums:** *Piazza Castello, Tel. 62083191.* A series of museums with collections of art antiquities, applied arts and engravings, and musical instruments.

HISTORY MUSEUMS

- **Municipal Archeological Museum (Civico Museo Archeologico):** *Corso Magenta 15, Tel. 86450665.* Offers a large collection of Greek, Roman, and Etruscan pottery and bronzes.

- **Municipal Museum of Milan (Civico Museo di Milano):** Via Sant'Andrea 6, Tel. 76006245. Showcases illustrations and paintings of the city's history, dating from the 17th to the early 20th century.

- **La Scala Theater Museum (Museo Teatrale alla Scala):** *Piazza Scala 2, Tel. 8053418.* Illustrates the development and history of this famous theater.

- **The Toy Museum (Museo del Giocattolo):** *Ripa di Porto Ticinese, Tel. 8322103.* An interesting collection of 19th and 20th century toys and games.

- **The Leonardo da Vinci Science and Technology Museum (Museo Nazionale della Scienza e dela Tecnica Leonardo da Vinci):** *Via San Vittore 21, Tel. 48010040.* This huge museum complex, housed in three buildings, illustrates the history of science and technology. Includes modern physics, optics, clock making, telecommunications, metallury, rail transport, naval science, paintings, and furniture.

- **Cinema Museum (Museo del Cinema):** *Palazzo Dugnani, Via Manin 2/B, Tel. 6554977.* Includes exhibits illustrating the period before the invention of motion-pictures (use of magic lanterns, daguerrotypes, and phenakistoscopes) as well as the origin and development of the cinema.

- **Municipal Aquarium and Hydrobiology Center (Acquario Civico):** *Via Gadio 2, Tel. 86462051.* Includes 38 tanks displaying both freshwater and saltwater species.

- **Municipal Natural History Museum (Museo Civico di Storia Naturale):** *Corso Venezia 55, Tel. 62084505.* Includes a large collection of insects, birds, minerals, and fossils, including a life-size reconstruction of a Triceratops (dinosaur).

CHURCH MUSEUMS

- **The Cathedral Museum (Museo del Duomo):** *Piazza del Duomo 14, Tel. 860358.* Located across the piazza in the Royal Palace (Palazzo Reale) where the Museum of Contemporary Art (Museo d'Arte Contemporanea) is also housed, this newly renovated museum includes exhibits illustrating the construction, as well as the reconstruction, of this massive and intricately designed cathedral.

- **The Museum of the Basilica of Sant'Ambrogio (Museo della Basilica di Sant'Ambrogio):** *Piazza Sant' Ambrogio, Tel. 86450895.* Offers a collection of artifacts illustrating the history of the Basilica. Includes the crypt of Saint Ambrose and two paintings by Bernardino Luini.

- **The Museum of the Basilica of Santa Maria della Passione (Museo della Basilica di Santa Maria della Passione):** *Via Conservatorio 16, Tel. 76021370.* Includes ornaments, vestments, and paintings illustrating the rich artistic tradition of Milan's second largest church.

ACCOMMODATIONS

Since Milan is a major center for business and commerce, hotels in Milan tend to cater to the business crowd and the numerous trade fairs that are held in this city each year. You'll find elegant five-star luxury hotels along with several five and four star hotels that represent some of the finest hotels in all of Italy.

Hotels in Milan are classified as five-star luxury (★★★★★L), five-star (★★★★★), four-star (★★★★), three-star (★★★), two-star (★★), and one-star (★).

Not surprising, given the nature of their market, Milan's hotels tend to be expensive and fully booked much of the year, except during August when several small hotels actually close. Five-star hotels can cost US$400-500 a night. You are well advised to book accommodations far in advance. If you plan to visit the city during March or October, the two busiest trade show months, expect to find most major hotels fully booked.

If you arrive at Linate Airport without a reservation, try using the centralized computerized reservation system (HRM, Hotel Reservation Milano, Tel. 76007978) which includes nearly 100 hotels by category. The same reservation system is available at the provincial tourist offices or Azienda di Promozione Turistica (APT): Palazzo del Turismo, Via Marconi 1, Tel. 809662 (Piazza Duomo) and Stazione Centrale.

Here are some of best hotels in Milan. Most of them are centrally located so you will be within close walking distance to most major shops, restaurants, and sights.

- **The Four Seasons:** *Via Gesù 8, Tel. 77088, Fax 77085000.* This is Milan's finest hotel and centrally located for shopping. A beautifully restored 14th century monastery, it exudes elegance and class that is the hallmark of the Four Seasons name. Most of its 98 rooms face a quiet courtyard. Very expensive (★★★★★L).

- **Principe di Savoia:** *Piazza della Repubblica 17, Tel. 6230, Fax 6595838.* Located just north of Milan's most upscale shopping area, this grand, elegant, and comfortable hotel is a favorite of many seasoned visitors to Milan. Favored by business travelers, the rooms are large and lavishly decorated with wood marquetry and sumptuous fabrics. Impeccable service. The renowned Galleria Restaurant serves Italian cuisine and regional specialties. Try the Café Doney for a typical Milanese breakfast or afternoon tea. 287 rooms. Very expensive (★★★★★L).

- **Palace:** *Piazzo della Repubblica 20, Tel. 6230, Fax 6595838.* Located next to the elegant Principe di Savoia, this understated and elegant hotel caters to a similar upscale clientele found next door. Many travelers select this hotel for its fine location, excellent amenities, yet slightly lower price than it's sister CIGA hotel located next door. Very expensive (★★★★★L).

- **Duca di Milano:** *Piazza della Repubblica 13, Tel. 6284, Fax 6555966.* Formerly an annex of the Principe di Savoia, the Duca di Milano is now a separate hotel. This all-suite hotel features bedroom/sitting room suites that can be especially conducive to small business meetings or working lunches. Close to business and shopping districts. Very expensive (★★★★★).

- **Excelsior Hotel Gallia:** *Piazza Duca D'Aosta 9, Tel. 6785, Fax 66713239.* A grand hotel with its imposing facade is located near the central train station. Rooms were recently redecorated recreating its original art nouveau style but providing the most modern facilities. Tradition, charm and cosmopolitan facilities combined with discreet, yet efficient service appeals to discerning clientele. 242 rooms. Very Expensive (★★★★★).

- **Pierre Milano:** *Via de Amicis 32, Tel. 72000581, Fax 805-2157.* Located west of the Duomo near the medieval church of Sant'Ambrogio. Each room is elegantly decorated in a different style and furnished with a variety of antique furnishings, a mix of classical and modern art plus all amenities expected of four-star hotels. 47 rooms. Expensive (★★★★).

- **Hotel de la Ville:** *Via Hoepli 6, Tel. 867651, Fax 866609.* Central location coupled with good service make this a choice of many travelers. A soft palette to the decor as well as the balconies and view of the Duomo offered in some rooms bring visitors back. 105 rooms. Expensive (★★★★).

- **Duomo:** *Via San Raffaele 1, Tel. 8833, Fax 86462027.* This popular hotel has one of the most central locations in Milan—at the Duomo. Some rooms with a view make this a popular hotel with upscale travelers. 160 rooms. Closed during August. Expensive (★★★★).

- **Jolly President:** *Largo Augusto 10, Tel. 7746, Fax 783449.* A popular business hotel centrally located one block directly east of the Duomo. The rooms are modern though basic and the service is attentive and professional. With 220 rooms one stands a better chance of getting a room here when trade shows are in full swing. Expensive (★★★★).

- **Manin:** *Via Manin 7, Tel. 6596511, Fax 6552160.* Centrally located for shopping, this small hotel is popular with the fashion show crowds. Expensive to moderate (★★★★).

- **Casa Svizzera:** *Via San Raffaele 3, Tel. 8692246, Fax 72004690.* The location doesn't get much better for this popular small hotel which is located next to the Duomo and a stone's throw from the Galleria shopping arcade. Considered good value so make reservations early. 45 rooms. Closed August. Expensive to moderate (★★★).

- **Manzoni:** *Via Santo Spirito 20, Tel. 76005700, Fax 784212.* Centrally located in relation to the Montenapoleone/Spiga shopping area, this small hotel, recently remodeled, offers excellent value. 50 rooms. Credit cards not accepted. Moderate (★★★).

- **Carlton-Senato:** *Via Senato 5, Tel. 76015535, Fax 783300.* Perfectly located for shopping in the Montenapoleone/Spiga area, and housed in a lovely palazzo, this friendly modern hotel offers peace and quiet—especially the rooms facing the Via della Spiga. 79 rooms. Expensive to moderate (★★★).

- **Gritti:** *Piazza Santa Maria Beltrade 4, Tel. 801056, Fax 89010999.* Located at the north end of Via Torino within a few hundred yards of the Duomo. Colorfully decorated lobby. 48 rooms. Moderate (★★★-★★).

If you're traveling on a tight budget and prefer less expensive accommodations, consider staying at one of these hotels. While they lack many of the amenities expected of first-class and deluxe hotels, many of these places offer good value for those who spend most of their time outside the hotel:

★★★

- **Cairoli:** Via Porlezza 4, Tel. 801371, Fax 72002243.
- **Lombardia:** Viale Lombardia 74, Tel. 2824938, Fax 289-3430
- **Mennini:** Via N. Torriani 14, Tel. 6690951, Fax 6693437.
- **New York:** Via Pirelli 5, Tel. 66985551, Fax 6697267.
- **Teco:** Via Spallanzani 27, Tel. 29510028, Fax 29404595.

★★—★

- **Boston:** Via Lepetit 7.
- **Brera:** Via Pontaccio 9.
- **London:** Via Rovello 3, Tel. 72020166, Fax 8057037.
- **Paradiso:** Via B Marcello 85
- **Roma:** Corso Lodi 4.
- **San Francisco:** Viale Lombardia 55, Tel. 23610009, Fax 26680377.
- **Tonale:** Via Tonale 14.

RESTAURANTS

Milan also boasts some of Italy's best restaurants, offering everything from local Milanese cuisine to fine dishes from all over Italy—Abruzzi, Neapolitan, Piedmont, Sardinian, Sicilian, Apulian, Venetian, and Tuscan cuisines—as well as international cuisine and fast foods (Burghy, Wendy, Quick). Like in so many other Italian cities, you'll find numerous food shops offering everything from pastries to cheeses and ice cream parlors. And like Milan's shopping and accommodations, dining out can become a very expensive experience. It's not difficult to spend US$30-$60 per person for lunch and US$150-$250 per person for dinner, if you dine in some of Milan's finest establishments.

Some of Milan's best restaurants include the following:

- **Boeucc:** *Piazza Belgioioso 2, Tel. 760-20224. Reservations required. Closed Saturday and Sunday lunch and August, Christmas, and Easter.* Milan's oldest restaurant exudes understated elegance with its cream colored fluted columns, chandeliers, plush carpeting and even a garden for warm weather dining. Serving typical Milanese food, it's an excellent place to try some of the risotto dishes Milan is known for such as *costoletta alla milanese*. The dessert cart will tempt even the most avid diet conscious or try their chestnut ice cream with hot zabaglione.

- **Savini:** *Galleria Vittorio Emanuele, Tel. 72003433. Closed Saturday and Sunday lunch, August, Christmas, and Easter.* Diners chose Savini as much for the elegant surroundings and ambience as for the food. Its three floors occupy a conspicuous place in the Galleria Vittorio Emanuele—the wonderful iron and glass domed gallery across from the Duomo. Try the *risotto giallo* or *costoletta di vitello*, but save room for a selection from the dessert cart.

- **Scaletta:** *Piazza Stazione Genova 3, Tel. 58100290. Reservations suggested 2-4 weeks in advance in high season. Closed Sunday and Monday, August, Christmas & Easter. No credit cards.* Located near the train station and up a small stairway that leads to a cozy dining room that could be part of a comfortable home, the menu offers unconventional and distinctive, yet truly Italian food. Prepared by chef/owner Pina Bellini the exciting blend of flavors keeps the local clientele coming back for more. Both Pina and her son Aldo take time to offer suggestions on the menu which changes frequently as well as the wine selections.

- **Antica Trattoria della Pesa:** *Viale Pasubio 10, Tel. 655-5741. Dinner reservations advised. Closed Sunday and two weeks* *in August. No credit cards.* With antique furniture, dark wood paneling, and traditional lamps this trattoria offers the ambience of a by-gone era reminiscent of the time over 100 years ago when this restaurant was first opened. Offers Milanese cuisine with a hearty focus. If you have room for dessert, try the vanilla souffle.

❑ **Bistrot di Gualtiero Marchesi:** *La Rinascente, Piazza Duomo, Tel. 877120. Closed Sunday lunch, Monday and August.* This bistro offers two bonuses: a close-up view of the Duomo from the 7th floor of the Rinascente Department Store and cuisine prepared under the supervision of well-known chef Gualtiero Marchesi. For prices that are inexpensive to moderately expensive one gets the expertise of a chef who also operates a lavish Relais et Chateaux establishment. There is a wide range to the menu which features many fish and vegetarian dishes. The entrees, main courses and desserts are each held to a high standard. When Rinascente is open enter through the store and take the elevator. During the evening enter from Via San Raffaele 2.

❑ **La Libera:** *Via Palermo 21, Tel. 8053603. Closed Saturday and Sunday lunch, August and December 22-January 1. No credit cards.* Located in the heart of the Brera district, this beer cellar with kitchen is popular with the young clientele who come for the creative menu, draft beer and lively conversation. The soft jazz background music adds to its charm.

❑ **Calajunco:** *Via Stoppani 5, Tel. 2046003. Reservations necessary. Closed Saturday lunch, Sunday, and some holidays.* The restaurant is decorated in light and chic blue and white. Start by sampling from the wide range of hot and cold antipasto. Calajunco excels in seafood and though the menu changes frequently, try the pumpkin-stuffed ravioli if it is available. If you prefer meat dishes try their veal scaloppine alle Setta Isole prepared with mozzarella, tomatoes and fresh basil. Everything is fresh and well presented. For dessert the almond semifreddo with chocolate or the chocolate and ricotta cassatella are good choices.

❑ **Nabucco:** *Via Fiori Chiari 10, Tel. 860663. Reservations suggested. Closed Sunday and Monday lunch.* Located in the Brera district, this moderately priced restaurant offers an excellent rage of salads as well as homemade pastries and assorted other desserts. Their *prix-fixe* lunches are priced even lower and offer good value. Try their *risotto con porcini.*

- **Trattoria Milanese:** *Via Santa Marta 11, Tel. 86451991. Reservations recommended. Closed Tuesday, August, and Christmas.* Located near the Duomo this small trattoria has been operated by the same family for over 80 years. The food is regional, prepared in the traditional manner and nicely presented. If you like veal, try the *costoletta alla milanese.*

- **San Vito da Nino:** *Via San Vito 5, Tel. 8377029. Closed Monday and August*. Lovely ambience accented with elegant place settings of fine crystal and china. Patrons feel like celebrities as they are greeted with warm welcomes and lavished with attentive service. Menu features Italian food with a strong French influence. The meat dishes are a real strength here: grills, braised beef in wine, or game in season. Try the risotto flavored with champagne. For dessert, consider a delectable chocolate souffle or orange scented crepes Suzette.

ENJOYING YOUR STAY

Being a sophisticated international business community, Milan offers numerous entertainment venues for its visitors. You'll have no problem finding things to do at night in Milan.

ENTERTAINMENT

There's always lots going on in Milan. Opera season runs from December 7 through June 7. Major ready-to-wear women's fashion shows take place during March and October. International trade fairs, festivals, and shows are held in the city each month. Art exhibits, concerts, theatrical performances, and sporting events take place daily. Numerous parks and gardens provide opportunities to enjoy the city's many open spaces.

If you enjoy evening entertainment, Milan has much to offer in this department from discos to piano bars. Music lovers should head for the Brera and Navigli areas where young artists and musicians tend to gather. The Brera area, especially along Via Madoninna and Fiori Oscuri, has several music bars and jazz clubs. The Navigli area, especially at the Darsena basin and the two streets along the main canals (Naviglio Grande and Naviglio Pavese), offers similar entertainment opportunities. The area around the Duomo is usually lively during evening.

Some of Milan's most popular places for nightlife include:

BARS

- **American Bar Coquetel:** *Via Vetere 14, Tel. 8360688. Open 8am-2am. Closed Sunday, August 1-September 6.* Located in the Navigli area.

- **Bar Giamaica:** *Via Brera 32, Tel. 876723.* A favorite for artists and intellecturals.

- **Manhattan:** *Via Verri 3, Tel. 76023566.* Serves lunch and late dinners. Pianist entertains in the evening.

DISCOS

- **City Square:** *Via Castelbarco 11, Tel. 58310682. Open Friday and Saturday, 11pm-3am; Sunday 3pm-6:30pm. 20,000 Ilira cover charge on Friday and 25,000 Ilira cover charge on Saturday.* Milan's largest disco. Occasionally has live entertainment.

- **Shocking Club:** *Bastioni di Pota Volta 12, Tel. 6595407. Opens at 10:30pm. Closed Mondays. 20,000 Ilira cover charge Tuesday-Thursday and Sunday and 25,000 Ilira on Friday and Saturday.* Milan's most popular disco.

LIVE ENTERTAINMENT

- **Capolinea:** *Via Lodovico il Moro 119, Tel. 89122024. Open 8pm-1:45pm. Closed Mondays.* Popular spot for some of the best Jazz musicians passing through Milan.

- **Tangram:** *Via Pezzotti 52, Tel. 89501007. Open 9pm-2am. Closed Sundays.* Includes quality jazz, blues, funk, and rock groups.

NIGHTCLUBS

- **William's:** *Foro Bonaparte 71, Tel. 877218. Open 10:30am-4am.* One of the city's most popular nightclubs, complete with Las Vegas acts and 40 hostesses.

PIANO BARS

- **Magia Music Meeting's:** *Via Salutati 2, Tel. 4813553. Open 10am-3m and 7pm-3am (Saturday 7pm-3am). Closed*

Sundays. Good place to review emerging musical talent, from solos to groups.

- **Ponte di Brera:** *Via Brera 32, Tel. 876723. Open 10pm-2am. Closed Sunday.* One of the oldest and most popular piano bars. Located above the Bar Giamaica.

ON TO COMO AND ITS LAKES

If you make only one trip outside Milian, be sure you do what the Milanese do—visit Como and its lakes. Located just 25 miles north of Milan in the foothills of the beautiful Alps, Lake Como can be easily reached by car (take A9 autostrada) or train within 40 minutes. You may want to rent a car in Milan to leisurely explore this delightful area. Along the way you will be able to visit factory outlets and explore other lakes in this region, especially Lake Maggiore and its lakeside town of Stresa, Garda, and Orta. However, you may want to avoid the months of July and August when thousands of Italians and Europeans descend on the lake region. Spring and fall are the best times to visit. We recommend a minimum of two days for this area. Four days would make a wonderful trip to this relaxing and colorful area.

Lake Como is to Milan what the Riviera is to the French—a place for rest and relaxation. It's the most popular lakeside destination. It's where many of Milan's wealthy maintain lavish villas and homes and where they escape to on weekends. But the lakeside town of Como, which is located at the southern end of Lake Como, also is an important textile center that is especially well known for producing beautiful silk fabrics which are exported throughout the world. It's a charming city offering interesting shopping opportunities for silk, fashion, jewelry, and leathergoods. You should start at the center of the town, the Piazza del Duomo, and proceed along Via Vittorio Emanuele and the parallel Via Bernardino Luini where you will find most shops offering the treasures of Como. For beautiful silk fabrics, try **Seterie Moretti** at Via Garibaldi 69 and **Mantero** at Via Volta 68.

On a calm day you also may want to take a boat to explore other areas around the lake (tickets cost 1,500 to 12,000 lira for various destinations) or take the funicular to Brunate where you can get a panoramic view from an altitude of 2,000 feet.

If time permits, go on to the town of Stresa which is located alongside Lake Maggiore. While not as popular a destination as Como, nonetheless, it draws thousands of tourists from all over Europe, and especially from Germany.

5

Florence

Few cities in the world captivate the imagination as much as Florence. It's simply an architecturally beautiful, artistically vibrant, and culturally seductive city. Above all, it's an extremely romantic city that challenges the senses and excites the imagination. Next to Venice, this is Italy's most interesting and beautiful city. It's a visual feast jam-packed with tourists. Chances are you will join millions of other people who become enthralled with this unique city.

Spread along the gently flowing River Arno, Florence rises like a medieval movie set complete with narrow cobblestone streets and densely populated commercial and residential areas. Here's where the Renaissance was born and where history, art, and culture remain enshrined in magnificent old stone buildings, monuments, and museums. It's also where 19 million visitors flock each year in search of the real Italy—the one that is associated with so much of 15th and 16th century Western science, literature, art, music, and architecture. It's also the one Italian city visitors are most likely to return to—or never leave!

Not surprising, everyone seems to fall in love with this wonderful city. We suspect you will too. Once you return home, your thoughts of Italy will often take you back to the many fond memories of Florence.

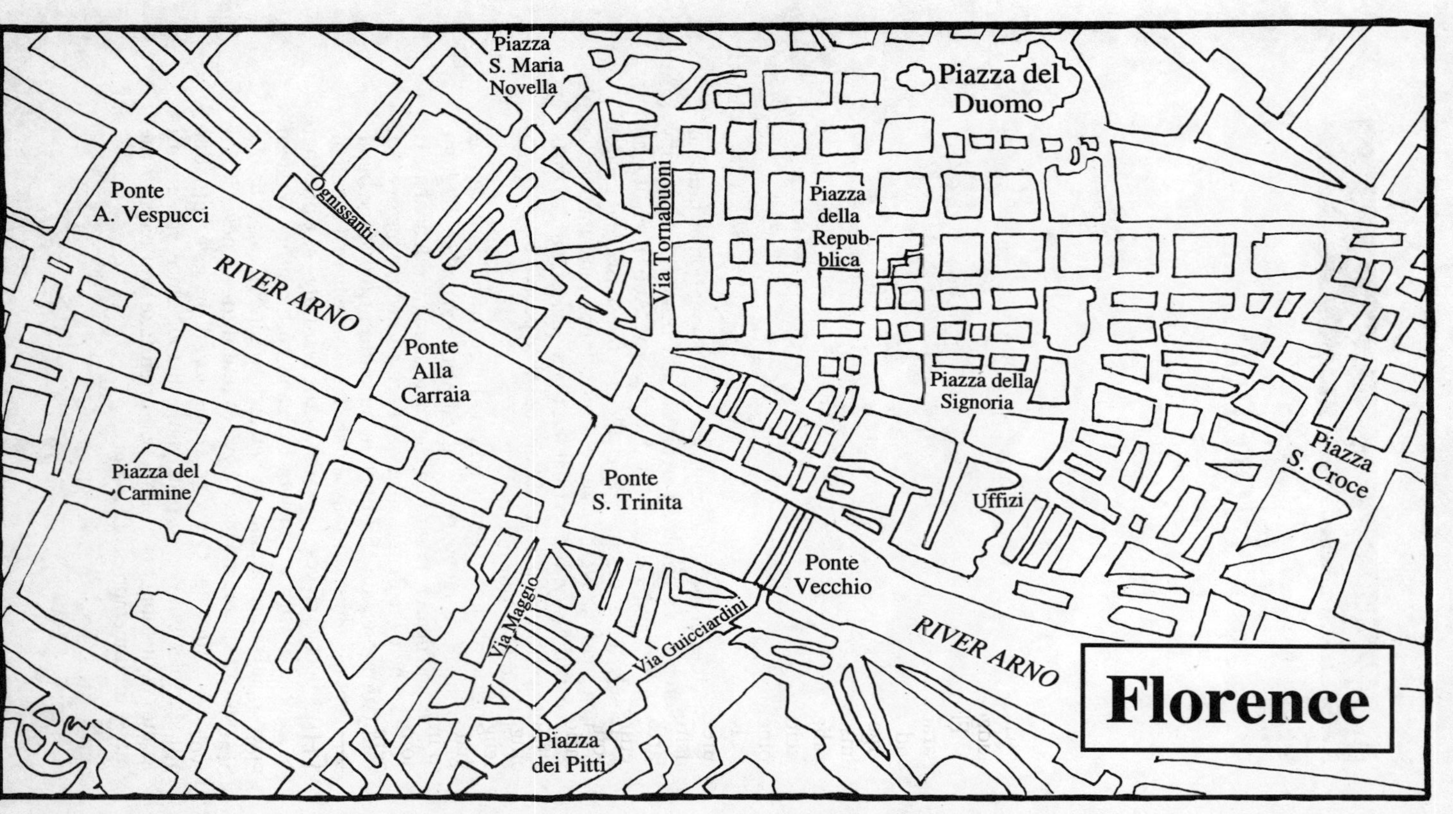
Florence
Piazza S. Maria Novella
Piazza del Duomo
Ponte A. Vespucci
Ognissanti
Via Tornabuoni
Piazza della Repub-blica
RIVER ARNO
Ponte Alla Carraia
Piazza della Signoria
Piazza S. Croce
Piazza del Carmine
Ponte S. Trinita
Uffizi
Ponte Vecchio
Via Maggio
Via Guicciardini
RIVER ARNO
Piazza dei Pitti

THE PERFECT TRIP

Here's the perfect and sometimes bewildering trip. A beautiful medieval city straddling the picturesque River Arno; one million local residents hosting 19 million visitors each year with 400 hotels; thousands of art treasures housed in museum after museum; historic monuments at every street bend; numerous squares, palaces, and churches; restaurants and eateries galore; hotels crammed with visitors; a tourist season that never seems to end; and hundreds of shops and market stalls crammed with a wide range of products appealing to every type of taste and budget.

Florence is unquestionably both a traveler's and shopper's paradise. It's especially appealing to lovers of Renaissance art and architecture, those who appreciate large doses of Western history and museums, and shoppers in search of quality Italian products. If you don't find many exciting treasures and pleasures here, something may be wrong with you!

- ❑ **Spread along the gently flowing River Arno, Florence rises like a medieval movie set.**
- ❑ **This city of 1 million local residents hosts 19 million visitors each year.**
- ❑ **Florence is the ideal travel destination for beauty, romance, ambience, history, art, culture, lifestyle, and shopping.**
- ❑ **Florence is home to 15,000 Americans who have made this city their permanent residence.**

Few places on earth evoke such pleasure and emotion as Florence. For many visitors, this is their favorite place on earth. Back home they often dream of returning to romantic Florence. And no wonder. Florence is the ideal travel destination for beauty, romance, ambience, history, art, culture, lifestyle, and shopping. Nowhere else will you find such a delightful "big city" travel destination that evokes such emotions. Some people come here and want to immediately return. Others never leave. Indeed, Florence is home to 15,000 Americans who have made this city their permanent residence.

THE BASICS

Florence is halfway between Milan and Rome. Located in the beautiful Tuscany region, it has played critical roles in the evolution of Europe and Italy. Forged through a combination of Roman conquest and a litany of powerful local rulers who shaped its medieval character, Florence has played one of the most influential roles in the evolution of art, culture, science, and politics in world history. This is the city of Michelangelo, Galileo, Machiavelli, and Dante. It's the city of the powerful

Medici family that served as the patron of the arts and helped usher in the Renaissance. Florence has given to the world art, architecture, culture, political thought, and lifestyle like few other cities in history.

Today Florence continues to give to the world a sense of history, culture, and style. It also educates the world in the fine art of living, from its exquisite fashion design houses to its culinary arts. This is the Italian city you will most likely fall passionately in love with and plan to return to in years to come. Florence simply gets under your skin.

But keep in mind that this is overwhelmingly a city of tourists. While you will encounter some Florentines in shops and restaurants—most are very elegantly dressed—for the most part you will encounter hordes of tourists wherever you go. They're everywhere. Indeed, aside from viewing lots of art treasures, you may have difficulty meeting local people. One of the best ways to meet the locals is to go shopping.

- **The closest international airport is in Pisa, 80 kilometers to the west.**
- **Many visitors prefer arriving by train because of the densely populated nature of the city.**
- **Most cars are prohibited entry into the city center between 7:30am and 6:30pm, Monday to Saturday.**
- **You'll probably need to take a taxi to get to your hotel, even though your hotel appears nearby on a map.**
- **Beware of pickpockets and panhandlers around the train station, San Lorenzo Market, and the Duomo.**

GETTING THERE

Florence is easily reached from Rome, Milan, Venice, Bologna, and other cities by road or train. It does have a small domestic airport (Peretola) which is located 10 kilometers northeast of the city. The closest international airport is in Pisa (Galileo Galilei Airport) which is located 80 kilometers west of Florence. If you are entering Italy by air, we recommend first flying into Rome or Milan and then taking a train to Florence. In fact, many visitors prefer arriving by train because of the densely populated nature of this city. If you drive to Florence, it's best to park your car outside the city since Florence's narrow streets and pedestrian zones do not permit much vehicular traffic aside from bicycles and racing Vespa motorscooters. In fact, most cars are prohibited entry into the city center between 7:30am and 6:30pm, Monday to Saturday. This is a walking city that is best experienced on foot. However, buses and taxis do traverse certain sections of the city.

The main train station, Stazione Santa Maria Novella, is located a short distance northwest of the city center. Nonetheless, you'll probably need to take a taxi to get to your hotel, even though it may appear on a map to be nearby. The taxi stand is located to your left as you leave the train track. Given the numerous narrow and one-way streets, an ostensibly short taxi ride can take some time and will probably be expensive.

GETTING AROUND

Since you'll need to navigate most of Florence on foot, it's best to get a map of the city as soon as you arrive as well as information on various museums (hours, admission prices) and upcoming events. Maps and other tourist information should be available at your hotel or through one of these tourist offices:

- **Consorzio I.T.A.**: located in the train station near track #16. This office also will book a room for you should you arrive without reservations (charges a 3,000-10,000 lira commission). Open 8:30am-9pm.

- **Informazione Turistica**: Located just outside the station, this office offers information on Florence. Open April-October, 9am-7pm, and November-March, 9am-2pm.

- **APT**: Via Cavour 1r. Open Monday-Saturday, 8am-7pm (Tel. 2760381 or 290832). Conveniently located near the Palazzo Medici-Riccardi and the Duomo. Also has offices at Piazzetta Guelfa 3 and Via Martelli which are open Monday-Saturday 9am-7pm and Sunday (summer only) 8:15am-1:15pm.

- **Consortium Italian Tourist Association**: Viale Gramsci 9a.

MANAGING YOUR MONEY

Banks give the best exchange rates. Most are open Monday-Friday, 8:30am-1:20pm and 2:45-3:45pm. Some are open on Saturdays. The American Express office at Via Dante Alighieri, 20-221 (Tel. 50-981) is open Monday-Friday, 9am-5:30pm and Saturday 9am-12:30pm.

BEWARE OF PICKPOCKETS AND PANHANDLERS

Florence has it share of pickpockets and panhandlers who prey on tourists, especially in and around the train station, San Lorenzo market, and the Duomo. Keep a firm grip on your purse or wallet wherever you go. Be particularly suspicious of bands of gypsy girls who are known for distracting and attacking tourists as they engage in bold daytime robberies.

HOURS

Most shops are open from 9am to 1pm and from 3:30pm to 7pm each day. Many shops also stay open between 1pm and 3:30pm, especially department stores and supermarkets. Most shops close on Sunday and many are closed Monday morning.

SPENDING TIME

It's difficult to advise how much time you should spend visiting Florence. It all depends on your travel style and preferences. If, for example, you love art, museums, and history, plan to spend a week or two here. You'll think you've died and gone to cultural heaven! It simply doesn't get much better than Florence for art and history buffs. But if you are a contemporary type of traveler—enjoy meeting people, shopping, dining, and enjoying local entertainment—Florence can easily be done in three to four days. You may find all the art, history, and culture both excessive and boring. But you won't be disappointed by Florence's many other treasures and pleasures.

- ❑ **Banks give the best exchange rates.**
- ❑ **Watch out for pickpockets and panhandlers in and around the train station, San Lorenzo Market, and the Duomo.**
- ❑ **Most shops are open from 9am to 1pm and 3:30pm to 7pm each day.**

THE PLEASURES OF SIX FLORENCES

Even though you can get around by bus, taxi, motorbike, and bicycle, plan to arm yourself with a good map and really walk the city. Since this is a very compact city, you simply must approach it on foot. This is definitely the best way to get around and really see the city and its many attractions. In fact, there is so much to see and do in Florence that you may become overwhelmed with your choices!

Art, museums, and churches seem to reign supreme as the major tourist attractions in Florence. The crowds tend to be dense and the lines are often long and slow. If you are a real connoisseur of 15th and 16th century Italian art, architecture, and history, you can easily spend several days trying to absorb

Florence's numerous aging treasures. They are everywhere. Indeed, many visitors quickly become overwhelmed by Florence's over-abundance of art and architecture; some experience sensory overload! If you have only a passing interest in such treasures, you may want to focus on a few of the city's historic highlights, such as the huge Duomo, the Ponte Vecchio, the Church of Santa Croce, the Galleria dell' Accademia, the Piazza della Signoria, the Palazzo Vecchio, the Uffizi Gallery, and the Palazzo Pitti.

While Florence's narrow and crowded streets can easily become disorienting for first-time visitors, it is a relatively easy city to navigate once you orient yourself to the city's six major sections. The first thing you need to know about the geography of the city is the east-west River Arno. It dissects the city into four northern sections (Centro Storico, Santa Maria Novella, San Lorenzo, and Santa Croce) and two southern sections (Oltrarno and Colli). Each section yields its own unique set of treasures and pleasures.

CENTRO STORICO

This is the historical and symbolic center of Florence and the Renaissance. It's literally filled with fascinating history, art, architecture, and monuments as well as crammed with interesting shops and restaurants. The great concentration of art and architecture here may overwhelm you. This is the area that gave birth to much of the Renaissance and all its accompanying politics and craft guilds. Stretching from the famous Ponte Vecchio (bridge) spanning the River Arno in the south to the imposing Duomo (cathedral) in the north, the area is peppered with a fascinating concentration of churches, palaces (palazzi), squares (piazze), and galleries that distinguish it from other parts of Florence. While most of this area is a pedestrian zone, keep an eye out for the many bicycles, speeding Vespas, and cars and trucks that often enter the narrow streets. This is a very noisy and congested area. Major highlights in this area are:

- ❑ **Piazza del Duomo and the Duomo:** This famous piazza includes the imposing Duomo, Campanile (tower), and Battistero di San Giovanni (Baptistry of San Giovanni). The Duomo (officially called the Cathedral of Santa Maria del Fiore or Saint Mary of the Flower), constructed in 1296-1436, visually dominates the city and countryside. Its remarkable red-tile dome, designed by the talented Filippo Brunelleschi, has become a symbol of Florence, Italy, and the Renaissance.

- **Ponte Vecchio:** Originally constructed in the 12th century and subsequently rebuilt several times, this famous bridge is another great symbol of Florence. It has real character and is a major shopping center. It's constantly crowded with tourists who enjoy viewing the gently flowing River Arno, taking pictures, chatting with friends, eating another gelato, or window shopping the numerous gold shops that line both sides of this aging bridge. You'll also encounter an occasional street artist who provides inexpensive entertainment. Stop at T. Ristori (1-3r), U. Gherardi (5r), or Cassetti (52r) for a sampling of the gold goodies that make this bridge so famous.

- **Bargello:** Museo del Bargello or Museo Nazionale. This 14th century palace has been at the center of Florencc's history, from politics to public hangings. Today, it houses the world's most important collection of Renaissance sculpture. Look for the works of Michelangelo, Donatello, Jacopo Sansovino, Benevenuto Cellini, Gian Lorenzo Bernini, Filippo Brunelleschi, Desiderio da Settignano, and Mino da Fiesole.

- **Piazza della Signoria:** This is one of Florence's most popular and architecturally important squares. It's literally an outdoor museum of impressive, though somewhat oppressive, sculptures. Here you'll find Giambologna's equestrian figure, Bartolommeo Ammannati's fountain, and copies of Michelangelo's *David* (go to the Accademia for the original) and Donatello's *Judith and Holofernes* (go to the Signoria for the original). It's dominated by the fortresslike Palazzo Vecchio, one of Florence's most important landmarks which now functions as the seat for Florence's municipal government. From here you can hire a horse-drawn carriage to take you leisurely through many parts of the city.

- **Palazzo Vecchio:** Old Palace or Palazzo della Signoria. Serving once again as Florence's City Hall, this former palace (built in 1229) includes several works of art—as well as much appreciated public restroom facilities. The most important works are found in two adjacent rooms on the second floor—Sala dei Cinquecento and Studiolo. Its impressive 94-meter high clock tower punctuates as well as contrasts sharply with Florence's Duomo-dominated skyline.

- ❑ **Galleria degli Uffizi:** Uffizi Gallery. Located south of Palazzo Vecchio and across the street from the River Arno, this is one of Italy's most popular museums. Housing the greatest collection of Italian paintings, this is also Italy's most important museum. If you visit only one museum in Florence, or Italy, make sure it's this one. Here you'll marvel at some of the great works of Michelangelo, Leonardo da Vinci, Raphael, Rembrandt, Uccello, Lippi, Botticelli, Caravaggio, and Titian. Expect to encounter long lines and huge crowds since this is the highlight attraction for most visitors to Florence. If you want to avoid the longest lines, it's best to visit in the early morning, noon, or late afternoon. Better still, beginning in September 1996, the museum started to experiment with a new reservation system. Each day 300 tickets are set aside for individuals who call ahead to make reservations. With a reservation, you can by-pass the long lines altogether. From the United States, call this number to make a reservation: 011-39-55-471-960.

SANTA MARIA NOVELLA

Located directly west and northwest of the Centro Storico and adjacent to the River Arno, this also is a heavily touristed area especially noted for its train station, upscale shopping, famous hotels and restaurants, and American presence. If you've burnt out on the art, architecture, monuments, museums, and crowds in other sections of the city, this area may be just what you need to refocus your travel senses around contemporary Florence and Italy—the one offering fine quality hotels, restaurants, and shops. Most of this area is open to vehicular traffic, although parking is often impossible. This area is the mecca for dedicated upscale shoppers who head for one of Italy's most famous and elegant shopping streets—Via dei Tornabuoni—where dreams can indeed come true for rather hefty prices. You'll find lots of designer clothes, accessories, and jewelry here. Shops along adjacent streets offer fine quality art, antiques, and linens. Major highlights in this area include:

- ❑ **Santa Maria Novella:** This unique Renaissance and Gothic church dominates the popular Piazza Santa Maria Novella. Its Gothic interior makes it the most important Gothic church in Tuscany. Includes numerous art treasures, from stained-glass windows (*The Coronation of the Virgin*) and statuary to frescos and paintings (Masaccio's *Holy Trinity With Two Donors*).

❑ **Via dei Tornabuoni:** Shopping doesn't get any better than along this famous street dominated by upscale boutiques and jewelers. Start at the southern end of this street at the fabulous flagship Ferragamo store (16r), adjacent to the obelisk, and keep moving north. Welcome to Gucci, House of Florence, Cartier, Buccellati, Crisci, Versace, Trussard, Yves Saint Laurent, Cadadei, Ugolini, and Faraone-Settepassi. Watch your wallet. If the gypsy kids don't get you near the Duomo, the shops along this street may do the job to the tune of "big bucks". You'll become captivated by the incredible selections!

- **Centro Storico is the historical and symbolic center of Florence and the Renaissance. It's where the action is for most visitors to Florence. The real highlights here are the Duomo, Piazza della Signoria, Palazzo Vecchio, Galleria degli Uffizi, and Ponte Vecchio.**
- **The Santa Maria Novella area includes the city's most up-scale shops.**
- **San Lorenzo is noted for its markets, museums, and students.**
- **The Church of Santa Croce is Florence's Pantheon—burial site for four of the world's great figures in politics, science, and art—Michelangelo, Galileo, Machiavelli, and Ghiberti.**
- **The Oltarno area, on the southern side of the River Arno, is much quieter and less crowded. It offers good shopping opportunities for top quality antiques and jewelry.**
- **The Colli area attracts the fewest tourists. It's most noted for the huge Palazzo Pitti.**

❑ **Excelsior and Grand Hotels:** Facing each other at Piazza Ognissanti, these are two of Florence's top hotels. The Excelsior is the grandest of them all. Part of the CIGA hotel chain, both hotels offer old world ambience. Try Il Cestello Restaurant at the Excelsior for superb dining. Turn the corner and visit some of Florence's best art and antique shops.

SAN LORENZO

Located directly north of the Centro Storico and northwest of Santa Maria Novella, the San Lorenzo area is especially noted for its markets, museums, and university students.

❑ **Piazza San Lorenzo and San Lorenzo Church:** The Piazza San Lorenzo is the center for the outdoor vendor market (Mercato di San Lorenzo) as well as one of Florence's oldest and most important churches, San Lorenzo. While originally built in the 4th century, it was subsequently rebuilt in the 11th and 15th centuries. You'll be looking at the 15th century rendition. Designed by Brunelleschi and completed in 1460, many of Florence's most famous artists (Michelangelo and Donatello) worked on its interior; the facade of the church remains unfinished. The church is an excellent example of early Renaissance architecture and another major Brunelleschi project (he also designed the Duomo and Sagrestia Vecchia).

- ❑ **Galleria dell'Accademia:** Located off the beaten tourist path at Via Ricasoli 60. Thousands of visitors come here each day to see one statue—Michelangelo's *David*. The gallery also houses fine paintings by lesser known artists and other noted sculptures by Michelangelo. But for most visitors, it's all about *David*. If you don't arrive early (40 minutes before the doors open at 9am, Tuesday thru Sunday), the lines can be long and slow.

- ❑ **Mercato di San Lorenzo:** San Lorenzo Market. Located one block north of the baptistery (Duomo), this bustling street market with hundreds of stalls offering a wide range of products extends for several blocks around Piazza San Lorenzo, from via Nazionale along via dell' Ariento and Canto dei Nelli to B.S. Lorenzo (Piazza San Lorenzo).

SANTA CROCE

Located directly east of Centro Storico and southeast of San Lorenzo, the Santa Croce area also borders the River Arno. This area is especially noted for the famous church of Santa Croce, the leather shops surrounding the Piazza Santa Croce, and the numerous small shops and restaurants found throughout this increasingly gentrified area.

- ❑ **Church of Santa Croce:** Many observers consider this to be Florence's most important church. Judged by the remains it contains, at least many of Florence's notables thought this to be true. This is really the closest Florence gets to its own Pantheon. Indeed, in tombs beneath the floors and in elevated sarcophagi of this Gothic church lie the remains of 270 Florentines, including four of Italy's most famous names in the fields of art, science, and politics—Michelangelo, Galileo, Machiavelli, and Ghiberti. It also includes a memorial to Florence's great poet, Dante. Elaborate sarcophagi and frescos enhance an otherwise drab interior of vaulted ceilings. The church facade is decidedly 19th century in origin.

- **Piazza Santa Croce:** This large piazza lined with palazzi is a popular tourist stop for those interested in visiting the church of Santa Croce. The piazza is surrounded by numerous shops selling leather goods, art, and souvenirs. Look for several leather shops along Borgo dei Greci, a major shopping street leading into the piazza.

OLTRARNO

Located on the southern side of the River Arno, directly across from Centro Storico and Santa Maria Novella, the Oltrarno area has a different character from these other more heavily touristed areas. It's quieter, less crowded, and the pace of life is slower. Most tourist activity in Oltrarno is centered around three major streets that are immediately reached via the Ponte Vecchio and adjacent to the Pitti Palace: Via Guicciardini, Via Maggio, and B.S. Jacopo. Lined with antique, jewelry, accessory, and art shops as well as hotels and restaurants, these three streets form a convenient shopping triangle. Much of the area is populated by craftsmen who can be seen and heard operating in their workshops. Major highlights in this area include:

- **Piazza Santo Sprito:** This large and pleasant piazza becomes a morning produce center during the weekdays. It also becomes a flea market every second Sunday of the month.

- **Santo Spirito:** Piazza Santo Spirito. Designed by Filippo Brunelleschi, this 15th century church boasts one of Florence's best Renaissance interiors. Includes noted paintings by Aurelio Lomi (*Adoration of the Magi*) and Filippino Lippi (*Madonna and Child With Saints*).

- **Santa Maria del Carmine:** Piazza del Carmine. This 15th century church contains several noted frescos by Masolino, Masaccio, and Lippi.

COLLI

Located on the southern side of the River Arno, directly across from the Santa Croce area, Colli attracts fewer tourists than other areas in Florence. Most shops are found along Via de Guicciardini which separates the Colli area from the Oltrarno area. Several hills in this area afford excellent views of Florence and the surrounding areas. Major attractions in Colli include:

- **Palazzo Pitti:** Originally built in the 15th century and subsequently enlarged during the 18th and 19th centuries, this is Florence's largest and grandest palazzo. It's home to several museums and galleries displaying everything from tapestries and home furnishings to costumes and paintings: Royal Apartments, Museo degli Argenti, Galleria del Costume, Galleria d'Arte Moderna, and Galleria Palatina.

- **Giardino di Boboli:** Boboli Gardens. Located on the hillside behind the Palazzo Pitti, these intriguing gardens include several major statues, an amphitheater, fountains, grottoes, and a cypress avenue. Good example of fine Italian landscaping.

- **Forte di Belvedere:** Via di San Leonardo. This 16th century fortress offers one of the best and most panoramic views of Florence and the surrounding countryside.

- **San Miniato al Monte:** Via del Monte alle Croci 34. Built in the 11th and 12th centuries, this is one of Florence's favorite churches. Perched at the top of the city's highest hill, San Miniato, it yields numerous architectural and artistic treasures, from Romanesque architecture to fine mosaics, frescos, and tombs.

WHAT TO BUY

After you've done your historical and cultural sightseeing, it's time to explore what contemporary Florence has to offer the world. Florence has a long tradition of fine craftsmanship and commercial talent dating from medieval times. It continues today in Florence's many workshops, stores, and market stalls that offer a wide variety of Florentine products.

Florence is famous for many types of products, from designer clothes and accessories to exquisite arts, crafts, and antiques. Florence is justly famous for these products:

DESIGNER CLOTHES AND ACCESSORIES

While Florence used to be the Italian center for designer clothes and accessories, until Milan displaced it over 20 years ago, it still is a major center for buying these products. You only need to go to one street to see most everything of quality Florence has to offer in this department—Via Tornabuoni. This street is to Florence what Montenapoleone is to Milan and Via Condotti is to Rome—a street of high fashion and quality accessory shops. Here you'll find **Salvatore Ferragamo**, **House of Florence** (the new "Gucci" shop), **Gucci**, **Gianni Versace**, **Trussard**, and **Yves Saint Laurent**. Just around the corner, along Via della Vigna Noova, is **Valentino**, **Georgio Armani**, **Ermenegildo Zegna**, and **Laurèl**. Prices are very high but so is quality. For relatively inexpensive clothes, try the stalls at San Lorenzo Market and the Straw Market.

LEATHER GOODS

Florence is one of Italy's premier centers for leather goods. You'll find everything here, from leather coats, shoes, and handbags to briefcases, gloves, and belts. Quality, however, can vary greatly. You'll find top quality leather goods in the designer shops along Via Tornabuoni: **Ferragamo**, **House of Florence**, **Gucci**, **Trussardi**, and **Casadei**. Other top quality leather shops include **Cellerini** (Via del Sole 37r), **Raspini** (Via Roma 25-9r, Via Martelli 5-7r, Via Por Santa Maria 72r), and **Beltrami** (Via dei Calzaiuoli 31r and 44r, Via dei Pecori 16, Via Calimala 9, Via Tornabuoni 48r). For one of the best factory shops for leather gloves, be sure to visit **Madova** (Via Guicciardini 1r, Tel. 2396526) which is located just beyond the southern end of the Ponte Vecchio in the Colli area. Tourist quality leather goods are readily available in the many vendor stalls of the **San Lorenzo Market** (Piazza San Lorenzo) as well as in and around the Piazza Santa Croce, especially at the eastern end of Borgo dei Greci (try **Bottega Fiorentina** at Borgo dei Greci 5r). If you're interested in seeing a working leather factory, stop at **The Leather School** in the Monastery of Santa Croce (enter through the Santa Croce church) which functions as both a leather factory and shop.

- **Top quality clothes and accessories are found in several shops along Via Tornabuoni.**
- **Florence is one of Italy's premier centers for leather goods.**
- **The largest concentration of gold shops is found on the Ponte Vecchio.**
- **Marbleized paper products make excellent and relatively inexpensive gift items.**
- **Most antique shops are concentrated along Via Maggio and Borgo Ognissanti.**

JEWELRY

Florence is especially famous for its unique gold jewelry as well as fine designs using precious and semi-precious stones. The largest concentration of gold shops is found on the **Ponte**

Vecchio, a four-century old tradition of selling gold jewelry from small shops overlooking the River Arno. Despite the ostensible tourist nature of this bridge trade (throngs of tourists window-shopping on both sides of the bridge), the shops here offer good quality and unique designs. Some shops may even extend a small discount for cash purchases. Some of the best gold shops here include **U. Gherardi** (5r), **Manelli** (14r), **Piccino** (23r), **Melli** (44-6r), and **Cassetti** (52r). Several other excellent jewelers are found in other parts of the city, especially in the Centro Storico and Santa Maria Novella areas. The finest quality gold and silver jewelry will be found at **Mario Buccellati** (Via Tornabuoni 71r), the famous Milanese jeweler. Other terrific jewelers include **Settepassi** (Via Tornabuoni 25r), **Befani & Tai** (Via Vacchereccia 13r, 7n), and **Maria Grazia Cassetti** (Via Por S. Maria 29r). For excellent reproduction Etruscan gold jewelry, be sure to visit **Quaglia & Forte** (Via Guicciardini 12r). You'll find two excellent jewelers producing creative and modern designs: **Gatto Bianco** (Borgo SS. Apostoli, 12r) and **Maggie Maggi Gioielli** (Piazza Pitti, 6r). We especially like the unique gold designs of Maggie Maggi Gioielli. Her prices appear to be very reasonable for the quality of designs and workmanship. For a good selection of reasonably priced jewelry, visit **Blue Point** (Via de´Calzaiuoli 39r). For costume jewelry, visit **Bijoux Cascio** (Via Tornabuoni 32r and Via Por Santa Maria 1r), **Angela Caputi** (Borgo San Jacopo 82), and **Freon** (Via de Guicciardini 118r).

MARBLEIZED PAPER

First introduced into Venice from the Orient in the 12th century, this is one of the great craft traditions Florence has adopted and become so well known for. Immersing papers in trays of liquid swirled colors, craftsmen practicing this age-old art form produce colorful book bindings, papered gift items, and stationery. You'll find everything from photo albums and greeting cards to bookplates, address books, picture frames, small boxes, and pencils produced in this medium. If you want to buy something that truly represents Florentine craftsmanship, and is relatively inexpensive, make one of these small purchases. You'll find many of the marbleized paper products available in the San Lorenzo market stalls as well as in specialty shops throughout the city. The single best source for these products is **Giannini e Figlio** (Piazza Pitti 37), a shop founded in 1856. Other shops worth visiting include **Pineider** (Piazza della Signoria 14r), **Bottega Artigiana del Libro** (Lungarno Corsini 3840r), **Fantasie Fiorentine** (Borgo San Jacopo 50r),

Il Papiro (Via Cavour 55r, Piazza del Duomo 24r, and Lungarno degli Acciaiuoli 42r), **Il Torchio** (Via dei Bardi 17), and **Cartoleria Parione** (Via Parione 10r).

CERAMICS, PORCELAIN, AND CRYSTAL

Florence doesn't offer a great deal in this department. However, one of our favorite Florentine shops is **Galleria Machiavelli** (Via Por S. Maria 39r, Tel. 2398586). They offer a nice selection of colorful ceramic bowls, jars, and small gift items. They also do excellent packing and shipping. Try **Armando Poggi** (Via Calzaiuoli 105r, 116r) for an excellent selection of both Italian and international porcelain, crystal, and silver. **Ditta Luca Dellas Robbia** (Via del Proconsolo 19) is good for pottery. If you're not planning to visit Venice, you might want to see the nice glass selections at **La Bottega dei Cristalli** (Via dei Benci 51r) which is located just around the corner from Piazza Santa Croce.

ARTS, ANTIQUES, AND FURNITURE

Florence abounds with shops offering paintings, decorative arts, antiques, and furniture. For one of the largest selections of quality oil paintings, visit **Galleria Masini** (Piazza C. Goldoni 6r, Tel. 294000) near the Grand and Excelsior hotels. Also look for **Ken's Art Gallery** (Via Lambertesca 15/17r, Tel. 2396587) and **Florence Art Gallery** (Via Tornabuoni 3, Tel. 211213). For gorgeous, but very expensive, inlaid mosaics produced with semi-precious stones, try **Art del Mosaico** (Largo Bargellini 2-4, Tel. 241647, adjacent to the Santa Croce church), **Pitti Mosaici** (Guicciardini 60r, Pitti Square 16r, and Pitti Square 18r, Tel. 282127), and **Bottega del Mosaico** (Via Guicciardini 126r, Tel. 210718). Most of Florence's major antique shops tend to be concentrated along Via Maggio in the Colli area and along Borgo Ognissanti in the Santa Maria Novella area which also has several furniture shops. Like antiques elsewhere in Italy, Florentine antiques can be extremely expensive.

LINENS

Several shops offer excellent quality bed, bath, and table linens. Try **Pratesi** (Lungarno Amerigo Vespucci 8r) and **Frette** (Via Cavour 2). **Loretta Caponi** (Borgo Ognissanti 12r) offers a good selection of linens, lace, and lingerie.

TRAVEL MAPS AND GUIDES

Forgot to pack the right travel resources to get you through the rest of Italy or Europe? Don't worry. If you need maps or travel guides, you won't do any better than **Libreria Il Viaggio** (Borgodegli Albizi 41r, Tel. 240489). They offer an excellent selection of English language travel resources on Florence, Italy, Europe, and the rest of the world.

SHOPPING FIVE FLORENCES

Shopping in Florence is best approached in terms of five distinct shopping districts. Each has its own unique mix of sites, shops, restaurants, and neighborhood ambience.

CENTRO STORICO

As noted earlier, this is the historical center of the city where most visitors immediately head for sightseeing and strolling. This section houses the major museums, works of art, the famous Duomo, and the popular bridge spanning the River Arno—the Ponte Vecchio. Here you will bathe in medieval Florence and all the art that represents its glorious past. This also is where you will encounter huge crowds, indeed wall to wall waves, of tourists in search of the same popular sites from March to November. Major hotels, such as the Savoy, are located in this area. Numerous shops, catering mainly to middle class tourists, line the many streets of this area as well as the Ponte Vecchio.

The major shopping streets in this area connect the Duomo to the Uffizi and Ponte Vecchio. **Via dei Calzaiuoli**, for example, is the main shopping street linking the Duomo with the Uffizi; the area between Piazza della Signoria and the Uffizi is primarily a pedestrian mall lined with varying quality clothing, accessory, jewelry, and gift shops.

The second major shopping street in this area is **Via Roma** which, as it continues south changes it name to Via Calimala and Via Por S. Maria, connects the Duomo to the Ponte Vecchio. This is the main walking thoroughfare for most tourists visiting Florence. These contiguous streets take you past the Piazza della Repubblica and the Savoy Hotel. Here you will find the **Straw Market** with its many small stalls selling inexpensive leather goods and clothes along with more upscale shops selling everything from jewelry to the latest in fashionable clothes, shoes, and accessories. This area also has the greatest concentration of ice cream (gelato) shops anywhere in Florence. At night, hundreds of people stroll the cobblestone streets enjoying the latest combination of ice cream flavors. If you look hard enough, you can even find some excellent shopping in this area that goes beyond the typical tourist shops. In fact, the best quality shopping is found in a two-block area adjacent to the Ponte Vecchio. Some of our favorite places include:

- ❑ **Galleria Machiavelli:** *Via Por S. Maria 39r, Tel. 2398-586.* A small two-storey shop offering an excellent selection of colorful and fun ceramic pieces—bowls, jars, planters, and small gift items. The frog and duck bowls are simply adorable! Does excellent packing and reliable shipping.

- ❑ **Befani & Tai:** *Via Vacchereccia 13r, 7n, Tel. 287825.* A small but exclusive jeweler with an extremely productive workshop upstairs. Produces one-of-a-kind designs. While its window and showcase inventory may seem sparse, this is the ultimate understated jeweler. Trust us; it produces top quality jewelry.

- ❑ **Maria Grazia Cassetti**: *(Via Por S. Maria 29r, Tel. 2396977).* Another excellent jewelry shop offering unique designs. Tends to specialize in large gold pieces and those made with precious stones (necklaces and bracelets). Also has two shops on the nearby Ponte Vecchio (on the right-hand side at the southern end of the bridge) which offer a different line of jewelry.

- ❑ **Bijoux Cascio:** *Via Por S. Maria 1r, Tel. 294378.* Located just across from the foot of the bridge, this shop offers one of the best selections of costume jewelry. You might swear the pieces are real!

- ❑ **Blue Point:** *Via dei Calzaiuoli 39r, Tel. 210791.* Offers distinctive jewelry (rings, bracelets, necklaces, pins, earrings) in gold, silver, amathyst, pearls, coral, and turquoise. You'll find a good range of jewelry here, from inexpensive gold plated chains to expensive gold and pearl jewelry. What's particularly nice about this shop is the way it displays its jewelry—everything is on display and with price tags. In fact, the whole shop is organized for easy window-shopping. You can't help but find something here in your price range.

- ❑ **Gatto Bianco:** *Borgo SS. Apostoli 12R, Tel. 282989.* located just off the main street (Via Por S. Maria) and near the Ponte Vecchio, this unique jewelry shop offers the creative designs of Walter E. Carla Romani who has his workshop in the back of the shop. You'll find very modern necklace, bracelet, earring, and pin designs using pearls, onyx, agate, amber, lapis, and red coral.

- ❑ **Martelli:** *Via Por S. Maria 18r, Tel. 2396395.* A small but excellent shop for gloves, neckties, and scarves. The leather gloves are good buys for both quality and price. Neckties and scarves come under such popular brand names as Giorgio Armani, Gianni Versace, Kenzo, Mazzoleni, Missoni, and Valentino.

- ❑ **Gold and jewelry shops along the Ponte Vecchio:** Step onto this popular bridge and you can easily spend an hour window shopping in what is Italy's most unique shopping bazaar for gold and jewelry. Each of the tiny shops lining both sides of the bridge displays most of their stock in their windows. Look for such shops as U. Gheradi, Gheradi & Gheradi, Capelli, L. Vaggi, Rajola, L. Vettori, P. Fallaci, P. Venturi, Marchi, Bellini, Soldi, Cerrini, and Cassetti. Abitazione (#36) also offers a good selection of gloves, scarves, and neckties. Don't be turned off by all the tourists. Contrary to what others may say about this shopping area, the shops here are a great place to do comparative window shopping for both designs and prices. You may find something very special here. Some shops may give you a discount for cash.

SANTA MARIA NOVELLA

This is Florence's most upscale shopping area and the place where you will find some of the city's finest hotels (Excelsior and Grand) and restaurants. It's also the area of the main train station and one of Florence's largest piazze, the **Piazza Santa Maria Novella**. The Santa Maria Novella area is where you can stroll along the banks of the lovely River Arno, stop at numerous upscale clothing and jewelry shops, visit art galleries and antique shops, and enjoy some of Florence's finest restaurants. While history abounds in this area, it has little to offer in comparison to the highly concentrated monuments and art galleries in the Centro Storico area. For many visitors, the Santa Maria Novella area is a shopper's paradise for the best of the best that Florence has to offer. Walk it's two main shopping streets—**Tornabuoni** and **Vigna Nouva**—and you will discover Italy's major designer boutiques and jewelry shops that have made Florence such a leader in the world of fashion design: **Louis Vuitton, Gucci, Gianni Versace, Trussard, Cartier, Yves Saint Laurent, Valentino, Georgio Armani, Ermenegildo Zegna,** and **Laurel**. Discover the new **House of Florence** (Via Tornabuoni 6r, Tel. 288162) for exciting new designs in leather goods and scarves by Gucci family members. Pass by the always exciting **Mario Buccellati** (Via dei Tornabuoni 71r, Tel. 2396579) for fabulous one-of-a-kind jewelry. The workmanship in gold is without parallel, except by other Buccellati family members. And look for **Nai-Oleari** (Via della Vigna Nuova 35r) which offers uniquely designed fabrics and accessories (purses, bags, children's backpacks, umbrellas, neckties). Walk into the flagship **Salvatore Ferragamo** shop that heads Via Tornabuoni (in front of the Column of Justice, Piazza S. Trinita), just after a bus load of Japanese tourist invade this shop to snap up armfuls of Ferragamo shoes and accessories, and you'll quickly discover why Florence has such a worldwide reputation for quality products. This shop oozes with quality shoes, handbags, scarves and accessories.

Then stroll down the adjacent Via del Parione and Borgo Ognissanti and you'll discover numerous antique and furniture shops as well as art galleries, jewelry stores, and linen shops. Near the facing Grand and Excelsior hotels you can rent a car from the major rental agencies headquartered in this area.

SAN LORENZO

Located immediately north, northwest, and northeast of the Duomo, San Lorenzo is best noted for its huge indoor and outdoor markets. Its two-story covered indoor market offers a large variety of food. Here's where the locals buy their fresh produce and cuts of meats. Like many similar wet markets throughout the world, it's of most interest to those who are intrigued with a pre-supermarket shopping style. This is the closest you'll get to the slaughter house, and you may need a stomach to go with it! Not our type of shopping but a cultural experience nonetheless.

The most interesting shopping lies just outside the wet market, surrounding the building and stretching several blocks from Via Nazionale along Via dell'Ariento and Canto dei Nelli to B.S. Lorenzo (Piazza San Lorenzo). This area comprises one of Italy's largest street markets, the famous **San Lorenzo Market**. Hundreds of vendor stalls line these streets. Taken together, they offer a wide variety of products for shoppers interested in a bazaar-style shopping experience. Here you will find leather coats, bags, belts, shoes, and wallets; sweaters; marbleized paper products; scarves; gloves; shirts; hats; T-shirts, sweatshirts, and aprons; neckties; and even suits. Many of the stalls display "fixed price" signs as well as accept major credit cards. Others only accept cash and will bargain. Since most of the stalls sell the same things, this is a good place to do comparative shopping. However, be forewarned that the prices here may not be better than in the many street shops elsewhere in the city. Furthermore, the quality of goods varies and some items are of questionable quality—especially leather coats. On the other hand, many leather gloves selling in the US$25 to $60 range appear to be of similar quality as those found in some of the better street shops. Inexpensive scarves (US$15 to $30) and neckties (US$10 to $15) also appear to be good bargains here. In other words, you may or may not get a good deal here. Just because goods are being sold from mobile vendors and stalls in bazaar fashion does not necessarily mean they offer the best buys. Nonetheless, this is still a fun place to shop and soak up some of the local shopping color.

- **Contrary to what others may say, the jewelry shops on the Ponte Vecchio can be good places to both window shop and shop.**
- **For bargain shopping and tourist trinkets, head for the open-air San Lorenzo Market and Straw Market.**
- **Many of the vendor stalls in the San Lorenzo Market display "fixed price" signs and accept major credit cards. Be forewarned the prices here may be no better than elsewhere in the city.**
- **One of the largest concentrations of leather shops is found within one block of the Piazza Santa Croce.**
- **Florence's best ice cream shop, Vivoli, is located at Via Isola delle Stinche 7r in the Santa Croce area.**
- **Madova (Via Guicciardini 1r) is one of Florence's oldest and most popular leather glove shops.**

But there is much more to this area than just the San Lorenzo market. Several streets running north of the Duomo, such as B.S. Lorenzo, V. Martelli, V.C. Cavour, V. Ricasoli, and Via dei Servi are lined with shops selling the latest in fashion clothes, accessories, and jewelry. One of our favorite shops here is the **Mineral Shop** (Via dei Servi, 120r, Tel. 218281) with its excellent selection of fossilized stones and semi-precious jewelry. You'll find several unique designs in necklaces, bracelets, pins, and earrings in this small but good quality shop.

You'll also find lots of great restaurants and inexpensive eateries throughout this diverse area.

SANTA CROCE

If you're looking for leather, the Santa Croce area is the place to go. Most famous for the Piazza Santa Croce and its adjacent

Santa Croce Church, which houses the remains of such famous Florentines as Michelangelo, Machiavelli, and Galileo, this piazza also is the home for **The Leather School** which functions as both a leather factory and shop. Santa Croce includes several shops offering a wide selection of leather coats, handbags, shoes, and accessories. The main shopping street is Borgo dei Greci. Begin directly east of the Piazza Signoria and Palazzo Vecchio and walk this street until you come to the Piazza Santa Croce. Most of the leather shops are located within a block of the Piazza Santa Croce. However, you will find a few small shops along the way selling a wide variety of goods. One of our favorites is a tiny shop called **Alfreda e Manuela Evangelisti** (Borgo dei Greci 33r) or just "Evangelisti" on the sign above the door. This shop offers one of the best selections of inexpensive neckties and scarves, including ponchos, in Florence. The prices are comparable to those found in the vendor stalls of the San Lorenzo Market. And you even get friendly and helpful service here! Further down this street near the Piazza you will come to one of Florence's largest leather shops, **Bottega Fiorentina** (Borgo dei Greci 5r, Tel. 295411). Here you will find five large rooms offering a wide selection of leather coats, purses, belts, bags, shoes, wool ponchos, and silk neckties. This is a good one-stop-shop for buying small gift items. Several other leather shops are found up and down the street near Bottega Fiorentina. However, we found the prices to be a bit high compared to shops elsewhere in the city. As soon as you enter the Piazza Santa Croce, you'll find numerous leather and jewelry shops lining the square. Many tour companies send their clients to various shops in this square. One shop in particular stands out here. Just to the left side of the church is **Arte del Mosaico** (Largo Bargellini 2-4, Tel. 241647) which has a large selection of mosaic paintings using semi-precious stones. The shop also has a workshop in the back where artists produce the pricy mosaics. These are real works of art—not tourist quality. And the prices reflect the excellent quality work. Expect to pay 1.5 million lire for a very small mosaic. Larger ones go for 10 million lire and higher. You may not feel you're getting much for US$5,000, but you are offered an exquisite work of art. If we were to buy a mosaic anywhere in Florence, we would make this shop our very first and last visit for comparing motifs and quality.

While you're in the Santa Croce area, don't forget to try Florence's best ice cream shop, **Vivoli**, which is located at Via Isola delle Stinche 7r. Somewhat difficult to find (near the corner of Vigna Vecchia), it's well worth the walk if you want to experience the best of the best in Florentine ice cream. For

5,000 lire, you can treat yourself to the creamiest and most unique combination of flavors in town. No cones served here—only cups. And you can even sit down at a counter for the price of the cup!

The Santa Croce area also yields a few other excellent shops. You'll discover many small antique shops along such streets as Vigna Vecchia and Via Ghibellina. For the best travel book and map store in Florence, stop at **Il Viaggio** at Borgo degli Albizi 41r (Tel. 240489). You'll find an excellent collection of travel guides and maps here on Florence and other parts of Italy as well as other places in Europe, Africa, and Asia. If you're missing something for the rest of your trip to Italy or Europe, make sure you visit this shop. You'll also find an excellent art gallery along this same street—**Navanazati Galleria d'arte** (Borgo deglil Albizi 67r) which includes a good selection of modern ceramics, sculptures, and paintings. Look for special exhibitions here. Via Dei Benci also yields several antique shops as well as a very nice Venetian glass shop—**La Bottega dei Cristalli** (Via dei Benci 51r, Tel. 2344891). It includes a unique selection of unusual glass trays along with a large selection of attractive bowls and glasses.

The rest of the Santa Croce area yields a large variety of small shops and restaurants. We recommend spending an hour or two just walking the streets in this area. You're likely to discover something unique.

OLTRARNO

The Oltrarno area is located on the south side of the River Arno. Adjacent to the Colli area, it's sometimes referred to as the "Pitti area" because of the presence of the huge Plazzo Pitti complex. It's best to enter this area from the Ponte Vecchio—just cross the bridge and you're immediately in the area. While somewhat less hectic than highly touristed areas on the other side of the river, the Oltrarno area offers some excellent shopping for jewelry, antiques, mosaics, clothing, and accessories. It's best to view this area as a shopping triangle consisting of three intersecting streets—**Via Guicciardini**, **Via Maggio**, and **Borgo Jacopo**. The major historical landmark bordering this area is the Palazzo Pitti. If you enter the area by crossing the Ponte Vecchio, just look straight ahead and you'll see the first shop worth visiting—**Madova** (Via Guicciardini 1r, Tel. 2396526). This is one of Florence's oldest and most popular leather glove shops. The selection is huge and the quality is good. The shop also has its own catalog. Just step up to the counter and get fitted. Across the street is one of Florence's oldest and most exclusive jewelry stores, **Quaglia & Forte** (Via Guicciardini 12r, Tel. 294534). They produce excellent quality 18k gold reproductions of Etruscan jewelry as well as beautiful angel skin coral jewelry. Further down this street look for **Freon** (Via de Guicciardin 118r, Tel. 2396504) for uniquely designed costume jewelry. They produce very modernistic designs which may or may not appeal to your tastes. Freon also has another shop across the street (#45) which primarily sells handbags. On the same side of the side of the street you'll see two shops selling mosaic "paintings" and table tops—**Pitti Mosaici** (Guicciardini 60r, Tel. 282127) and **Bottega del Mosaico** (Guicciardini 126r, Tel. 210718). Pitti Mosaici also has a workshop further down the street across from the Piazza dei Pitti where you can see the craftsmen practice their trade. You'll see some beautiful, but extremely expensive, inlaid work being done here with hard and semi-precious stones. The quality of the craftsmanship is excellent. Expect many of the small framed pieces to cost US$2,000 to US$10,000. You may want to avoid asking the price of the table tops!

As you pass by the piazza, look for a small jewelry shop called **Maggie Maggi Gioielli** (Piazza Pitti 6r, Tel. 292704). This is a real gem of a shop. The talented Maria Grazia Maggi designs some truly unique gold and silver jewelry. A gold jeweler and fine art sculpturist, she has won several awards for her distinctive designs which combine East (India) and West traditions with traditional Florentine craftsmanship. You'll find her own interpretations of Etruscan designs worked into rings, bracelets, and necklaces. This is one of our favorite small jewelry shops that you may want to include on your "must visit" list. Best of all, her prices are very reasonable. She crafts her jewelry in the back of this small shop.

As you leave Maggie Maggi Gioielli, turn right and go around the corner to **Via Maggio**. This is Florence's major antique street. From the Piazza di San Felicia to the Ponte S. Trinita, both sides of the street are lined with more than 25 antique shops selling very expensive antiques. This is the street for discerning collectors who should know what they are doing in the world of fine Italian antiques.

Just before you come to the end of Via Maggio, turn right onto **Borgo Jacopo**, the final street that completes our shopping triangle. This street has a few antique shops, clothing and accessory stores, and one of Florence's best restaurants—Osteria del Cinghiale Bianco (Borgo San Jacopo, 43r, Tel. 215706, cash only)—for both lunch and dinner. Although crowded (reservations recommended), this restaurant offers good value and is an excellent place to stop for lunch. Try their fresh boar. At the end of this street you will again come to the Ponte Vecchio which has an excellent ice cream shop at the foot of the bridge.

IN SEARCH OF QUALITY

Quality shopping abounds in Florence along with mediocre shopping. If you're primarily in search of top quality shopping, you'll find that quality shops tend to congregate along the same streets and areas: **Via Tornabuoni** (Ferragamo, Gucci, House of Florence, Versace, Trussard, Yves Saint Laurent, Cartier, Casadei, Buccellati, Settepassi-Faraone); **Via della Vigna Nuova** (Laurèl, Valentino, Georgio Armani, Ermenegildo Zegna); **Borgo Ognissanti** (antiques and furniture); **Via Maggio** (antique shops); **Via Guicciardini** (jewelry and art shops); and the **Duomo** (gifts, clothes, accessories, jewelry).

If you're looking for bargain shopping and tourist trinkets, head for the **San Lorenzo Market** and the **Straw Market** as well as the moderately priced department stores—**Coin** (Via dei Calzaiuoli), **Standa** (Via Panzani), and **Upim** (Piazza Repubblica). These places offer relatively inexpensive clothes, leather goods, accessories, and gift items.

ACCOMMODATIONS

Old villa hotels abound in Florence and many are architectural delights that have been restored to their former glory while being fitted with modern amenities desired by today's travelers. There are more than 400 hotels in Florence but with a daily average of 20,000 visitors a day actually staying in the city, hotels are often fully booked—especially during the busy summer season and at Easter. So it behooves one to book ahead—especially in high season. Because of problems with "no-shows" many hotels will request payment for the first night when the reservation is made.

The constant stream of visitors means that hotel prices are generally kept high, and although it is easier to make reservations between November and March, you may find that prices do not vary much. The city streets can be noisy, so if you are a light sleeper, you may want to request a room away from the street or ask whether the rooms are soundproofed. Hotels with restaurants often include the cost for breakfast whether or not you want it, and some may also insist that you take a main meal in the hotel restaurant.

There are also many small, inexpensive yet charming hotels

and pensiones in Florence. Sandra Gustafson's ***Cheap Sleeps in Italy*** is a good guide to many of Florence's small hotels from no stars to three stars. These hotels offer good value and often an opportunity to feel as if one is living in the city rather than merely a visitor in a hotel.

If you arrive without a reservation there are several organizations that can help you find a room in almost any price range for a small commission. **ITA** is located in the Santa Maria Novella station, Tel. 282893, open 9-8:30; they will not take bookings over the telephone. **Florence Promhotels**, located on Viale A. Volta 72, Tel. 2478543, will take bookings by phone or mail. **Toscana Hotels 80** located at Viale Gramsci 9, Tel. 247-8543, will take bookings by phone or mail.

The following are some of the best hotels in Florence. All are in or close to the city center so that you are within walking distance of museums, restaurants, and shops.

- ❑ **Excelsior:** *Piazza Ognissanti 3, Tel. 264201, Fax 210-278*. The best of the best, the Excelsior exudes old world elegance—Napoleon's sister, Caroline, once lived here. A short walk from the city center or along the Arno from the Ponte Vecchio it is situated on a small piazza. From its gilt and marble lobby to its luxurious rooms and baths complete with heated towel bars, the Excelsior is classical, plush, well staffed and efficiently managed. Many of the rooms overlook the Arno as does the roof garden terrace. Its terrace restaurant, Il Cestello, with its river view is one of the best in the city and one of the few restaurants that stays open all week. Very expensive (★★★★★L).

- ❑ **Grand:** *Piazza Ognissanti 1, Tel. 288781, Fax 217400*. Situated across the piazza from the Excelsior, some regulars prefer the smaller size (109 rooms) to its CIGA sister's (205 rooms). Whatever the reason, the expected personalized service does not disappoint. Designed by Brunelleschi, the Renaissance decor evokes visions of a by-gone era. Provides the amenities expected of a luxury hotel. Very expensive (★★★★★L).

- ❑ **Savoy:** *Piazza della Repubblica 7, Tel. 283313, Fax 284-840*. Centrally located amid both the monuments for sightseeing and shopping, the location may be a double-edged sword as some patrons say noise can be a problem—even with double-glazed windows. This grand old hotel, a member of The Leading Hotels of the World, lives up to the expectations of service expected by those with this exclusive membership. Rooms are variously decorated in Venetian, Florentine and some in contemporary style. Very expensive (★★★★★L).

- **Helvetia & Bristol:** *Via dei Pescioni 2, Tel. 287814, Fax 288353.* This centrally located hotel set on a quiet street behind the Piazza della Repubblica, is a member of the exclusive Relais & Chateaux group. Considered one of Italy's finest hotels, it has recently been renovated and incorporates antique furnishings and oil paintings to provide individual character to each room as well as to the public areas. The marble bathrooms have Jacuzzis. Very expensive (★★★★★L).

- **Regency:** *Piazza Massimo d'Azeglio 3, Tel. 245247, Fax 2342938.* This small hotel is set in a 19th century villa on a quiet street within walking distance of town. A member of the Relais & Chateaux group, the rooms and public areas are graciously furnished with antiques. Room size varies, and some are truly spacious. Impeccable service, a private garage and a lovely garden are noteworthy. Features an excellent restaurant—Relais le Jardin. (★★★★★L)

- **Villa Cora:** *Viale Machiavelli 18, Tel. 2298451, Fax 229086.* An exquisite neo-classical villa, its 56 spacious rooms and suites are complemented by a beautiful garden with a heated pool. It is about 2 miles from the city center. The Taverna Machiavella, an expensive and formal restaurant, is a part of the hotel. Service lives up to the expectations of a 5-star hotel. (★★★★★L)

- **Villa Medici:** *Via del Prato 42, Tel. 2381331, Fax 2381336.* Located between the railroad station and the Arno within walking distance from town, this luxurious villa occupies a reconstructed 16th century palace. Rooms are spacious and some have balconies. Impeccable service. Although consisting of only 110 rooms, the hotel includes shops, a pool, garden, and restaurant—you wouldn't ever have to leave the hotel. (★★★★★L)

- **Brunelleschi:** *Piazza S. Elisabetta 3, Tel. 562068, Fax 219653.* Located on a piazza off a quiet street near the Duomo, a 6th century Byzantine tower, a church and a third building are combined to form this architecturally unique hotel. Soundproofed rooms, many with good views, are comfortable, accented with contemporary decor and feature generous sized travertine baths. There are great city views from the rooftop terrace. The hotel has its own museum that displays ancient Roman foundations and pottery shards found during the restoration of the hotel. Expensive (★★★★).

- **Sofitel:** *Via Cerretani 10, Tel. 2381301, Fax 2381312.* This relatively new hotel, opened its doors in 1992 and is sited in a 17th century palazzo. It is in an unbeatable central location with soundproofed rooms. Those who yearn for clean contemporary design rather than another old world look will find this modern hotel offers a refreshing change. Service is good and there is a good restaurant which serves an American style buffet breakfast which is included in the room rate. (★★★★)

- **Roma:** *Piazza Santa Maria Novella 8, Tel. 210366, Fax 215306.* Positioned in a 16th century palazzo on one of Florence's most important squares this 50 room hotel features stained glass windows, frescoed ceilings, and inlaid marble floors. Many rooms overlook the piazza and a church. There is a restaurant. (★★★★)

- **Anglo-American:** *Via Garibaldi 9, Tel. 282114, Fax 268513.* Set in an old villa, the public areas are light and airy and decorated in an English garden style. Mirrored galleries give a feeling of spaciousness. Room sizes vary and some are quite spacious. All are decorated in period furnishings or replicas. Includes a restaurant. (★★★★)

- **Calzaiuoli:** *Via Calzaiuoli 6, Tel. 212456, Fax 268310.* The greatest strength of this hotel is its ideal location midway between the Duomo and the Piazza Signoria on Florence's largest pedestrian street. Its contemporary decor of fabric covered walls with coordinating curtains and bedspreads are eye pleasing but not noteworthy. Most rooms are large by standards in this part of town. The lobby is unexciting. No restaurant. This is location, location, and location. (★★★)

- **Grand Hotel Cavour:** *Via del Proconsolo 3, Tel. 282461, Fax 218955.* Centrally located 2 blocks from the Duomo, this restored palazzo has kept the best of its architectural heritage. Some rooms have the original brick archways or beamed ceilings while others have great city views. Rooms have large closets and nice baths with heated towel racks. The dramatic lounge has a fountain in one corner. There is an excellent restaurant next door—Beatrice—in an old chapel that serves good food with great ambience. (★★★)

- **Il Guelfo Bianco:** *Via Cavour 57, Tel. 288330, Fax 295203.* Only 2 short blocks from the Duomo on one of the best shopping streets, this hotel has recently been renovated and the rooms are soundproofed. There are two sections to the hotel and some rooms are very spacious in the section that is accessed from an outside entrance beside the lobby area. The baths are more spacious than many in the city center hotels. Includes a lovely breakfast room and an outside courtyard used for breakfast in nice weather. (★★★)

- **Morandi alla Crocetta:** *Via Laura 50, Tel. 2344747, Fax 2480954.* This small and relatively inexpensive hotel is a gem. Located in a restored 16th century convent, it's an oasis of quiet. Each room is different and they vary in size, but the smaller rooms are considered singles, so there is a good amount of space. There are frescos which have been carefully uncovered, exposed parts of the old structure incorporated into decorating decisions, and pieces used creatively from other old buildings to give a real sense of history. There is a comfortable sitting room and wherever you are in the hotel it feels more like a home than a hotel. Offers only ten rooms at present, but the owner is working to expand as areas are restored downstairs. About a fifteen minute walk from the city center.

If you are on a tight budget and prefer spending your cash on shopping rather than sleeping, also consider these hotels:

- **Albergo Firenze:** Piazza Donati 4, Tel. 268301, Fax 212370.

- **Hotel Archibusieri:** Vicolo Marzio 1, Tel. 282480, Fax 219367.

- **Hotel Bellettini:** Via dei Conti 7, Tel. 231561, Fax 283551.

- **Hotel La Scaletta:** Via Guicciardini 13, Tel. 283028, Fax 289562.
- **Hotel Lombardi:** Via Fiume 8, Tel. 283151, Fax 284808.
- **Hotel Italia:** Via Faenza 26, Tel. 287508, Fax 210941.
- **Hotel Azzi:** Via Faenza 51, Tel. 213806, Fax 213806.
- **Hotel Anza:** Via San Zanobi 45, Tel. 490990.
- **Hotel Nazionale:** Via Nazionale 22, Tel. 2382203.
- **Hotel Visconti:** Piazza degli Ottaviani 1, Tel. 213877.
- **Pensione Accademia:** Via Faenza 7, Tel. 293451.

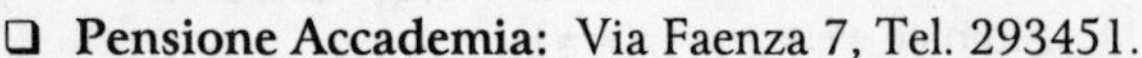

RESTAURANTS

Florence has a few outstanding restaurants and a lot of very good ones. Residents like to tell that Catherine de'Medici took a cadre of Florentine chefs with her to Paris and that began international haute cuisine. However, most Florentine food is simple fare made with the freshest ingredients. Four courses are the norm: an antipasto consisting of cold meats or a liver pate spread on small pieces of toasted bread are most likely starters. Primi piatti usually consists of a risotto or pasta dish with the secondi piatti often a meat or fish main course. Dessert may be cheese, cookies or zuccotto—a liqueur-soaked cake with a creamy chocolate filling. There are few sauces, few spices; yet at its best, Tuscan cooking is a joy.

Dining in Florence takes place earlier than in Rome—12:30pm for lunch and from 7:30 in the evening for dinner. Many of the best restaurants close in August. Reservations are wise—even a day or two in advance.

- **Terrazza Brunelleschi:** *Hotel Baglioni, Piazza Unita Italiana 6, Tel. 215642. Reservations suggested. Jacket and tie.* You'll get one of the best views in town from this rooftop restaurant as the wraparound picture windows frame Brunelleschi's dome. The outdoor terrace for summer dining provides lots of ambience. Known for traditional Tuscan dishes. Try their minestra di fagiola (bean soup).

- ❑ **Enoteca Pinchiorri:** *Via Ghibellina 87, Tel. 242777. Reservations Required. Jacket and tie. Closed for lunch Sunday and Monday and closed in August and 1 week in December.* An outstanding restaurant, generally considered one of the best in Italy, set in a magnificent Renaissance palace. The menu is definitely Italian, but the wine cellar is stocked with wines from every major wine producing region worldwide. The range as well as the caliber of wines available is superb.

- ❑ **Il Verrocchio:** *Villa La Massa, Via La Massa 6, Candeli, Tel. 6510101. Reservations advised. Jacket and tie. Closed Monday and Tuesday from November to March.* Located about 20 minutes from Florence by car, most patrons would say it was worth the trip. Set in an 18th century villa, the dining room has a large fireplace, classical columns and a vaulted ceiling. Adding to the ambience, in good weather there is a terrace for dining that overlooks the Arno. Although this restaurant recently received a negative review from one of the foremost restaurant rating guides, you may wish to give it a try with the expectation that the chef just had a bad night that evening. You may want to try the lamb with apricot sauce or one of the usually excellent pasta dishes.

- ❑ **Relais Le Jardin:** *Hotel Regency, Piazza Massimo d'Azeglio 5, Tel. 245247. Reservations required for non-guests of hotel. Jacket and tie. Open lunch and dinner Monday to Saturday. Closed Sunday.* One of Florence's top restaurants, there are two dining rooms—one overlooking the garden. Features various regional Italian cuisines. You might try the risotto alla milanese, medallions of veal with rhubarb or crepes filled with zucchini.

- ❑ **Angiolino:** *Via Santo Spirito 36r., Tel. 2398976. Dinner reservations advised. No credit cards. Closed Sunday dinner, Monday and last 3 weeks in July.* A charcoal grill and wood burning stove gives a warmth—both literally and figuratively—to this informal restaurant. Tuscan cuisine.

- ❑ **LaLoggia:** *Piazzale Michelangelo 1, Tel. 2342832. No reservations. Closed Wednesday and August 10-25.* For a wonderful view you may want to try this informal restaurant. There are tables outdoors in nice weather when you may find it crowded. Try the porcini mushrooms or another of their Florentine classics.

- **Harry's Bar:** *Lungarno Vespucci 22r, Tel. 2396700. Reservations required. Closed Sunday and December 15-January 8.* If you've tired of pasta and want an American hamburger, this is the place! In addition to familiar American fare, the menu also includes two Tuscan dishes which change daily. Popular and lively place for American expatriates. Along the Arno, but no view.

- **Mario da Ganino:** *Piazza dei Cimatori 4r, Tel. 214125. Reservations advised. Closed Sunday and August 15-22.* This informal, rustic restaurant is located between the Duomo and the Palazzo Vecchio. Select from many pasta dishes. You might try Gnudoni—a ravioli without the pasta casing—or try the cheesecake for dessert.

- **La Capannina di Sante:** *Piazza Ravenna and Ponte da Verrazzano. Tel. 688345. Dinner only. Closed Sunday and 1 week in August.* This restaurant by the Arno is not heavily frequented by tourists, so you are likely to encounter mostly Florentines here. It is known for its well prepared fresh seafood and a good white wine selection.

- **Sabatini:** *Via Panzani 9a, Tel. 282802. Closed Monday and some holidays.* Set in an elegant old villa near the Duomo, this restaurant has a retractable roof that allows dining under the stars in good weather. Try the cannelloni, the bow-tie pasta with broccoli, or lamb.

- **Il Profeta:** *Borgo Ognissanti 83, Tel. 212265. Closed Sunday and last two weeks of August.* In this restaurant near the Arno, comfortable informality prevails. Select from the pastas on the menu or try fritto misto—crispy morsels deep-fried in olive oil. If you have room try their house dessert—zuppa del Profeta—a cake and custard combination.

ENJOYING YOUR STAY

Florence offers an over-abundance of things to see and do. While much of the tourist activity centers on standing in lines to visit museums and churches and dining in restaurants, many of Florence's treasures and pleasures are relatively hassle free—just walking the streets, watching people, exploring intriguing piazzas, visiting colorful markets, strolling along the banks of the River Arno, or attending an outdoor concert.

Because the city is spread out over six districts with no coherent core, planning where to go first, second, and third can be a daunting task. Our advice: head first for the Ponte Vecchio or Duomo and then work your way along the major streets within each district that lead to various piazzas, churches, museums, and shops. Otherwise you may exhaust yourself by going from one end of the city to another each day in an effort to visit similar types of sites that are spread throughout the city.

In addition to visiting many of Florence's churches, museums, galleries, shops, and restaurants, you may want to sample Florence's nightlife and explore some interesting areas nearby. Unlike Venice, which is relatively dead at night, Florence is alive both day and night.

ENTERTAINMENT AND NIGHTLIFE

If you enjoy dining, dancing, theater, music, and movies, Florence will not disappoint you. There's always something going on in Florence which further enhances its paramount cultural image. Check with your hotel concierge, pick up tourist literature, look for posters, or survey Florence's daily newspaper, *La Nazione*, or monthly magazines, *Time Off* and *Firenze Spettacolo*, for information on what's happening in Florence.

SPECIAL EVENTS

If you're in Florence during May and June, you'll have an opportunity to see some of the world's most famous conductors perform, listen to fabulous concerts with old and new compositions, and watch operas at Italy's oldest and most important music festival, **Maggio Musicale** or May Music Festival, which also includes a film festival. While most events are held in the Teatro Communale (Corso Italia 16, Tel. 2779236), to the delight of tourists, some of the concerts are held outdoors in the sculpture-rich Piazza della Sognoria, Teatro Romano, Santa Croce, and Palazzo Pitti. July is the season for special theatrical performances, ballets, and concerts. Between June and late August several chamber and symphony concerts take place as part of another festival, **Estate Fiesolana**, which also includes theater, dance, and film. September begins Opera Season. If you're in Florence during December, be sure to attend the ballet for a special performance of the *Nutcracker Suite*. Tickets to these and other performances can be obtained through box offices, travel agents, major hotels, and central ticket agencies.

CLASSICAL MUSIC

Florence's concert season is by no means confined to the summer festival months. Other concerts take place throughout the year at the Teatro dellas Pergola, Palazzo dei Congressi, Teatro Communale, and Teatro Verdi.

CONTEMPORARY MUSIC

Florence has its share of visiting international rock and pop stars and bands that perform in the Palasport stadium at Viale Paoli, the Teatro Verdi, Teatro Tenda, Palazzo dei Congressi, and the Auditorium Flog. Major international jazz performances are held at the Auditorium Flog. Popular jazz clubs include the **Jazz Club** (Via Nuova dei Caccini 3, tel. 2479700) and **Salt Peanuts** (Piazza Santa Maria Novella 26r).

NIGHTCLUBS AND DISCOS

If you enjoy nightclubs and discos, Florence offers several options in this department. Florence's largest and most popular discos include: **Tenax** (Via Pratese 46a, Tel. 308160, open Wednesday to Saturday); **Space Electronic** (Via Palazzuolo 37, Tel. 293082, open nightly); **Manila** (Piazza Matteucci-Campi Bisenzio, Tel. 894121, open Friday to Sunday); and **Andromeda** (Piazza de´ Cerchi 7a, Tel. 292002, open Monday to Saturday). Other alternatives include: **Jackie O´** (Via Erta Canina 24, Tel. 2344904); **Caffè Voltaire** (Via della Scala 9r, Tel. 218255); **Meccanò** (Viale degli Olmi 1, Cascine Park, Tel. 331371); **Marcacanà** (Via Faenza 4, Tel. 210298); and **Full Up** (Via della Vigna Vecchia 21r, Tel. 293006).

One of the best piano bars in the city is at the **Excelsior Hotel** (Piazza Ognissanti 3, Tel. 2674201). Its rooftop garden location offers an excellent view of the River Arno.

BEYOND FLORENCE

If time permits, you may want to venture beyond Florence. Within the immediate vicinity of Florence, you'll find several interesting villas and convents, many of which are open to the public and can be reached by bus.

If you rent a car, you'll have more flexibility to explore several intriguing cities, towns, and villages within a 100 kilometer radius of Florence. Some of the most interesting places to visit include:

- **Seina:** Located 68 kilometers south of Florence, this is perhaps Italy's most beautiful medieval city with its own unique style of art and architecture. Indeed, many visitors to Florence prefer staying in Seina and then commuting to Florence by train. It's one of the most frequently visited cities in all of Italy. This Gothic city is filled with wonderful treasures and pleasures, including a beautiful main square (Piazza del Campo), a gorgeous Gothic cathedral, the Duomo, and several interesting museums. Shoppers should look for local ceramics.

- **Pisa:** Located 80 kilometers west of Florence, this is the famous city of the Leaning Tower of Pisa. Heavily touristed because of the tower, Duomo, and baptistery, you'll find lots of tourist shopping opportunities near the town, especially for T-shirts and knick knacks. For good quality shopping, especially for Venetian glass and jewelry, stop at **G. Barsanti & Figli** a small, but nice shop along the Piazza Duomo.

- **Lucca:** Located 65 kilometers west of Florence and 25 kilometers north of Pisa, this is one of Tuscany's most beautiful fortress towns which is filled with Romanesque churches, museums, and monuments. A great walking town.

- **Other Towns:** Several towns dot the Tuscan countryside. You might enjoy visiting the following places:

  - **Arezzo:** Located 88 kilometers northeast of Siena. Visit the church of San Francesco at the center of town.

  - **Cortona:** Located 30 kilometers south of Arezzo. Known for its excellent art and antique shops.

  - **Fiesole:** Located 8 kilometers northwest of Florence, this hill town offers and excellent view of Florence and its surrounding countryside. Also has a few interesting churches and museums.

  - **Montepulciano:** Located 35 kilometers southeast of Siena, this attractive hill town boasts numerous churches, palaces, shops, and cafés.

- **San Gimignano:** Located 31 kilometers northwest of Siena. If you have time to visit only one hill town, make sure it's this one. An impressive town of high walls, narrow streets, and unique towers.

- **Volterra:** Located 29 kilometers southwest of San Gimignano, this is a famous town for alabaster. Look for shops selling alabaster jewelry, boxes, and souvenirs.

6

Rome

Welcome to wonderful and romantic Rome. If you enjoy history, ancient ruins, powerful art and architecture, fine restaurants, delightful sidewalk cafés, terrific shopping, and lots of varied things to see and do, you're gonna love Rome. If you can tolerate charming chaos and adjust well to the ambience and relaxing lifestyles of southern Italy, Rome may well become one of your favorite "big city" destinations.

Rome was not built in a day, so don't expect to see it all at once. Take your time, even indulge yourself by spending some leisurely time in sidewalk cafés watching the world go by. Like a fine wine or meal, Rome is to be savored. Enjoy what you can in the limited time you've scheduled for this city. If you try to see and do everything on a tight schedule, you may quickly become frustrated with this city of rich history, culture, art, architecture as well as great shopping and dining. Plan to come back sometime to explore its remaining treasures and pleasures.

An Eternal and Dramatic City

Eternal and dramatic Rome—where all roads lead and where more than 26 centuries of history appear well and alive—offers

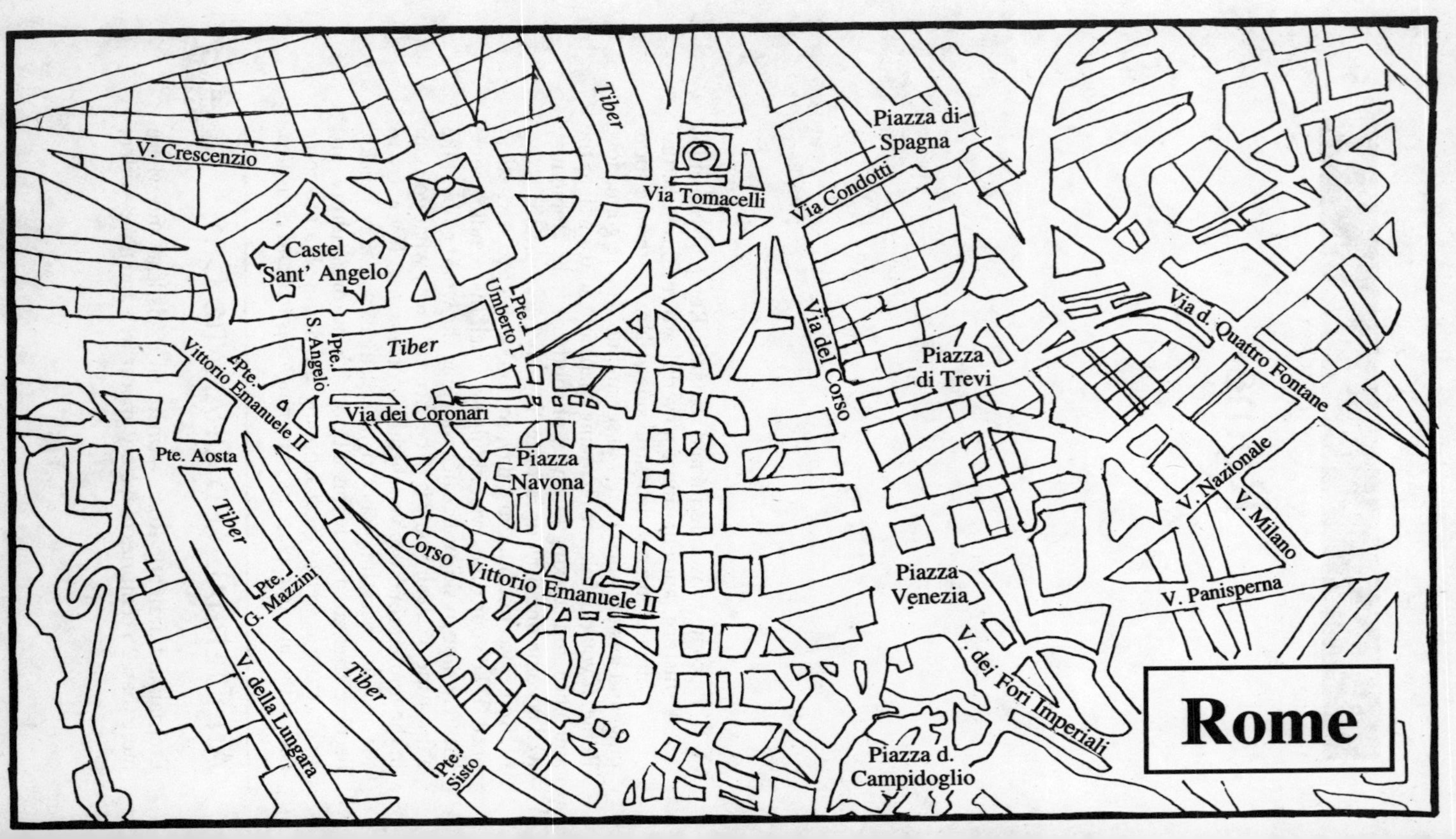
Rome
V. Crescenzio
Tiber
Piazza di Spagna
Via Tomacelli
Via Condotti
Castel Sant' Angelo
Pte. Umberto I
Via d. Quattro Fontane
Pte. S. Angelo
Tiber
Via del Corso
Piazza di Trevi
Pte. Vittorio Emanuele II
Via dei Coronari
Pte. Aosta
Piazza Navona
V. Nazionale
V. Milano
Tiber
Corso Vittorio Emanuele II
Piazza Venezia
V. Panisperna
Pte. G. Mazzini
V. della Lungara
Tiber
V. dei Fori Imperiali
Pte. Sisto
Piazza d. Campidoglio

an incredible number of treasures and pleasures for discerning travelers. No doubt about it. This is still a glorious and romantic city that once ruled the Western world. It's a pageant of history. It's the city of the fabled Colosseum, Forum, Pantheon, Vatican, River Tiber, Piazza Navona, Trevi Fountain, and Spanish Steps as well as lawyers, civil servants, and hordes of tourists in search of this city's many treasures and pleasures.

Rome also is the city of the Etruscans, Julius Caesar, popes, Bernini, Raphael, Michelangelo, Goethe, Keats, Byron, Shelley, Mussolini, and great political and cultural dramas that helped shape Western civilization. Home for the Vatican, the city continues to define religion for millions of Roman Catholics worldwide. A living museum, Rome is chock-full of history, monuments, fountains, architecture, statues, churches, museums, parks, piazzas, crumbling antiquities, excavations, tombs, art, and culture as well as the living chaos of people, traffic, noise, pollution, and inefficiencies. Travelers in search of quality will discover some of Italy's finest restaurants, hotels, and shopping in Rome.

- ❑ **Rome wasn't built in a day, so don't expect to see it all at once. Rome is to be savored. Plan to come back some day to further explore its many treasures and pleasures.**
- ❑ **This is still a glorious and romantic city displaying more than 26 centuries of history through powerful ruins, architecture, and art.**
- ❑ **Rome is the city of the fabled Colosseum, Pantheon, Forum, River Tiber, Piazza Navona, Trevi Fountain, and Spanish Steps—a big city with a very big history.**

Rome is a big city with a big history. One of the world's great magnets for tourists, the city is many things to many different people. There's Etruscan Rome, Early Christian Rome, Ancient Rome, Medieval Rome, Baroque Rome, Neoclassical Rome, Papal Rome, and Modern Rome—all seemingly defined by distinct historical, cultural, and artistic periods. But there are many other Romes which are best defined by their restaurants, cafés, shops, piazzas, churches, and fountains. Spend three days, a week, a month, or even a year here and Rome will not disappoint you. You'll marvel at its numerous ruins, savor its unique ambience, and indulge in its many gastronomic pleasures and shopping treasures. Hang around the Spanish Steps, Piazza Navona, or the Trevi Fountain and you'll find yourself surrounded by hordes of tourists in search of today's real Rome. Walk its narrow streets and dark-cobbled pathways and you'll also discover elements of a medieval Rome. Or get in line at the Vatican to see the many treasures accumulated by the powerful Catholic Church that once ruled much of the Western world as well as tour this city within a city.

If you're like many other visitors to Rome, you'll add this city to your "most favorite" list of places you hope to return to again and again. It may well become your Eternal City, the one that continues to capture your imagination and characterize Italy as a wonderful Roman holiday.

THE BASICS

Located in central west Italy in the heart of the Lazio region just 16 miles from the Mediterranean (Tyrrhenian Sea) and bisected by the meandering River Tiber, Rome was built on seven hills, the tallest of which reaches 462 feet above sea level. Situated in marshy and steamy lowlands, Rome boasts an area of nearly 10 square miles, a population of 3.3 million, over 5,000 restaurants and trattorie, and nearly 1,000 fountains. Come here in the heart of summer when the heat, traffic congestion, and tourists meet and you'll discover one very hot and humid city. It's an enormous city of grand Renaissance and baroque architecture whose landscape is dotted with domes, spires, monuments, and museums alongside layers of ruins and excavations. Pleasing to the eye and savoring to the soul, Rome is a sensual and dramatic city whose long history seems to constantly come alive amidst its many famous historical sites and imposing architecture.

- **The city encompasses 10 square miles, a population of 3.3 million, more than 5,000 restaurants and trattorie, and nearly 1,000 fountains.**
- **While all roads may lead to Rome, they also seem to often stop functioning in Rome. Too many cars, buses, and trucks vie for too little street surface.**
- **The main airport (Fiumicino) is located 18 miles from the city center.**
- **Taxis from the airport to the city center costs 65,000 lira (US$39). The airport to city train costs less and is very convenient if you're traveling lightly.**

Rome is not the easiest place to navigate. Indeed, this is where southern Italy begins with its attendant living chaos, amusing attitudes, charming street life, and leisurely lifestyle. While all roads may lead to Rome, they also seem to often stop functioning in Rome. After all, a city preserving many centuries of its history tends to preserve its narrow and circuitous streets which, in turn, contributes to overall traffic and transportation problems. Like most large cities, everyone seems to complain about Rome's traffic. Too many cars, buses, and trucks vie for too little street surface, and an underground subway can't be completed because of all the antiquities being excavated. Italy's famous lethargic bureaucracy seems to grind on and on as thousands of additional people pile onto Rome's congested streets each year. But in the midst of all this chaos is a living city of grand sites and sounds. Indeed, what a wonderful and dramatic setting for traffic jams!

ARRIVAL

Most visitors to Rome arrive at the **Leonardo da Vinci International Airport** (also called **Fiumicino Airport**) which is located about 18 miles from the center of the city. A second airport, **Ciampino**, is located about the same distance from the city as Fiumicino; several charter flights use this airport. Assuming you will be arriving through Fiumicino Airport, the quickest way to get into the city is by **taxi** which takes about 30-40 minutes, depending on the traffic situation. If you're traveling alone, this is the most expensive way to go—costs approximately 65,000 lira (US$39). Taxis are available just outside the baggage claim area. The **train** costs less and takes about 30 minutes to reach the center of the city; it's especially convenient if you're traveling lightly. Two trains run from the airport to the city. The first and fastest train, the nonstop Airport-Termini express (marked FS), departs hourly between 7:50am and 10:25pm and will take you directly to the main rail station, Stazione Termini (Termini Station), for 12,000 lira. From there you can catch a taxi, bus, or the Metro to your hotel. The second and slower line, FM1, departs from the airport every 20 minutes between 6:55am and 8:15pm; it makes stops in Rome (Trastevere, Ostiense, and Tiburtina stations) and goes on to suburban Monterotondo. It costs 7,000 lira. You can easily get to the airport train station from the baggage claim area: walk through the underpass and take the escalator to the train station where you can purchase a ticket from a vending machine near the turnstiles.

Hotel courtesy vans also are available at the airport. However, be sure to contact your hotel prior to arrival to arrange for this transportation service.

If you arrive by train, you will stop at Rome's main terminal, Stazione Termini. Centrally located, this station is serviced by taxis, buses, and the Metro.

If you are in a driving mood, you can contract for a **rental car** at either Fiumicino Airport or Stazione Termini. You'll find Hertz, Avis, Europcar, and Maggiore represented at these locations. However, be forewarned that driving a car in Rome may be more trouble than it's worth. You'll be dealing with narrow streets, congested traffic, and difficult parking. Our recommendation: use public transportation within Rome and rent a car for traveling outside the city.

GETTING AROUND

Rome is a big city with many important sites spread out over a large area. While you will probably do a great deal of walking within each area (be sure to wear comfortable walking shoes), plan to take buses, trams, taxis, or the subway (Metro) between areas. Orange ATAC **buses and trams** operate throughout the city between 6am and midnight. If you avoid rush hour, the buses and trams are good way to get around the city. Tickets cost 1,500 lira (90¢) for unlimited use for 1½ hours. You also can purchase a special one-day (6,000 lira) or one-week (24,000 lira) tourist pass good for unlimited use of all ATAC buses and trams as well as the subway. Purchase these tickets at the Stazione Termini or at tobacco shops (*tabacchi*) and bus terminals; the one-week ticket is only available at ATAC booths. Be sure to enter at the front or back of the bus; you must punch your ticket at the back and exit from the middle of the bus. The first bus you enter will validate your ticket.

- **Bus tickets cost 1,500 lira for unlimited use for 1½ hours; a one-day pass costs 6,000 lira; and a one-week pass costs 24,000 lira. If you're staying in Rome for at least 5 days, purchase the one-week pass.**
- **Enter buses at the front or rear, get your ticket punched at the back, and exit from the middle.**
- **The underground Metro is the fastest, cheapest, and most convenient way to get around the city.**
- **Taxis are neither cheap nor readily accessible along the street or at taxi stands. They are most plentify at the Stazione Termini and Piazza San Silvestro.**
- **You're well advise not to drive in Rome. The traffic is terrible and it's difficult to find parking spaces.**

The **subway or Metro** is the easiest way of getting around the city. Its two underground lines (A and B) stop at most major tourist sites as well as intersect at Stazione Termini, the central train station. Look for the big red "M" signs for entrance into the subway. The subway costs the same as the buses and trams. You can purchase tickets at vending machines in the stations and at tobacco shops and terminals. Be sure to carry small change to feed the vending machines (they accept 50, 100, and 200 lira coins) or you can purchase books of 10 tickets for 6,000 lira. However, you may be better off purchasing the special one-day or one-week tourist pass that allows you to use the complete ATAC transportation system, including the Metro.

While **taxis** are available, they are neither cheap nor readily accessible along the street or at taxi stands. The best places to find taxis are at the Stazione Termini and Piazza San Silvestro. You or your hotel also can call a taxi (Tel. 3570, 3875, 4944). Taxis are metered with the flag falling at 6,400 lira ($3.80) and each additional 800 feet costing 300 lira (20¢). Taxis also add surcharges on Sundays as well as daily between 10pm and 7am.

You really don't want to drive a **car** in Rome. Not only is the traffic terrible, you'll have difficulty finding a parking place. However, you may want to rent a car if you plan to tour outside the city. Most major car rental firms, such as Hertz (Tel. 547991), Avis (Tel. 4701216), and Budget (Tel. 484810), have offices in the city. In fact, it's cheaper to pick up your car in the city because the rental firms must impose a 10% government tax on cars picked up at the airport. Car rentals arranged while you are in Rome can be expensive. Like in the rest of Europe, it's always cheaper to reserve a car in advance (call their toll-free numbers) before you arrive in Rome.

SAFETY AND SECURITY

While we've had no problems in Rome, we know others who have encountered expert thieves and pickpockets. Please watch your purse and wallet. Be especially wary of those ostensibly cute bands of gypsy kids who may surround and distract you as they pick your pockets. They are very good at their trade. Even watch yourself in the crowded Vatican. Pickpockets literally "work the room" in the Sistine Chapel!

GETTING TO KNOW YOU

The living chaos of Rome's narrow and congested streets, juxtaposed with ancient ruins, dramatic monuments, and heady Renaissance and baroque architecture, give this city a very unique character. For many visitors, spending three days, one week, or even a month here is not enough to discover the many treasures and pleasures of this grand city. Not surprisingly, Rome grows on you over time. Every time you return, you'll probably discover another Rome.

When getting oriented to Rome, it's best to follow these basic tips:

1. **Stay at a hotel near the center of the city or at one within convenient access to public transportation.** While several of Rome's sites are spread out over a large area and thus require taking public transportation, most of the major sites are centrally located and within relatively easy walking distance. Try to stay near the center of the city, on the east side of the River Tiber, from where you can easily walk to most places. If you stay outside the city, you may have a long and expensive commute.

2. **Wear a good pair of sturdy and comfortable walking shoes.** If you're planning to visit many sites and do a lot of shopping, you will do a great deal of walking. Rome's streets are jam-packed with wonderful sites, shops, and restaurants as well as people. Indeed, the best way to see Rome is on foot. Since many of Rome's cobblestone streets can be hard on the feet, wear a good pair of walking shoes.

3. **Orient yourself to the city in relation to the River Tiber.** The River Tiber meanders from north to south through the city, dissecting it into eastern and western sections. Most major sites (Forum, Colosseum, Pantheon, Spanish Steps, Piazza Navona, Trevi Fountain) are located on the eastern side. The western section is primarily noted for being home to the Vatican City.

4. **Purchase a good map and guidebook or join an English-speaking tour to visit the major sites.** Most popular sites in Rome are not well explained for individuals who wish to visit them on their own. Don't arrive at a site, for example, and expect to find brochures and signs explaining the history and significance of the site. Since so many of Rome's sites are rich in history, you are well advised to acquire a detailed guide to the various sites or join a local tour which provides in-depth information on individual sites. Travel guides such as the green ***Michelin Guide to Rome*** and the ***Blue Guide to Rome and Environs*** provide enormous details on most major Rome sites. You might want to acquire these or similar guides before arriving in Rome. Several tour companies such as American Express (Tel. 67641), Appian Line (Tel. 4884151), and CIT (Tel. 47941), offer half-day bus tours to various parts of Rome. The city bus company, ATAC, also offers a tour of Rome. Bus No. 110 (no guide) departs from Piazza dei Cinquecento (in front of the Stazione Termini) at 3:30pm (2:30pm in winter) and passes 45 major sites over a 3-hour period.

5. **Use the bus, tram, or Metro to get around the city.** While many sights and activities are within easy walking distance, you'll find the bus, tram, and Metro to be the cheapest and most convenient way

to get around the city. Since buses and trams suffer through the same traffic jams as do taxis and cars, you may want to use the faster underground Metro. The system is relatively easy to use and quickly puts you near most major sites.

6. **Plan to spend an intense three to four days seeing Rome's major sites.** Sightseeing in Rome can be very time consuming given the enormous complex of ruins, museums, and churches awaiting the uninitiated visitor. Visiting the Vatican alone can take a better part of one day. For many people, three to four days of sightseeing only scratches Rome's rich historic and artistic surface; many seasoned travelers recommend a minimum of five days. Even a week devoted to such activities may not be enough. If you feel overwhelmed with so much to see and do in Rome, make a detailed plan of what you want, need, and can do in the limited time available. Then plan to come back again some day to see Rome in greater depth.

- **One of the best places to start your Rome adventure is at Victor Emanuel II Monument, a monolithic example of architectural bad taste.**
- **The Spanish Steps and Via Condotti constitute Rome's most upscale shopping area.**
- **Rome's most popular tourist attractions—the Colosseum, Roman Forum, Imperial Forums, Circus Maximus—are found along Via dei Fori Imperiali.**
- **The Vatican is located outside the central city on the west side of the River Tiber.**

Central Rome is best approached in terms of two major streets, **Via del Corso** and **Corso Vittorio Emanuele II**, which intersect at Piazza Venezia as Via del Corso and Via del Plebiscito (the extension of Corso Vittorio Emanuele II), and a series of major piazzas—Piazza Navona, Piazza Venezia, Piazza del Colosseo, Piazza Campo dei Fiori, Piazza del Popolo, and Piazza di Spagna. One of the best places to start your Rome adventure is at the monolithic, gaudy, and somewhat tacky **Victor Emanuel II Monument** (Monumento di Vittorio Emanuele II which is located at Piazza Venezia, the intersection of Via del Corso and Via del Plebiscito. Rome's embarrassing example of bad taste in 19th century architecture, this monument dominates what has become one of Rome's most hectic traffic arteries. The area west and northwest of this monument constitutes the old city (*centro storico*). Here you will discover Piazza Navona with its many sidewalk cafés and Bernini fountains; the awesome Pantheon; the antique shops of Via dei Coronari; the art galleries of Via Giulia; and numerous interesting narrow streets, medieval pathways, and piazzas teeming with restaurants, cafés, bars, shops, and markets.

The area north of Victor Emanuel II Monument and east of Via del Corso includes two of Rome's most popular attractions—**Spanish Steps** (Piazza di Spagna) and **Trevi Fountain** (Fontana di Trevi). Via del Corso links Piazza Venezia to Piazza del Popolo. This is also Rome's most upscale shopping area, especially along Via Condotti and its adjacent streets which lead from the Spanish Steps. One of Rome's most popular tourist areas, it's filled with wonderful shops, restaurants, and sidewalk cafés. It's a great place for people-watching. Window shop at the exquisite shops lining Via Condotti, walk up the Spanish Steps for a good view of the city, and stroll to the nearby Trevi Fountain where you can throw the obligatory coin in the fountain. If you do all this, you'll quickly discover why so many visitors fall in love with Rome. This whole area exhudes a certain ambience and energy not found elsewhere in Rome or Italy.

The area southeast of Victor Emanuel II Monument, along Via dei Fori Imperiali, is rich with ruins and antiquities of ancient Rome that constitute some of Rome's and Italy's most popular tourist attractions. This is the area of the **Roman Forum**, **Imperial Forums**, **Colosseum** and its adjacent **Arch of Constantine**, and **Circus Maximus**. All are within easy walking distance of each other. Here's where Roman history comes alive, especially in the impressive Colosseum which is perhaps Italy's most recognizable symbol. Expect to encounter large tourist crowds and heavy traffic throughout this popular area.

West of the River Tiber stands another major symbol of Italy, the **Vatican**. Literally a city and state unto itself, the Vatican attracts millions of visitors each year who enjoy strolling around St. Peter's Square. Most end up standing in long lines to visit St. Peter's Basilica and the Vatican Museums with its popular Sistine Chapel. A monument to the history, wealth, and power of the Catholic Church, the Vatican is one of those *"must visit"* when-in-Rome attractions that often overwhelms visitors who are not prepared for the sheer density of treasures displayed here. However, watch your wallet here. While this may be the closest place to God, it also attracts godless pickpockets who can have a field day amongst the dense crowds whose attention is diverted to viewing all the godly and gaudy forms that make up this impressive complex.

Rome boasts numerous other attractions both within and outside the city. For us, the real pleasures of Rome lie in walking its many streets and squares where we discover all kinds of treasures that make this such a delightful place to visit. Not surprising, our Roman treasures are found in the numerous shops and markets that yield many shopping treasures that further define our eternal Rome.

SHOPPING TREASURES

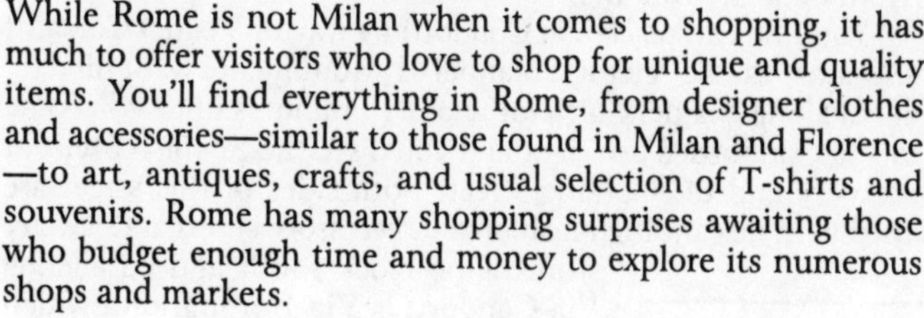

While Rome is not Milan when it comes to shopping, it has much to offer visitors who love to shop for unique and quality items. You'll find everything in Rome, from designer clothes and accessories—similar to those found in Milan and Florence—to art, antiques, crafts, and usual selection of T-shirts and souvenirs. Rome has many shopping surprises awaiting those who budget enough time and money to explore its numerous shops and markets.

MAJOR SHOPPING AREAS

As tourists quickly discover, any city with lots of tourist attractions also offers lots of shopping opportunities for tourists. Rome will not disappoint you, from the tacky to the terrific. Your choices are endless. Go to any of the major sites and you'll find the ubiquitous T-shirts (good prices), knick knacks, and souvenirs. But look a little harder and you'll discover that some of Italy's best quality shopping can be easily found in Rome. Better still, most of this shopping is confined to a central area and can be easily covered on foot within a day or two.

Rome's major shopping areas radiate north, northwest, west, and southwest of Victor Emanuel II Monument (Piazza Venezia). You may want to start your shopping adventure at Victor Emanuel II Monument, the Spanish Steps, or Piazza Navona. All three of these major landmarks make excellent departure points for discovering Rome's many shopping treasures. Our recommendation: start out at the Spanish Steps. It doesn't get much better than the Spanish Steps and its adjacent streets.

SPANISH STEPS AND VIA CONDOTTI

For quality shopping, you only need to head for one tourist attraction—the **Spanish Steps** or Piazza di Spagna. This is where the Rome's quality shopping both begins and ends. Largely a pedestrian zone crowded with people enjoying the ambience and views from the 137 travertine steps that define this piazza, the Spanish Steps sit at the top of Rome's classiest shopping street—**Via Condotti**—and beneath one of its classiest hotels—**Hassler**. Milan's Via Montenapoleone may be better but Rome's Via Condotti is Italy's second best along with Florence's Via Tornabuoni. Via Condotti is to Rome what Fifth Avenue is to New York City, what Rodeo Drive is to Hollywood, or what rue du Faubourg-Saint-Honoré and Avenue Montaigne are to Paris.

You also can reach Via Condotti by way of Via del Corsa. If you start at the Victor Emanuel II Monument, walk directly north along Via del Corsa for about 15 minutes until you come to Via Condotti. Turn right and you'll see the Spanish Steps at the very end of this long street. Both sides of this street are lined with elegant high-fashion and accessory shops and jewelry stores. One block south and paralleling Via Condotti is **Via Borgognona** which also includes several upscale shops. Just north of the Spanish Steps is **Via del Babuino** with antique shops and **Via Margutta** with art galleries.

- **Some of Italy's best quality shopping can be easily found in Rome.**
- **While many shops are closed on Sunday, some stay open for tourists, especially near the Spanish Steps.**
- **Some of Italy's top jewelers, clothing boutiques, and specialty shops are found along Via Condotti, Rome's most upscale shopping area.**
- **Via dei Coronair, near Piazza Navona, is lined with attractive and expensive antique shops.**
- **Campo dei Fiori boasts Rome's most colorful food market, Mercato Campo dei Fiori.**

Via Condotti is a great place to do window-shopping as well as to treat yourself to some of the best of the best shopping Italy has to offer. While many shops are closed on Sunday, some do stay open for the tourist trade. The street is basically a pedestrian mall, although watch out for an occasional car, motorcycle, or horse-drawn carriage entering this area. Here's where you will find Italy's top jewelers, clothing boutiques, and specialty shops. All the major designers are here—**Salvatore Ferragamo** (74), **Giorgio Armani** (75), **Louis Vuitton** (15), **Valentino** (13), **Gucci** (8), and **Prada** (91)—along with lesser-known high quality shops—**Mariselaine** (70), **Campanile** (58), and **Rogani** (47). The Gucci shop is Rome's most famous leather and accessory shop; it's usually packed with Japanese. Via Condotti is home to major jewelers: **Bulgari** (10), **Buccellati** (31), and **Cartier** (80-82). Our favorite here is Buccellati who produces fabulous jewelry, especially in gold in silver. For a wonderful selection of ceramics and glassware, be sure to stop at **Modigliani** (24).

Via Borgognona includes several additional upscale boutiques such as **Fendi** (36-40), **Gianfranco Ferré** (6), **Laura Biagiotti** (434), and **Polidori**.

Via Bocca di Leone is home to the famous designers **Valentino** and **Gianni Versace**.

Several nearby streets within this area also offer excellent shopping opportunities: **Via Margutta** is known for its art galleries; **Via Babuino** has several antique and clothing shops; shops along **Via del Corso** and **Via Giubbonair** offer medium-range clothes and accessories; look for food and delicacies along **Via della Croce**; and **Via Frattina** includes jewelry, leather goods, clothes, and accessories with shops such as **Byblos, Castelli**, and **Tiffany**. Also explore **Via del Gambero**. At the top of the Spanish Steps and southeast of the Hassler Hotel are some of Rome's smartest couturiers along **Via Gregoriana** and **Via Sistina**. If you walk directly south of the Spanish Steps, you'll come to the **Trevi Fountain** within 10 to 15 minutes. Several cafés, restaurants, gelatos, and souvenir shops are found around this popular tourist site.

PIAZZA NAVONA

One of the Rome's most popular piazzas for tourists, artists, and merchants, this charming baroque neighborhood yields numerous shops offering everything from art and antiques to clothes and jewelry. The main shopping street here is the lovely **Via dei Coronari**. Lined with attractive and expensive antique shops, this is the street for antique hunters in search of quality treasures. Nearby streets, such as **Via dei Soldati, Vicoli della Palomba**, and **del Cancello**, are filled with young artisans producing engravings, prints, furniture, jewelry, and gift items.

PIAZZA DEL POPOLO/PANTHEON

Located immediately west of Via del Corso and running from Piazza del Popolo in the north to the Pantheon and Corso Vittorio Emanuele II in the south, this shopping area is filled with small artisan shops offering a wide variety of specialty items, from candles to clothes. The narrow and winding streets, as well as interesting morning street markets, provide added character to this area. Look for elegant antique shops along Via Fontanella Borghese. Near the Pantheon, along Via dei Cestari, you'll find several shops offering ecclesiastic articles.

PIAZZA CAMPO DEI FIORI

Located south of Piazza Navona and between Corso Vittorio Emanuele II and the River Tiber, this colorful shopping area includes several small shops, talented artisans, and narrow medieval shopping streets. It also includes one of Rome's best and most colorful food markets, the **Mercato Campo dei Fiori** (open Monday through Saturday, 7am to 1:30pm) which operates at Piazza Campo dei Fiori. Watch your valuables here since this area is reputed to be a favorite haunt for pickpockets. From the piazza, explore several adjacent streets and their numerous shops: **Via dei Banchi Vecchi** for hat makers; **Via Monte de Pietà** for pawnshops; **Via dei Pettinari** for antique jewelry; **Via dei Giubbonari** for inexpensive clothes; **Via dei Balestrari** for dressmakers; and **Via Giulia** for antique stores. This area also includes the **Jewish Ghetto**, Rome's oldest Jewish quarter, which begins at Via delle Botteghe Oscure (southwest of Piazza Venezia). While this area has little to offer shoppers other than inexpensive clothes, notions, and housewares, it's especially noted for its interesting history; indeed, this is one of Europe's oldest Jewish communities.

While you may discover several other neighborhood shopping areas that yield interesting shopping, the areas radiating within a 10 to 15 minute walk north, northwest, west and southwest of Victor Emanuel II Monument constitute Rome's major shopping areas. Shopping in these places takes on a very special Roman character as you walk along the labyrinth of narrow cobblestone pathways, congested streets, and crowded sidewalks dramatized by old stone buildings, baroque architecture, and colorful piazzas. You'll encounter a wide range of shopping treasures here, from clothes and accessories to antiques, arts, crafts, and souvenirs.

MARKETS

If you enjoy exploring open air markets with all their attendant fresh fruits, vegetables, meats, flowers, and inexpensive goods, Rome will accommodate your interest with several such markets. Be sure to do what the locals do—bargain for everything. While you may not find much to purchase in these markets (what's a tourist to do with a freshly killed chicken or octopus?), you may enjoy the colorful and entertaining outdoor shows. Here are some of Rome's best such markets:

- ❑ **Mercato Campo dei Fiori:** *Piazza Campo dei Fiori. Open Monday through Saturday, 7am to 1:30pm.* This is Rome's largest fresh fish, vegetable and fruit market. Get here early for the haggling shows as chefs, housewives, and others make their morning purchases of everything from octopus and oysters to cheeses and flowers.

- **Mercato Vittorio:** *Piazza Vittorio Emanuele II. Open Monday through Saturday, 7am to 2pm.* This popular open-air food market includes numerous stalls offering fresh meats, fish, poultry, fruits, and vegetables. It also includes numerous stalls selling souvenirs, clothing, leather goods, and shoes.

- **Mercato di Porta Portese:** *Between Viale di Trestevere and the River Tiber (stretches for about 1 mile along the Tiber, from Ponte Sublicio to Ponte Testaccio and about half way down Viale di Trestevere). Open Sundays, 6am to 2pm.* This is Rome's popular Sunday flea market, one of the largest in Europe. Hundreds of vendors offer everything from clothes and household goods to new antiques and auto parts. Watch out for the clever pickpockets who work the massive crowds.

- **Mercato Sannio:** *Via Sannio at Porta San Giovanni. Open Monday through Friday, 8am to 1pm, and Saturday, 8am to 7pm.* This weekday flea market includes many of the same items found at the Sunday Mercato di Porta Portese. Indeed, many of the vendors here move to Porta Portese on Sunday. Lots of clothes, leather goods, shoes, and new antiques.

- **Mercato dei Fiori:** *Via Trionfale 47-49 (at Via Paolo Sarpi). Open Tuesday, 10am to 1pm.* If you like flowers and don't mind making a trip outside the city center, you'll enjoy this popular flower market. A daily wholesale flower market, it opens to the public on Tuesday mornings.

Rome also has its share of antique markets and auctions, including regular Christie's and Sotheby's auctions. If you love to hunt for antiques, collectibles, and objets d'art, be sure to visit several of the antique markets which are usually held on Sunday. Check the "Arts and Antiques" section of the *Where Rome* tourist magazine for specific dates, places, and offerings.

DEPARTMENT STORES

Rome has the usual complement of well-known Italian department stores. Look for the following:

- **Coin:** *Piazzale Apio 15; Via Togliatti 2; Viale Libia 61; and Via Mantova 1f-1h. Open 9am to 1pm and 3:30 to*

7:30pm. Closed Monday mornings. A good solid department store offering lots of clothes and accessories.

- **La Rinascente:** *Piazza Colonna (off Via del Corso); and Piazza Fiume. Open 9:30am to 7:30pm. Closed Monday mornings.* The only department store serving the city center. Rome's most upscale department store with a good range of merchandise. Well stocked with clothes, perfumes, cosmetics, and household goods.

- **Standa:** *Cors Francia 124; Corso Trieste 200-226; Via Cola di Rienzo 173; Viale Regina Margherita 117-123; and Viale Trasteveree 60. Open 9am to 1pm and 3:30 to 7:30pm.* Italy's answer to K-mart. Stocks a wide selection of basic department store goods. Average quality, modest prices.

- **Upim:** *Piazza Sant Maria Maggiore; Via Alessandria 160; Via Nazionale 211; and Via del Tritone 172. Open 9am to 7:30pm. Closed Monday mornings.* Similar to Standa in terms of selections, quality, and prices.

WHAT TO BUY AND WHERE

Rome has numerous top quality shops displaying the *"best of the best"* Rome and Italy have to offer. Most of the shops are within easy walking distance of each other as well as near many of Rome's famed attractions. If you centrally locate yourself at the Spanish Steps, Piazza Navona, or Victor Emanuel II Monument, you'll be within a 10-20 minute walk of most shops.

Most of Rome's major shops keep the same ubiquitous shopping hours: open Monday through Friday, 9:00am to 1pm and 3:30pm to 7:30pm; closed all day Sunday and some Monday mornings. However, more and more shops in the central tourist areas, especially along Via Condotti and the Spanish Steps, remain open on Sundays and Mondays. Some shops vary their hours during the heat of the summer (June to September) but reopen in the afternoon at 4 or 4:30pm and close at 8pm.

ART

- **Associazione Culturale Valentina Moncada:** *Via Margutta 54, Tel. 6797909. Open Tuesday to Saturday, 3-7pm.* This art workshop and gallery includes the works of European and American artists.

- **Galleria Bonomo:** *Piazza Santa Apollonia 3, Tel. 581-0579. Open Tuesday to Friday, 4:30am to 8pm.* Includes the works of famous Italian artists.

- **Galleria Ecate:** *Via della Scale 13, Tel. 5894741. Open Tuesday to Saturday, 4:30 to 8:30pm and Thursday 4:30 to 11pm.* One of Rome's most interesting galleries offering the contemporary works of many famous international artists.

ANTIQUES

- **Ad Antiqua Domus:** *Via Paola 25-27, Tel. 6861530 and Via dei Coronari 227, Tel. 6875384. Open 9am to 1pm and 4pm to 8pm. Closed Monday mornings.* Offers an excellent selection of antique Italian furniture.

- **Antichita' Davide Sestieri:** *Via Margutta 57, Tel. 320-7590. Open 9am to 1pm and 4:30 to 7:30pm. Closed Sunday and Monday mornings.* Offers an outstanding selection of 18th and 19th century Italian and Chinese porcelain.

- **Antique Armoury:** *Via del Babuino 161, Tel. 3614158. Open 9am to 1pm and 4:30 to 7:30 pm. Closed Sunday and Monday mornings.* Specializes in military antiques: firearms, helmets, uniforms, miniature soldiers, bronzes, prints, posters, equestrian items, and metals.

- **Enrico Camponi:** *Via della Stelletta 32, Tel. 6865249. Open 9am to 1pm and 4:30 to 7:30pm. Closed Sunday and Monday mornings.* Noted for its antique Italian glassware, especially chandeliers and vases from Murano.

- **Luciano Coen:** *Via Margutta 63/65, Tel. 3201274. Open 9am to 1pm and 4:30 to 7:30pm. Closed Sunday and Monday mornings.* Includes a unique collection of 16th to 18th century French and Flemish tapestries as well as 19th century European and Oriental carpets.

BOOKS

- **Antiquaria Scarpignato:** *Via di Ripetta 156, Tel. 687-5923. Open 10am to 1pm and 4:30 to 7:30pm. Closed Monday mornings.* Good selection of old engravings, maps, and rare books.

- ❑ **Feltrinelli:** *Largo Torre Argentina 5a, Tel. 68803248; Via del Babuino 41, Tel. 6797058; and Via Vittorio Emanuele Orlando 83-86, Tel. 484430. Open 9am-8pm. Closed Monday mornings.* One of Rome's largest and best stocked bookstores.

- ❑ **Libreria del Viaggiatore:** *Via del Pellegrino 78, Tel. 68801048. Open 10am to 8pm (closed until 3pm on Monday).* A good source for travel guides and literature.

- ❑ **Rizzoli:** *Largo Chigo 15, Tel. 6796641, and Via Tomacelli 156, Tel. 68802513. Open 9am to 7:30pm. Closed Monday mornings.* Fabulous range of books in one of the city's largest bookstores. Includes English-language books.

FASHION—MEN'S

- ❑ **Giorgio Armani:** *Via Condotti 77, Tel. 6991460. Open 9:30am to 1pm and 3:30 to 7:30pm. Closed Monday mornings.* Outstanding quality fabrics and styles put this designer in a league of its own. Offers fashionable clothes for men, women, and children. The less expensive and trendier Emporio Armani line is found at Via del Babuino 140, Tel. 6788454.

- ❑ **Calderoni:** *Via Bisolati 4-10, Tel. 4741123; Via Bissolati 48-52, Tel. 4881915; Via Barberini 90, Tel. 483662; and Via del Tritone 57-58a.* This long-established clothier (since 1870) offers quality fabrics and elegant designs for men and women.

- ❑ **Caleffi:** *Piazza Montecitorio 53, Tel. 6793773.* One of Rome's best shops for quality suits, coats, shirts, and knitwear.

- ❑ **Ermenegildo Zegna:** (Adamshop) *Via Due Macelli 32, Tel. 6990865, and Via Lucrezio Caro 89, Tel. 3216342.* Famous fabrics and distinctive styling make this one of Italy's most famous men's shops for quality suits, jackets, ties, and accessories.

- ❑ **Schostal:** *Via del Corso 158, Tel. 6791240. Open 9am to 7:30pm. Closed Monday morning.* One of Rome's oldest and most well respected men's shops. Offers a wide selection of quality apparel, from underwear to suits. Good service and value.

FASHION—WOMEN'S

- ❑ **Etro:** *Via del Babuino 102, Tel. 6788257.* Offers beautifully designed bags, belts, jackets, ties, scarves, and waistcoats in attractive fabrics for both women and men. Classic elegance.

- ❑ **Fendi:** *Via Fontanella Borghese 57, Tel. 6876290; and Via Borgognona 36-40, Tel. 6797641. Open 9:30am to 7:30pm. Closed Monday mornings.* One of Italy's top names offering classy designer leather, furs, and accessories. Has seven shops in Rome, five of which are located along Via Borgognona.

- ❑ **Gianfranco Ferré:** *Via Borgognona 12c, Tel. 6790050.* This attractive shop offers the famous designer's exclusive line of clothing, knitwear, leather goods, and accessories.

- ❑ **Gucci:** *Via Condotti 8, Tel. 6789340. Open 10am to 7pm. Closed Monday mornings.* One of Rome's very best and most popular designer shops. This is Gucci's flagship shop. Filled with gorgeous leather and clothing for both women and men.

- ❑ **Hermès:** *Via Condotti 67, Tel. 6791882.* From Paris, this is one of the world's top designer shops offering the fabulous signature scarves along with their hallmark leather goods. Includes leather bags, belts, gloves, and numerous accessories.

- ❑ **Max Mara:** *Lido di Ostia. Via delle Baleniere 119/A. Tel. 5697202.* Trendy fashion clothes from one of Italy's most popular designers. Distinctive colors and designs for everything from casual wear to formal wear.

- ❑ **Missoni:** *Via del Babuino 96-97, Tel. 6797971; Piazza di Spagna 78, Tel. 6792555. Open 10am to 7:30pm (Via del Babuino); 9:30am-1pm and 3:30 to 7:30pm (Piazza di Spagna). Closed Monday mornings.* Famous for its distinctive knits, women's suits, and patterned stockings.

- ❑ **Prada:** *Via Nazionale 28-31, Tel. 4882413. Open 9am to 1pm and 3:30 to 7:30pm. Closed Monday mornings.* One of the finest names in Italian leather and fabrics.

- ❑ **Valentino:** *Via Condotti 22 (menswear), Tel. 6783656; Via Bocca di Leone 15-18 (women's wear), Tel. 6795862; Via del Babuino 61 (Oliver boutique), Tel. 6798314. Open 10am to 7pm. Closed Monday mornings.* One of the truly great names in the fashion world. Fabulous selections with prices that will knock your socks off!

- ❑ **Versace:** *Via Bocca di Leone 26 (women's wear and home décor), Tel. 6780521; Via Borgognona 24 (menswear), Tel. 6795292; and Via Borgognona 33/34 (Versus men's and women's wear), Tel. 6783977. Open 10am to 7:30pm. Closed Monday mornings.* Another great name in the fashion world with distinctive designs that are an acquired taste (a bit on the gaudy side of baroque).

- ❑ **Giorgio Sermoneta:** *Piazza di Spagna 61-71, Tel. 679-1960.* Excellent quality and selection of gloves.

JEWELRY

- ❑ **Brusco:** *Viale dei Colli Portuensi 590-592, Tel. 65742980.* This popular jeweler with Italian celebrities offers some of the most fabulous names in jewelry, from jewels and watches to pearls. Represents such famous names as Chopard, Breitling, Cartier, Buccellati, Baume & Mercier, and Mikimoto.

- ❑ **Buccellati:** *Via Condotti 31, Tel. 6790329. Open 10am to 1:30pm and 3pm to 7:30pm.* Definitely our favorite Italian jeweler. Simply fabulous designs in gold and silver by one of the world's master jewelers. The attention to detail and the emphasis on quality are remarkable. Prices may seem astronomical here, but at Buccellati you get the very very best in Italian craftsmanship and unique designs. Once you've been to Buccellati, all other jewelry doesn't seem the same. This shop looks very austere and forbidding. Don't worry; it's a security thing. Just ring the bell and enter for a wonderful treat in quality jewelry and understated but proper service.

- ❑ **Bulgari:** *Via Condotti 10, Tel. 6793876. Open 10am to 7pm. Closed Monday mornings.* One of Italy's finest jewelers. Look for outstanding quality and designs in diamonds, pearls, gold, and silver. Also includes a popular line of women's watches. Great understated but elegant window displays.

- **Cartier:** *Via Condotti 82-83, Tel. 6782582. Open 10am to 7pm. Closed Monday mornings.* Representing the finest in French jewelry, this elegant shop includes the full line of famous Cartier jewelry, from diamond studded pins, rings, and necklaces to elegant watches.

- **Cilla Bijoux:** *Via Francesco Crispi 72-74, Tel. 484594.* Offers a terrific selection of costume jewelry in classic and contemporary designs at affordable prices. Shop also functions as an artisan studio.

- **Massoni:** *Largo Carlo Goldoni 48, Tel. 6782679.* This long established (since 1796) jeweler produces some of Rome's best quality jewelry. Fine craftsmanship.

- **Petochi:** *Piazza di Spagna 23, Tel. 6791558. Open 9:30am to 1pm and 3:30 to 7:30pm. Closed Monday mornings.* Famous jeweler offering an exclusive collection of contemporary and classic designs. Includes china, crystal, and sterling flatware.

LEATHER GOODS

Rome abounds with fine leather shops that offer everything from exclusive designed handbags and coats to shoes, gloves, and accessories. While many of Rome's best leather shops are listed under the "Fashion—Women" shopping category, especially Gucci and Hermès, here we identify many other fine leather shops worth browsing for something special.

- **Artigianato del Cuoio:** *Via Belsiana 90, Tel. 6784435.* Produces own leather products on the premises: bags, belts, luggage, and accessories. Offers a wide range of attractive designs and colors. Also does custom work. Good prices.

- **Bottega Veneta:** *Via Sebastianella 18/A, Tel. 6782535.* Famous for quality leather suitcases, shoes, bags, and a wide range of small leather products, from diary covers to key rings.

- **Fellini:** *Via del Corso 340, Tel. 6785800, and Via di Pietra 90/91, Tel. 4467221.* Offers a good selection of quality belts and small leather items. Also does custom work.

- **Louis Vuitton:** *Via Condotti 15, Tel. 69940000.* World-famous for distinctive luggage and handbag designs as well as leather accessories.

- **Mandarina Duck:** *Via Propaganda 1, Tel. 69940320, and Corso Vittorio Emanuele 16, Tel. 6789840.* Offers quality luggage, bags, and briefcases with the districtive Mandarina Duck logo.

- **Sirni:** *Via della Stelletta 33, Tel. 68805248.* This small shop produces excellent quality copies of Chanel, Gucci and Hermès handbags. Also makes bags, belts, and wallets to your specifications.

- **Trussardi:** *Via Condotti 49, Tel. 6792151. Open 10am to 1:30pm and 2:30 to 7pm. Closed Monday mornings.* One of Italy's best names for top-quality leather handbags and clothes. Very popular and trendy.

SHOES

- **AVC:** *Piazza di Spagna 88, Tel. 69922355, Viale Parioli 172, Tel. 8070951.* Good quality shoes and boots as well as other leather goods.

- **Bruno Magli:** *Via del Gambero 1, Tel. 6793802, and Via Veneto 70/A, Tel. 464355.* Top quality shoes, boots and bags from this world-famous shoe maker.

- **Campanile:** *Via Condotti 58, Tel. 6783041. Open 9:30am to 7:30pm. Closed Monday mornings.* Produces own line of popular footwear of exceptional quality and design.

- **Dal Cò:** *Via Vittoria 65, Tel. 6786536. Open 9:30am to 1pm and 3:30 to 7:30pm. Closed Monday mornings.* Produces excellent quality custom-made shoes and boots for women. Styles range from classic to high fashion. Also offers coordinating handbags.

- **Ferragamo:** *Via Condotti 73-74, Tel. 6791565.* This popular Florentine-based designer is famous for offering gorgeous selections of classic and fashionable footwear. Also includes numerous accessories and fashion clothes for women and men.

- ❑ **Laudadio:** *Via Gregoriana 1-2, Tel. 6790583. Open 9am to 1pm and 3:30 to 7:30pm. Closed Monday mornings.* Produces excellent quality custom-made shoes.

- ❑ **Pollini:** *Via Frattina 22-24, Tel. 6798360. Open 9:30am to 1pm and 3:30 to 7:30pm. Closed Monday mornings.* Offers high quality and fashionable shoes, boots, and handbags.

HAUTE COUTURE

While Rome is not the haute couture capital of Italy—Milan takes this honor—it does offer numerous shops representing the great international haute couture names based in Italy. They represent the very best in Italian high fashion. As expected, these are extremely expensive shops. After all, Italian haute couture represents top quality and such quality has a very high price. Here are Rome's 16 top haute coutures:

- ❑ **Armani:** Via Condotti, 55, Tel. 6991460.

- ❑ **Renato Balestra:** Via Sistina 36, Tel. 6795424.

- ❑ **Roberto Capucci:** Via Gregoria na 56, Tel. 6792151.

- ❑ **Courreges:** Via Bocca di Leone 84, Tel. 6793321.

- ❑ **Gianfranco Ferré:** Via Borgognona 42, Tel. 6795361.

- ❑ **Raniero Gattinoni:** Piazza di Spagna 91, Tel. 6795361.

- ❑ **Givenchy:** Via Borgognona 21, Tel. 6784058.

- ❑ **Gucci:** Via Condotti 8, Tel. 6789340.

- ❑ **Lancetti:** Via Condotti 61, Tel. 6780907.

- ❑ **Les Copains:** Piazza di Spagna 33, Tel. 6788418.

- ❑ **Mila Schon:** Via Condotti 64-65, Tel. 6792151.

- ❑ **Trussardi:** Via Condotti 49, Tel. 6792151.

- ❑ **Ungaro:** Via Bocca di Leone 24, Tel. 6789931.

- ❑ **Valentino:** Via Bocca di Leone 15-18 (women), Tel. 6795862; Via Condotti 13 (men), Tel. 6783656.

- ❑ **Gianni Versace:** Via Bocca di Leone 26 (women), Tel. 6780521; Via Borgognona 29 (men), Tel. 6795292.

- ❑ **Yves Saint Laurent Rive Gauche:** Via Bocca di Leone 34-35, Tel. 6795577.

MAJOR ATTRACTIONS

Rome boasts Europe's largest concentration of sightseeing attractions—piazzas, palaces, churches, museums, ancient ruins and monuments. If you are an ancient history buff, Rome will enthrall you with its heady dose of history well preserved in excavations and powerful architecture. After all, a city with a grand history of over 2,500 years has inherited many stone and brick structures that have weathered centuries of political turmoil and environmental degradation.

- ❑ **Rome boasts Europe's largest concentration of sightseeing attractions.**
- ❑ **Start your sightseeing at one of the major piazzas.**
- ❑ **Today's piazzas function similarly to the forums in ancient Rome—popular centers for congregating, observing others, exchanging ideas, relaxing, or just "hanging out" when there's not much else to do.**
- ❑ **Most sites in Rome could legitimately share the same classification—museum.**

If you don't plan properly, you can easily become overwhelmed by the tremendous number of sights found through out the city. Start at one of the major departure points for seeing and doing things in Rome—a piazza. Indeed, today's piazzas function similarly to the forums in ancient Rome—popular centers for congregating, observing others, exchanging ideas, relaxing, or just "hanging out" when there's not much else to do.

Assuming you don't have a month or year to see all the sights in Rome, here are some of the *"best of the best"* that will keep you busy for a few days of sightseeing. We've classified them into six major categories for enjoying three different Roman experiences: Grand and Ancient Sites; Papal Rome and the Vatican; Piazzas and Fountains; Palaces; Churches; and Museums. As you will quickly discover, most sites in Rome could legitimately share the same classification—museum. Sites within each of these sightseeing categories offer a very different Roman experience.

GRAND AND ANCIENT SITES

Rome is home for some of the world's most famous ancient sites. Most are located in the center of the city within easy walking distance of each other. The major area of excavation and ancient structures is bounded by four of Rome's seven famous hills—Capitoline, Palatine, Esquiline, and Quirinal—which are located immediately south and southeast of Piazza Venezia. This was the center of ancient Rome's imperial palaces, courts, temples, commerce, entertainment, celebrations, markets, taverns, and brothels. It now serves as a center for heavy tourist traffic.

❑ **The Colosseum (Colosseo)**: *Piazza del Colosseo, Tel. 7004261. Open April to September on Monday, Tuesday, Thursday, Friday, and Saturday, 9am to 7pm; Wednesday and Sunday, 9am to 1pm; open October to March on Monday, Tuesday, Thursday, and Saturday, 9am to 3pm. Free admission to ground floor; 8,000 lira for visiting the upper levels. Take buses 11, 27, 81, 85, 87, or 186; tram 30 or 13; or the Metro to "Colosseo."* Visiting Rome without seeing the Colosseum is like going to Paris without seeing the Eiffel Tower. This is the greatest symbol of eternal Rome. Standing like a half-eaten round of Swiss cheese, it is 137 feet tall and 1719 feet wide. Construction of the Colosseum began by Vespasian in 72 AD and finished in 80 AD. Capable of seating more than 50,000 spectators, the Colosseum was the Roman stadium or arena for witnessing the death and destruction of men and animals. Numerous gladiators, criminals, slaves, and perhaps some martyred Christians, along with wild animals, met their deaths here before cheering crowds of blood-thirsty spectators. Used primarily during the first five centuries, it subsequently fell into disrepair and abuse; its marble and stones were cannibalized for building other structures (marble on the outer wall went to St. Peter's and various palazzi). While worn from nearly 2,000 years of harsh history (from weather to human destruction), nonetheless, what remains of the Colosseum will not disappoint you. Go to the top where you can get a panoramic view of the structure, including the exposed underground locker rooms and passages that housed men and funneled the wild animals into the arena. The Colosseum is an awesome display of stone and iron construction, although the iron has long

---

- ❑ **Visiting Rome without seeing the Colosseum is like going to Paris without seeing the Eiffel Tower.**
- ❑ **The Pantheon is the best preserved of all ancient Roman structures.**
- ❑ **The Vatican boasts some of the world's most fabulous works of art and architecture, including Michelangelo's frescos and Bernini's statues.**
- ❑ **Please be forwarned that a dress code is strickly enforced for entrance into St. Peter's Bascilia—no shorts, miniskirts, or bare shoulders.**
- ❑ **For a panoramic view of the Vatican and Rome, be sure to go the roof and dome of the basilica.**

---

disappeared as scavengers and others cannibalized the structure, leaving distinct pock marks in the aftermath. The adjacent **Arch of Constantine** was constructed in 315 AD, one of the last great monuments built in Rome.

- ❑ **Roman Forum (Foro Romano):** *Largo Romolo e Remo (Via dei Fori Imperiali), Tel. 6990110. Open April to September from Monday to Saturday, 9am to 6pm, and on Sunday 9am to 1pm; open October to March from Monday to Saturday, 9am to 3pm and on Sunday 9am to 1pm. Admission is 12,000 lira which also includes entrance into the Palatine Hills area. Take buses 11, 27, 81, 85, 87, or 186 or the Metro to "Colosseo."* This was the commercial, political, and religious center of ancient Rome, where the courts, temples, and businesses formed a union of powerful architecture. Extensively used between the second century BC and the 4th century AD, the Forum included an impressive array of temples, arches, and business and governmental buildings. Today most of these structures lay in ruins, abused by centuries of neglect. However, enough standing buildings, columns, and arches give a good idea of the once grand nature of this area. Look for the ruins of the Basilica Aemilla, Curia, Arch of Septimus Severus, Rostra, Temple of Saturn, Temple of Vespasian, Column of Phocas, Basilica Glulla, Temple of Castor and Pollux, Temple of Vesta, House of the Vestal Virgins, Temple of Antoninus and Faustina, San Lorenzo in Miranda, Temple of Romulus, Santi Cosma e Damlano, Basilica of Maxentius, Antiquarium Forense, and the Arch of Titus.

- ❑ **Palatine Hill (Palatino):** *Next to the Roman Forum on Via dei Fori Imperiali. Also can enter by way of Via di San Gregorio. Open Monday and Wednesday to Saturday, 9am to 6pm (9am to 3pm in the winter), and Tuesday and Sunday from 9am to 1pm. Admission charge to enter the Roman Forum includes entrance into this area. Take the same transportation as you would to the Roman Forum.* Here's where Rome began in the 8th century BC, the most famous of the seven hills. Located next to the Colosseum and the Roman Forum, Palatine Hill served as the residence for several Roman Emperors who built their palaces on this lovely hill overlooking the city. Today the hill still affords good views of the city and is a wonderful place to stroll amongst the ruins of once luxurious imperial villas and fields of flowers. Take special note to look for the

House of Livia, Domitian's Palace of the Flavians, and the stadium.

- ❑ **Imperial Forums (Fori Imperiali):** *Via dei Fori Imperiali (next to the Roman Forum). Open Monday, Wednesday, and Friday, 9am to 2pm; Tuesday and Thursday, 4pm to 7pm; Sunday, 9am to 1pm. Enter at Via 24 Maggio. Admission charge for entering Trajan's Market. Take buses 11, 27, 81, 85, 87, or 186 or the Metro to "Colosseo."* Originally built by Caesar (completed by Emperor Trajan) as an extension of the overcrowded Roman Forum, the Imperial Forums are now separated by Via dei Fori Imperiali (forums excavated and partly paved over by Mussolini when he constructed the road in 1932). The two major sights within the forums are the beautiful 138-foot marble Trajan's Column (includes an impressive spiral frieze of some 2,500 Roman army figures) and the three-story Trajan's Market (enter at 94 Via IV Novembre) which at one time housed nearly 150 shops. Only Trajan's Market is open to the public. You can view Trajan's Column from the sidewalk.

- ❑ **Circus Maximus (Circo Massimo):** *Located behind (south) Palatine Hill between Via dei Cerchi and Via del Circo Massimo*. This expansive arena was the center for chariot races. When flooded, it also could be used for boat races. Built in the 4th century BC and once capable of accommodating 300,000 spectators, today it retains a few impressive structures but is primarily a sunken field of grass with vague contours of a racetrack from a by-gone era.

- ❑ **Pantheon (La Rotonda):** *Piazza della Rotonda, Tel. 683-00230. Open Monday to Saturday, October to May, 9am to 5pm, and April to September, from 9am to 6pm; and Sunday, 9am to 1pm. Free admittance. Take bus 199 and all buses designated for Largo Argentina and Via del Corso.* The best preserved of all ancient Roman structures. Built by Emperor Hadrian in 119-128 AD to honor 12 important Roman deities, this huge domed structure, which forms a perfect interior circle, was transformed into a Christian church in 608. Services are still held here. Today the Pantheon includes the tombs of Raphael and Italy's first two kings. A remarkable architectural achievement, and one of the most beautiful ancient buildings in Italy. A 30-foot hole at the center of the dome provides the only source of light, and precipitation, for the interior of this impressive building.

- **Castel Sant' Angelo:** *Lungotevere Castello 50, Tel. 687-5036. Open Monday to Saturday, 9am to 3pm, and Sunday 9am to noon. Closed the second and fourth Tuesday of each month. Admission 8000 lira. Take bus 64 or 280 or the Metro to "Lepanto."* Facing the St. Angelo Bridge with its angelic Bernini statues, this 58-room castle was originally built in 130-139 AD as the tomb for Emperor Hadrian and his family. The structure has undergone a great deal of modification over the centuries—from a tomb, to a sanctuary, to a prison, to a fortress guarding the Vatican, to a museum. As a sanctuary it served as a refuge for popes (includes a secret passage connected to the Vatican). Today it's most famous for its lovely frescoes and its museum, the Museo di Castel Sant' Angelo, which includes an interesting collection of ancient arms, works of art, relics, a prison cell, and a 300-year-old papal bathroom complete with tub.

- **Appian Way (Via Appia Antica):** *Take bus 218 from San Giovanni in Laterano and get off at the catacombs; walk beyond this area.* Located on the outskirts of Rome, this ancient cobblestone road (2,300 years old) connected Rome to Brindisi on the southeast coast. The first ten miles of the road are especially famous for catacombs, ruins, and fortifications. Many of Rome's noted families were buried in this area. Also look for a small church, Domine Quo Vadis, which is reputed to be the place where Christ told St. Peter to return to Rome where he was subsequently crucified and became a Christian martyr.

- **Catacombs of St. Calixtus (Catacombe di San Callisto):** *110 Via Appia Antica, Tel. 5136725. Open 8:30am to noon and 2:30pm to 5pm (until 5:30pm between April and September); closed Wednesday. Admission 8,000 lira.* These are the most famous and best organized Roman catacombs for public view. Guided English tours include walking through subterranean tunnels and viewing crypts and galleries. Includes a small museum and shop area. Well worth visiting. Many tour companies conduct daily bus tours here or you can come on your own by car or public bus (#218).

PAPAL ROME AND THE VATICAN

If you've ever wondered where to find the treasures of the Catholic Church, look no further than Rome. Head straight for the Vatican and its wealth of treasures. Located immediately west of the River Tiber, across from the fortress Castel Sant' Angelo, the Vatican boasts some of the world's most fabulous works of art and architecture, including Michelangelo's frescos and Bernini's statues. A sovereign state unto it's own since 1929, with its own supreme ruler (the Pope), flag, government, and foreign policy, the Vatican draws millions of tourists each year in search of its major treasures: Piazza San Pietro (St. Peter's Square), St. Peter's Basilica, and the Vatican Museums with its forever popular Sistine Chapel. A real treat for many visitors, especially dedicated Catholics, is to have an audience with the Pope or at least get a glimpse of his physical presence.

The Vatican is another powerful symbol of Rome and Italy. But unlike the Colosseum, the Vatican has special meaning to millions of visitors who have a spiritual, emotional, and financial attachment to Catholicism's greatest power center. Plan to spend at least a half-day visiting the unique sights of the Vatican; many visitors plan a full day. Anticipate crowds and long lines during peak tourist season. Not surprising, the Vatican remains one of Italy's most popular tourist distinations.

Be sure to watch your dress and cameras in the Vatican. The "clothes cops" and "camera cops" are out in force trying to make visitors conform to their strict rules on how to "behave properly" in the Vatican. They are especially sensitive and zealous about dress: no shorts or T-shirts; no sleeveless dresses or low cut tops; no beach flip-flops on feet; and any backpacks will have to be checked before you will be allowed entry. They are hopelessly lost when it comes to enforcing camera rules.

PIAZZA SAN PIETRO

Constructed in 1667-1678, this magnificent square (St. Peter's Square) was designed by the famous Gian Lorenzo Bernini who was responsible for much of Rome's baroque style. Facing St. Peter's Basilica and capable of holding 400,000 people, the square is a true architectural masterpiece surrounded by two facing semicircles of four-deep colonnades topped by balustrades and statues of 140 saints. An 83½ foot obelisk with two nearby fountains mark the center of this impressive square.

St. Peter's Square is a good introduction to the Vatican. We recommend starting here. The square itself gives you an excellent introduction to the grandeur of the Vatican, especially its wealth and power. If you're lucky, you may even see the Pope granting an audience to a group on the square.

ST. PETER'S BASILICA

Please be forwarned that a dress code is strickly enforced for entrance into St. Peter's Basilica. If you arrive in shorts, a mini-skirt, or with bare shoulders, you will be disappointed for having come all this way and then denied admission by the "clothes cops" on the basis of your dress. Many people are turned away at the entrance each day because of this rule. The basilica is open from 7am to 7pm in the summer (April to September) and from 7am to 6pm in the winter (October to March).

The world's largest church, St. Peter's Basilica is indeed an impressive structure that attracts millions of visitors each year who marvel at its many treasures. But it's much more than just a big church. Above all, it's a symbol of the power of the Catholic Church. An original basilica was built here by emperor Constantine in 319 AD over the site where St. Peter was buried (now placed under the altar beneath the dome). Restored and reconstructed over the centuries, today the church is largely the product of a reconstruction begun in 1506 under the architectural guidance of Bramente and finally completed in 1626. It's a triumph to the Italian Renaissance and Italy's great 16th century artists. Measuring 636 feet in length, 138 wide, and with Michelangelo's dome reaching 435 feet high, it's simply a massive yet beautifully scaled structure filled with impressive paintings, sculptures, mosiacs, and decorations. Such great Italian architects and artists as Bramante, Raphael, Peruzzi, Conova, Della Porta, and Michelangelo contributed to its final form. While you can easily spend a couple of hours viewing the interior, be sure to look for Michelangelo's *Pietà* near the entrance (in a bulletproof case since a deranged spectator damaged it in 1972); Bernini's impressive seven-storey, 46-ton bronze Baroque canopy sculpture (combines architecture and decorative sculpture), *baldacchino*, over the papal altar (bronze

---

- **A good place to start your Vatican adventure is Saint Peter's Square (Piazza San Pietro).**
- **Beware of both the "clothes copes" and "camera cops" that patrol various sections of the Vatican. The "camera cops" are an utterly hopeless and ineffectual group who you can ignor with little consequence.**
- **St. Peter's Basilica is the world's largest church. It's simply a massive yet beautifully scaled structure filled with impressive painting, sculptures, mosiacs, and decorations.**
- **The Vatican Museums house a treasure-trove of fabulous artwork, an overwhelming display of art and memorabilia.**

---

originally came from the Pantheon); and Arnolfo di Cambio's 13th century bronze statue of St. Peter sitting on a marble throne. You also should visit three areas within the basilica:

- **Historical Museum (Museo Storico Artistico):** *Open April to September, 9am to 6:30pm and October to March, 9am to 5:30pm. Admission 3,000 lira.* Also known as the "Treasury." Offers a collection of sacred relics and Vatican treasures, including vestments, missals, pyxes, chalices, crucifixes, manuscripts, and the bronze tomb of Pope Sixtus V.

- **Vatican Grottoes:** *Enter by the pier of St. Longinus. Open April to September, 7am to 6pm, and October to March, 7am to 5pm. Free admission.* Includes the tombs of various popes and other notables. It's best to make this your last activity with the basilica because you must exit from St. Peter's once you've completed the Grotto tour.

- **Roof and Dome:** *Entrance to the roof and dome is by way of the courtyard which is located on your left when you leave the church. Open April to September, 8am to 6pm and October to March, 8am to 5pm. Admission is 6,000 lira if you use the elevator or 5,000 lira if you use the stairs.* For a panoramic view of the Vatican and Rome, be sure to go to the roof and dome of the basilica. You can reach it by elevator or via a very narrow and long staircase (take the elevator!). Once you reach the roof, you still need to climb a staircase to reach the foot of the dome from where you will get the best views.

VATICAN MUSEUMS

Here's where the Vatican's treasure-trove of fabulous artwork is found. From the paintings and sculptures lining corridors, to maps and tapestries adorning special rooms, to Michelangelo's frescoes in the Sistine Chapel and Raphael's frescoes in the Raphael Rooms, it's simply an overwhelming display of art and memorabilia. Most of the treasures are drawn from the 16th to 19th centuries but also include works of some noted 20th century artists such as Chagall, Dali, and Kokoschka. The Vatican Palace alone houses the world's largest collection of ancient sculptures (both originals and copies) thanks to the Renaissance popes who became great collectors of such art.

Depending on what you wish to see, you can spend anywhere from an hour to a full day or more touring the museums.

However, expect to spend some time waiting in line to enter the Vatican Museums—up to two hours on a busy day. After all, this is one of the most popular tourist destinations in all of Rome. Our advice: get in line early in the morning, perhaps a half hour before opening time which is 8:45am.

The main entrance to the Vatican Museums is on Viale Vaticano. The most convenient public transportation to this area is Bus 49 from Piazza Cavour which stops directly in front of the entrance. Alternatively, take Bus 81 or Tram 19 which stop at Piazza Risorgimento, or take Metro A to the "Ottaviano" stop and from there walk to the entrance.

- ❑ **The main entrance to the Vatican Museums is on Viale Vaticano. Get there early to avoid the long lines.**
- ❑ **If you're visiting the Vatican Museums early and want to avoid the crowds and tour groups, go directly to the Sistine Chapel which is at the end of most tours; you'll find few people crowding this room before 10:30am.**
- ❑ **Watch out for the "camera cops" who roam around the Sistine Chapel trying to stop visitors from taking pictures.**
- ❑ **Beware of potential pickpockets who literally "work the room" while visitors focus their attention to the heavenly depictions on the ceiling of the Sistine Chapel!**
- ❑ **If you are interested in touring the Vatican City and gardens, you'll need to join an official Vatican tour. Be sure to get tickets at least one day in advance.**
- ❑ **To arrange an audience with the Pope, you must have tickets which need to be arranged at least two weeks in advance. Private audiences must be arranged through your local bishop and may take one year to schedule.**

The Vatican Museums are open from October to June (except Easter), 8:45am to 1:00pm, Monday through Saturday, and from July to September, 8:45am to 4:00pm. They are closed on religious holidays, including all Sundays except the last Sunday of the month at which time admission is free. Regular admission costs 13,000 lira per person.

Once inside, except for the crowds, you should be able to easily find your way around. You can follow four color-coded tours, rent a tape recorder with English commentary, or just head off for the most popular attraction, the Sistine Chapel. The color-coded tours are organized by estimated time for completion: yellow (5 hours), green (3½ hours), beige (3 hours), and purple (1½ hours). They also are set up to regulate the flow of traffic throughout the museums. Unfortunately, you're destined to encounter numerous tour groups throughout the complex, many of which may hinder your progress in seeing the place. If you are visiting early and you are on your own, you might want to go directly to the Sistine Chapel which is at the end of most tours; you'll find few people there before 10:30am. If you take the longest tour (approximately 5 hours), you will visit many uncrowded rooms. Most visitors do the 1½ to 3 hour tours and thus crowd some of the major rooms.

All visitors to the Vatican Museum eventually end up in the **Sistine Chapel**. Located at the opposite end of the entrance (actually adjacent to St. Peter's Basilica), this is the room of Michelangelo's two famous frescoes—*Creation* (ceiling) and *The Last Judgment* (altar wall). Currently undergoing a slow yet extensive and controversial restoration to remove centuries of soot and grime, this room is usually packed with tourists gazing at the famous ceiling and attempting to evaluate the present state of the restoration. Many people linger here trying to identify the detailed figures and scenes in the paintings whereas others only need a few minutes to validate their *"been here, done this"* stop at the Sistine Chapel (it may be less impressive than your expectations would lead you to believe). Two tips on how to *"work the room"* or literally be worked on in the room. First, watch out for the "camera cops" who roam around the room trying to stop visitors from taking pictures. It's both a hopeless and hilarious task as hundreds of tourists continue snapping pictures in violation of the no-picture-taking rule. One would think the Vatican might either drop the rule or develop a better system for enforcing the rules. We have yet to see any film confiscated for violating this rule, especially amongst Japanese tourists who live by their cameras. Second, watch out for potential pickpockets who work this crowded room while the "camera cops" run around trying to stop picture-takers. What an easy way to make money—pick the pockets of those who focus all their attention upward to the heavenly depictions on the ceiling! Be sure to hold on to all your personal valuables while you focus your attention on the famous art decorating the ceiling and walls.

As you'll quickly discover, there's a lot more to the Vatican Museums than just the Sistine Chapel. Here's what else you can expect to see in this complex of museums, depending on the time you allot to this area:

- **Raffaello Rooms (Stanze di Raffaello):** Four rooms include some of the most beautiful frescoes in all of the Vatican mainly painted by Raphael Sanzio (second and third rooms) before his untimely death at age 37 but also includes works by Giulio Romano and other assistants. After the Sistine Chapel, this series of rooms is the most important for viewing the Vatican's impressive art works.

- **Egyptian Museum (Museo Gregoriano Egizio):** Offers a small collection of ancient Egyptian art from 3,000 BC to 600 BC, including painted mummy cases, statues, jewelry, and figurines.

- **Chiaramonti Museum (Museo Chiaramonti):** Includes several Roman statues, reliefs, and busts, including such noted ones as *Augustus of Prima Porta* and *Resting Satyr*.

- **Pio-Clementino Museum (Museo Pio-Clementino):** Displays the world's largest collection of classical sculptures in 16 rooms that occupy two floors.

- **Etruscan Museum (Museo Gregoriano-Etrusco):** Offers a collection of Greek, Roman, and Etruria art.

- **Candelabra Gallery (Galleria del Candelabri):** This room includes frescoes and several Roman marble statues with marble candelabra on both sides of the arches that divide this room into six sections.

- **Tapestry Gallery (Galleria degli Arazzi):** Three rooms display 10 huge Flemish tapestries woven from cartoons by Raphael.

- **Gallery of Maps (Galleria delle Carte Geografiche):** A lengthy gallery displaying a fascinating collection of maps, including regions, cities, towns, seaports, and islands, drawn by Antonio Danti between 1580-1583.

- **Borgia Rooms (L'Appartamento Boria):** Includes six rooms of frescoes with religious and classical themes. Incorporates the Gallery of Modern Religious Art in newly renovated rooms with works from numerous 20th century artists, such as Annigoni, Buffet, Chagall, Dali, Gauguin, Kandinsky, Klee, Kokoschka, Léger, Martini, Matisse, Picasso, Rodin, Siqueiros, Sironi, Sutherland, and Vlaminck.

- **Vatican Library (Biblioteca Apostolica Vaticana):** Displays a collection of over one million volumes, including 100,000 handwritten medieval manuscripts and books.

- **Picture Gallery (Pinacoteca):** Includes several religious paintings by noted artists, such as Giotto, Lippi, Raphael, and Leonardo. Many were recovered from France after being taken there by Napoleon. Includes paintings from the Byzantine School, Italian primitives, and 18th century Dutch and French masters.

- ❑ **Gregorian Museum of Pagan Antiquities (Museo Gregoriano Profano):** Display of Roman and neo-Attic sculptures, including Roman copies of Greek sculpture. Includes some original Greek sculptures.

- ❑ **Christian Antiquities Museum (Museo Pio Cristiano):** Displays early Christian and medieval antiquities, including carved sarcophagi.

- ❑ **Ethnological Missionary Museum:** Offers art and artifacts that illustrate life and religious practices from around the world. Includes displays from China, Japan, Korea, Tibet, Indochina, India, Indonesia, Philippines, Polynesia, Melanesia, Papua New Guinea, Australia, Middle East, Africa, North America, Central America and South America. Open on Wednesday and Saturday.

- ❑ **Historical Museum:** An interesting collection of carriages, uniforms, and arms.

You also will find a few shopping opportunities in the main passage areas of the Vatican Museums. Small booths and shops offer a range of cards, books, videos, crucifixes, and Vatican memorabilia.

VATICAN CITY AND GARDENS

If you are interested in seeing the Vatican City and gardens, don't expect to do so on your own. You must join an official Vatican tour to see these ostensibly private areas. Be sure to get tickets at least one day in advance. Contact the Information Office on the left side of St. Peter's Basilica. The tours, which combine bus and walking, take two to three hours. Two-hour tours depart at 10am on Tuesday, Friday, and Saturday and cost 16,000 lira. Three-hour tours, which also include the Sistine Chapel, depart on Monday and Thursday and cost 25,000 lira. You can only enter the city and gardens by joining one of these tours or with a special permit.

PAPAL AUDIENCES

Would you like to see the Pope? So would millions of other visitors. Indeed, the highlight of many visitors' trip to Rome and the Vatican is to attend a public or private audience with the Pope. The Pope gives an audience every Wedneday morning at 11am at the Sala Nervi. To arrange attendance at this audience, you need tickets which should be arranged at least two weeks in advance. You must request these tickets in writing by letter to:

Prefettura della Casa Pontificia
Città del Vaticano
00120 Roma
Tel. 69883273

Be sure to include your mailing address if you wish to have the tickets mailed directly to you. If you wish to arrange a private audience with the Pope, contact your local bishop who must then recommend you to the Vatican for such a visit. Allow plenty of time for a reply—from three months to one year.

If you miss these opportunities to see the Pope, you can get a glimpse of him on Sundays. He appears at his window on St. Peter's Square every Sunday morning.

- **Rome's piazzas are popular places to hang out for lunch, dinner, relaxing, evening entertainment, or people watching. They often change their character by the hour.**
- **Most palaces in Rome have been converted into museums, government offices, or embassies and are located on the major piazzas.**
- **It's difficult to classify museums in Rome as separate from churches and palaces. Most are museums.**
- **Piazza Venezia, Rome's major traffic center, is a good place to start your adventure.**
- **Piazza di Spagna (Spanish Steps) is one of Rome's most picturesque and vibrant squares. It's where you'll find the city's best shopping.**
- **The beautiful baroque-style Piazza Navona is the main plaza for Rome's *centro storico* and a popular meeting place for hundreds of people who come here daily to enjoy it.**

PIAZZAS AND FOUNTAINS

Like piazzas elsewhere in Italy, the ones in Rome are centers for architecture and activity. They include dramatic fountains, statues, palaces, churches, museums, restaurants, shops, and street vendors. They are popular places to hang out for lunch, dinner, relaxing, evening entertainment, or people watching. They often change their character by the hour, depending on the particular mix of individuals congregating or the type of activities underway. A great way to experience the ambience and character of Rome is to literally "hang out" at the city's popular piazzas. The most popular ones include the following:

- **Piazza Venezia and the Vittoriale:** Located in the center of the city, this square serves as a central traffic artery where Via del Corso meets Via dei Fori Imperiali and Via del Plebiscito. All traffic seems to converge on this square which is dominated by the strikingly ostentatious Vittoriale (Vittorio Emanuele Monument), the multi-tiered monument (some say a marble cake or typewriter) to the first king of Italy (Vittorio Emanuele II) and the site of the Tomb of the Unknown Soldier. From here you can easily walk to most major sights (Roman Forum, Imperial Forums, Colosseum, Palatino Hill, Circus Maximus) and shopping areas. On the west side of the square is the Palazzo Venezia, a Renaissance palace with an excellent collection of paintings, sculptures, and objets d'art. The central balcony of this palace served as Mussolini's pulpit for addressing large crowds gathered in the square.

- ❑ **Piazza del Campidoglio:** Located just south of Piazza Venezia at the top of Capitoline Hill (one of Rome's famous seven hills), this piazza was designed by Michelangelo with a distinctive star-patterned pavement. The piazza includes three palaces: Palazzo Nuovo, Palazzo dei Conservatori, and Palazzo Senatorio. The first two palaces constitute the Capitoline Museums which boast a fine collection of ancient sculptures.

- ❑ **Piazza di Spagna (The Spanish Steps):** Our favorite square; it simply looks and feels good. Built by the French in the 1720s to connect the French and Spanish quarters, one above the other, and a popular haunt of famous artists and literary figures, this unique piazza also is one of Rome's most picturesque and vibrant. During spring its 137 travertine steps are decked out with hundreds of colorful azaleas. Recently renovated, the steps have become a popular gathering place for hundreds of young people, caricature artists, musicians, and vendors. At the top of the steps is one of Rome's finest hotels, the **Hassler**. The restaurant Roof Restaurant in the Hassler Hotel serves a terrific Sunday buffet that also affords a wonderful view of the Spanish Steps and Rome. On the square look for the **Keats-Shelley Memorial House** (No. 26) which is a museum to English Romantic poets (Shelley, Keats, and Byron). This area also includes the famous **Caffé Greco**. Shoppers will be in heaven here. Rome's most upscale shopping street, **Via Condotti**, begins at the Spanish Steps and proceeds west. The street is now a pedestrian zone lined with some of the finest boutiques in all of Italy. Several other major shopping streets radiate from this piazza.

- **Piazza Navona:** Built on top of Emperor Domitian's stadium, this is the main plaza for Rome's *centro storico*. It's one of Rome's most beautiful baroque-style piazzas especially noted for its three fountains by Giacomo della Porta (Neptune) and Bernini (Fontana dei Quattro Fiumi and Fountain del Moro) and the Church of San Agnese in Agone. Fontana dei Quattro Fiumi (Fountain of the Rivers, representing the Nile, Ganges, Danube, and Plata) is one of Bernini's great masterpieces. The piazza is a popular meeting place for hundreds of people who come here daily to enjoy the cafés, pose for caricature artists, take pictures, and shop the stalls. Visit here and you will sample much of the pulse of Rome.

- **Piazza Campo dei Fiori:** Once a popular area for the city's major hotels, courtesans, and artisans, today this piazza is best known for being the center for Rome's best food market (6am to 1pm). A popular meeting area for hundreds of people who keep the piazza buzzing all day long, but especially in the mornings and late evenings, when restaurants and bars become the center of attention.

- **Piazza Farnese:** Adjacent to Campo de' Fiori, this piazza is dominated by the elegant Palazzo Farnese, considered by many to be Rome's finest Renaissance palace. Quieter and more elegant than its neighboring piazza.

- **Fontana di Trevi (Trevi Fountain):** Located on the tiny Piazza Trevi, this is Rome's most popular fountain whose massive dimensions and Rococo style are a bit out of scale for such a small piazza. It is literally a magnet for thousands of individuals who gather here each day, throw the obligatory coin over their shoulder into the noisy fountain, take pictures, visit the numerous adjacent souvenir shops and pizzerias, or simply "hang around" the fountain until late at night. Made especially famous in major movies (*La Dolce Vita*) and through popular music (Frank Sinatra).

PALACES

Most of the palaces in Rome were the palatial homes of the rich and famous from the 15th to 19th centuries. Many are architectural masterpieces designed by Italy's major architects. Most have been converted into museums, government offices, or embassies and are located on the major piazzas. Some are occasionally open to the public or require special permission for entrance. Rome's three most famous palaces include:

- **Palazzo Venezia:** Located on the west size of Piazza Venezia. A combination Medieval palace and fortress, this famous palace was built in 1455 for Cardinal Pietro Barbo (Pope Paul II) and has variously served as the embassy for the Venetian Republic and Austria as well as Mussolini's office. It now serves as a museum (Palazzo Venezia Museum) housing a large collection of art.

- **Palazzo Della Cancelleria:** Faces Piazza della Cancelleria and Corso Vittorio Emanuele II. Constructed between 1483 and 1513 for Raffaele Riario, this is one of best examples of early Renaissance architecture in Rome. Includes a beautiful interior courtyard ostensibly designed by Bramante.

- **Palazzo Farnese:** Located on Piazza Farnese which is adjacent to the popular Piazza Campo dei Fiori. This is probably Rome's most beautiful Renaissance palace. Begun in 1514 by Antonio da Sangallo the Younger and later completed by Michelangelo and Giacomo della Porta. The upper storeys and grand cornice along the roof are the work of Michelangelo. Since the 1870s the building has served as the French Embassy. Noted for its superb ceiling (second greatest after the Sistine Chapel), painted by Annibale Carracci between 1597 and 1604 in the Galleria vault. Open to the public on Wednesdays (but you will need a permit; write to: The Ambassador, French Embassy, Piazza Farnese 64, 00186 Rome).

- **Palazzo Doria Pamphili:** Located at Piazza del Collegio Romano 1/a, Tel. 6797233. Open to the public, Monday, Tuesday, Friday, Saturday, and Sunday, 10am to 1pm. 10,000 lira to tour picture gallery and 5,000 lira to tour the private apartments. One of the few palaces open to the public, this privately-owned palace includes some 1,000 rooms. Displays a treasure-trove of art for public view (the picture gallery tour) and examples of how the wealthy patricians lived in the 17th and 18th centuries (the private apartments tour).

CHURCHES

After visiting St. Peter's Basilica, all other churches in Rome pale in comparison. Nonetheless, Rome has many other churches you may wish to visit—just don't compare them all to St. Peter's. Most of these churches were designed by famous architects and are examples of various Roman architectural periods. Most also house important works of art.

- **San Petro in Vincoli:** Located just off Via Cavour along the narrow Via San Francesco da Paola, near Piazza Venezia and the Roman Forum. Includes the chains of St. Peter's and Michelangelo's *Moses*.

- **Santa Maria Maggiore:** Located on Via Cavour. This is one of Rome's oldest churches especially noted for its beautiful mosaics.

- **San Giovanni in Laterano (St. John Lateran):** Located at Piazza Porta San Giovanni. Founded by Constantine, this is Rome's cathedral. Reconstructed several times over the centuries, today this is a huge and imposing structure rich in statues, paintings, and tombs.

- **Sant' Andrea della Valle:** Located at Piazza Sant' Andrea. Designed by Carlo Maderno and Carlo Rainaldi, this 17th century church boasts Rome's second tallest cupola (St. Peter's is number one). Look inside for Giorgio Lanfranco's famous fresco, *The Glory of Paradise*.

- **San Luigi dei Francesi:** Constructed between 1518 and 1589, the exterior of this French church was supposedly designed by Giacomo della Porta. Chapels include frescoes by Domenichino and other important works of art.

- **Santa Maria della Pace:** Take Via della Pace to Piazza della Pace. An example of early Renaissance architecture, this church was built in the late 1400s under Sixtus IV. Includes paintings by Raphael (Sybils—the four prophets) and his disciplines along with one of Bramante's most important works, the small cloister.

- **Sant' Agostino:** Located just off of Piazza Navona along Via de Sant-Agostino on Piazza di Sant' Agostino. This early Renaissance church was built in 1479-1483 by Giacomo da Pietrasanta of Cardinal Augustine. Includes frescos by Pietro Gagliardi and Raphael and other works of art Jacopo Sansovino, Andrea Sansovino, and Guercino. Bernini designed the high altar. Look for Caravaggio's *Madonna of the Pilgrams* and Raphael's *Prophet Isaiah.*

- ❑ **Santa Maria Sopra**: Located at Piazza Santa Maria Sopra, famous for Bernini's marble elephant statue adjacent to a 6th century BC Egyptian obelisk, this church was initially built over a Roman temple to the goddess Minerva and then reconstructed in 1280 in its current Gothic style. Includes frescoes by Filippino Lippi and a statue of St. John the Baptist by Michelangelo.

- ❑ **Sant' Agnese in Agone**: Located on the west side of Piazza Navona, behind Bernini's popular Fountain of the Four Rivers. Built in the 17th century by Pope Innocent X, this is an excellent example of Baroque architecture. Especially noted for its intricate facade which was designed by Carlo Rainaldi and Francesco Borromini.

MUSEUMS

It's difficult to classify museums in Rome as separate from palaces and churches, especially after having visited the Vatican Museums. In one sense, they are all museums! Nonetheless, you will find other types of museums throughout the city. Many represent unique collections amassed by Rome's many popes, patricians, and politicians. We only include a few of the many museums found throughout Rome. If you enjoy museums, especially those depicting ancient sculptures and paintings, you'll find many additional museums with specialized collections to occupy your time in Rome. Most museums open at 9am and close at noon; many are closed on Monday; most have admission fees but waive the fees on Sundays.

- ❑ **Vatican Museums**: See our earlier discussion of this museum complex under the section on "Papal Rome and the Vatican."

- ❑ **Galleria Nazionale d'Arte Antica (National Gallery of Ancient Art)**: *Quattro Fontane 13, Tel. 4814591. Open 9am to 1:30pm (Tuesday, Thursday and Saturday, 9am to 6:30pm; Sunday 9am to 12:30pm). Closed on Monday. Admission 8,000 lira.* Housed in the exotically baroque Palazzo Barberini which was designed by Carlo

Maderno, Boromini, and Bernini. This gallery displays one of Rome's best art collections, especially on the first floor. Offers a good collection of 13th to 18th century paintings, including those by Raphael, Filippo Lippi, Holbein, Bronzino, El Creco, Caravaggio, Canaletto, Andrea del Sarto, Quentin Metsys, Tintoretto, Titian, and Guardi. Don't miss the beautiful frescos by Pietro da Cortona of *The Triumph of Divine Providence* in the first floor picture gallery. The second floor includes more paintings as well as clothes and furniture of the Barberini family who originally occupied this palace.

- **Galleria Nazionale d'Arte Moderna (The National Gallery of Modern Art):** *Viale delle Belle Arti 131, Tel. 3224152. Open 9am to 7pm, Tuesday to Saturday and 9am to 1pm Sunday and public holidays. Admission 8,000 lira.* Houses Italy's best collection of 19th and 20th century modern art, much of which is not well known outside Italy. Includes works by both Italian (Carolo Carrà, Marini, Modigliani) and noted international artists (Kandinsky, Cézanne, Moore, Klimt).

- **Musei Capitolini:** *Piazza del Campidoglio. Open 9am to 7pm, Tuesday to Saturday, and 9am to 1pm on Sunday. Admission 10,000 lira.* Includes the Museo Capitolino and the Museo del Palazzo dei Conservatori which are housed in the Palazzo Nuovo and Palazzo dei Conservatori respectively. Offers an outstanding collection of ancient sculpture along with some paintings from the 16th and 17th centuries.

- **Museo Barracoco:** *Piazza dei Baullari, Corso Vittorio Emanuele 168, Tel. 68806848. Open Tuesday to Saturday, 9am to 7pm and Sunday 9am to 1pm. Closed on Monday. Admission 3,750 lira.* Housed in the 16th century Palazzetto Farnesina, this museum includes a small but important selection of ancient Roman and Near East sculpture collected by Senator Giovanni Baracco. Look for Attic vases, Egyptian hieroglyphs, Babylonian stone lions, Greek sculptures, and Roman and Etruscan exhibits.

- **Museo Nazionale Etrusco di Valle Giulia (National Etruscan Museum of the Giulia Valley):** *Piazzale di Villa Giulia 9, Tel. 3201951. Open 9am to 7pm. Closed Monday. Admission 8,000 lira.* If you're interested in Etruscan art, this museum is for you. Housed in a 16th century palace cum villa built for Pope III, this museum includes statues, ceramics, jewelry, and objets d'art from the 6th, 7th, and 8th centuries BC. The grounds include attractive gardens, pavilions, fountains, and mosaics.

- ❑ **Museo Nationale Romano:** *Baths of Diocletian, Piazza dei Cinquecento, Tel. 4882364. Open 9am to 2pm Tuesday to Saturday and 9am to 1pm on Sunday; closed Monday. Admission 12,000 lira.* Displays a fabulous collection of ancient Roman, Helenistic, and Greek art, including sculptures, reliefs, mosaics, and frescos. Courtyard designed by Michelangelo in the 1560s.

- ❑ **Keats-Shelley Memorial House:** *Piazza di Spagna 26, Tel. 6784235. Open 9am to 1pm and 2:30pm to 5:30pm (summer 3pm to 6pm); closed Saturday, Sunday, and holidays.* Located just to the right of the Spanish steps, this small museum primarily displays the manuscripts, library, and memorabilia of Keats and Percy and Mary Shelley.

ACCOMMODATIONS

Rome offers a range of accommodations with the top end boasting luxurious palaces that rank among Europe's best hotels. In any price category one is likely to encounter modern amenities housed in older buildings—after all, Rome has a long history. This means that a hotel with an old and slightly worn facade may hide elegant and polished interiors. Most of the hotels housed in old buildings have great variety in the rooms within: size as well as decor frequently vary a great deal. If you are not thrilled with your assigned room, unless the hotel is fully booked, ask to see another.

Book well in advance—especially for stays at Easter or during the busy summer months. Even if you are visiting in the off-season, the hotels with the best value tend to be reserved well ahead. Consider the location you prefer. A hotel in the heart of the city will cost more than comparable accommodations on the perimeter. But you'll probably enjoy your stay more if you are within walking distance of sightseeing and shopping venues, and you are more likely to venture out in the evening and savor the romance of the "eternal city." Italian cities are walking cities and you'll quickly fall into the walking habit even if you hardly ever do at home. Consider a hotel near the Spanish Steps (Rome's best shopping is here) or the area near the Pantheon or the Colosseum.

Here are some of the best hotels in Rome. Most are centrally located to be within walking distance to many of the sights, shops, and restaurants.

- ❑ **Le Grand Hotel:** *Via Vittorio Emanuele Orlando 3, Tel. 06/4709, Fax 06/4747307.* This top hotel of the CIGA chain in Rome is just off the piazza della Repubblica and a few minutes from the via Veneto. It has a blueblood history as one of the great hotels of Europe and royalty as well as the ultra wealthy have and still stay here for both its grandeur and service. The exterior looks like a large Renaissance palace. Inside the floors are covered with marble and Oriental rugs complemented by crystal chandeliers, Louis XVI furniture and plenty of baroque plasterwork and high frescoed ceilings. The spacious rooms are luxurious and conservatively decorated and come with dressing areas and tiled baths. Each room differs from the rest and is soundproofed. The surrounding area is not as classy as when the hotel opened in the late 19th century. (★★★★★L)

- ❑ **Excelsior:** *Via Vottorio Veneto 125, Tel. 06/4708, Fax 06/4826205.* This CIGA property, considered by some to be the most splendid hotel in the city, with its palatial limestone facade and its corner tower has become a Rome landmark. The immense lobby is covered with marble floors, thick blue rugs, gilded walls, and accented with crystal chandeliers and Empire furniture. The spacious rooms are elegantly furnished and have marble baths. It is a favorite of many Americans who occasionally enjoy a glimpse of one of the movie stars or dignitaries who stay here. (★★★★★L)

- ❑ **Hotel Lord Byron:** *Via G. de Notaris 5, Tel. 06/3220404, Fax 06/3220405.* This secluded art deco villa is on an exclusive little street on a hilltop in a residential area of embassies and private villas. It is outside the city, but the quiet parkland area makes it worth the trips by car to the city center for those wanting quiet. With a feel that is more like a private house than a hotel, the lobby has flowers everywhere and a decor reminiscent of the 1930s. Rooms are comfortable with a large dressing area, closet and spacious bath. (★★★★★L)

- ❑ **Hassler:** *Piazza Trinita dei Monti 6, Tel. 06/6782651, Fax 06/6789991.* Set on the piazza above the Spanish Steps, the Hassler is the only deluxe hotel in this part of Rome. The location is great for shopping the Via Condotti and Via Borgognona and the view from the Hassler Roof Restaurant is a favorite with visitors and local clientele alike—especially for Sunday brunch. The lobby is ornate but it's glory is a bit faded. The rooms are decorated with Oriental rugs, brocade furnishings and these too have a faded charm. Most baths have double sinks and some rooms have balconies. (★★★★★)

❑ **Cavalieri Hilton International:** *Via Cadlolo 101, Tel. 06/31511, Fax 3151224.* Set a distance from the city center it has a view overlooking the city. There is a courtesy bus to town. Sunlight floods through massive windows into the marble lobby which boasts sculpture and 17th century art. Rooms are decorated in soft pastel colors complementing rich wood tones. Bathrooms are covered in marble with large mirrors. Most rooms have balconies. In many ways this seems like a resort hotel with its tennis courts, jogging track and large swimming pool. (★★★★★)

❑ **Hotel Atlante Star:** *Via Vitelleschi 34, Tel. 06/6873233, Fax 06/6872300.* Just a short distance from St. Peter's Basilica and the Vatican with great views from many of its rooms. The lobby is of dark marble accented by chrome trim and lots of lacquered wood. As is the case with most city center hotels, room size varies. The rooms are comfortable but some are smaller than what some may expect in a 4-star hotel. The lacquered surfaces and printed fabrics give an air of art deco. The staff is friendly and efficient. The upstairs restaurant offers spectacular views of St. Peter's.(★★★★)

❑ **Hotel Forum:** *Via Tor de Conti 25, Tel. 06/6792446, Fax 06/6786479.* Blessed with an exceptional location near the Circus Maximus, the Forum and the Colosseum and built around a medieval bell tower, this hotel exudes character. Housed in a former convent, the public areas have paneled walls with Italian and French styled furnishings. The rooms are nicely appointed with antiques, wood marquetry and Oriental rugs. Great view from the rooftop restaurant. (★★★★)

❑ **Ville Inter-Continental Roma:** *Via Sistina 67-69, Tel. 06/67331, Fax 06/6784213.* Located near some of the most upscale shops in Rome and near the Spanish Steps in a 19th century palace. The public areas are filled with marble, Oriental rugs, brocades and crystal. Rooms have been renovated and are decorated in classic style with the expected amenities. Some rooms have balconies and on the upper floors some have great views. The rooftop terrace provides a great view. (★★★★)

- ❑ **Hotel Raphael:** *Largo Febo 2, Tel. 06/682831, Fax 06/6878993.* A short walk from the piazza Navona in the heart of the city, the Raphael is in an old convent that was converted to a hotel in the sixties. The public areas are filled with antiques and Oriental rugs and display a unique collection of Picasso ceramics. The rooms vary in decor and size. Bathrooms are clad in marble. Some rooms have terraces. There is a panoramic view of Rome from the rooftop terrace. (★★★★)

- ❑ **Hotel d'Inghilterra:** *Via Bocca di Leone 14, Tel. 06/672-161, Fax 06/69922243.* Great views of the Piazza di Spagna neighborhood from its 12 suites. Some consider it the most fashionable small hotel (only 102 rooms) in Rome. Perhaps in part because of its size, a sense of quietude prevails. Recently renovated, the rooms are furnished ornately and all differ from one another in size as well as decor. Ask for a room that opens onto the upstairs terrace. (★★★★)

- ❑ **Scalinata di Spagna:** *Piazza Trinita dei Monti 17, Tel. 06/6793006, Fax 06/69940598.* The wonderful location directly above the Spanish Steps and across the piazza from the Hassler make this 3-star hotel a good value at about half the price of a room across the street. The lobby has the feel of a country inn with bright printed slipcovers adorning the furniture. Rooms vary: some have low ceilings with beams and antique reproductions while others have higher ceilings and a more contemporary look to the decor. Breakfast on the roof garden terrace offers a wonderful view of St. Peter's dome. (★★★)

- ❑ **Del Sole al Pantheon:** *Piazza della Rotonda 63, Tel. 06/6780441, Fax 06/69940689.* This 3-star hotel offers great value. The location overlooks the Pantheon in the heart of the old city. There is a large marble fireplace in the sitting room. Rooms are decorated with antiques and reproductions and with a recent remodeling, modern amenities have been added. Many rooms have Jacuzzis and double glazed windows. (★★★)

Rome also offers a good selection of less expensive two-star (★★) hotels. Some of the best in this category include:

- **Albergo Pomezia:** Via dei Chiavari 12, Tel. 06/686137.
- **Hotel Amalia:** Via Germainico 66, Tel. 06/3721968 or Fax 06/380168.
- **Hotel Dage:** Via due Macelli 106, Tel. 06/6780038 or Fax 06/679-1633.
- **Hotel Imperia:** Via Principe Amedeo 9, Tel. 06/481-4474.
- **Hotel Pensione Merana:** Via Vittorio Veneta 155, Tel. 06/4821797 or Fax 06/4821810.
- **Hotel Piccolo:** Via dei Chiavari 32, Tel. 06/6542560.

RESTAURANTS

Traditional Italian meals are hearty. We are not so much alluding to the calorie count but the number of courses. A traditional meal will consist of four courses: the antipasti or appetizers; primo piatto or first course which usually consists of pasta; secondo piatto or second course which is usually a meat or fish course; and dolce or dessert. It is possible to eat well and healthy, but you will need to pace yourself or you will find yourself eating far more than you are used to at home. Pasta is good for even those on a low cholesterol diet and the Italians do wonderful things with it. Don't be afraid to skip courses if you really don't want all that food. Order the pasta course—usually one of the best anyway—and skip the meat or fish course. Your budget as well as your bathroom scales will thank you for it when you return home.

If you are on a budget or short on time, for breakfast or lunch you may wish to grab a fast bite at a stand up counter like you see so many Italians doing. If you sit down at a table a table charge will be added to your bill. At many restaurants there will be an additional charge if you order bread although they are not supposed to charge if you did not order it. *Pane e coperto* refers to a cover charge and is levied per person. *Servizio* is the service charge and usually amounts to 10-15% of the total bill. *Servizio incluso* or *servizio compreso* means the cover charge is already included in the bill.

Few restaurants serve food on a continuous basis as Americans have come to expect. Most will have definite and limited serving hours for each meal. Lunches are sometimes long drawn-out affairs and dinner is served later than many travelers are used to. In fact some restaurants in Rome open at six to serve pre-arranged dinners to American tour groups. After the tour groups leave the staff cleans and sets up for dinner for the local clientele. If you want American fast food, McDonald's has come to Rome or you can try the local fast food burger chain—Burghys. Many restaurants close at least one day a week—usually Sunday or Monday—some close in August and some for a week or so in December. So if you are planning a very special evening, be sure to call ahead for reservations or have one of the hotel staff call for you. Reservations are a good idea at any popular restaurant anyway.

The following restaurants are some of the best in Rome. Some have been selected because the food, service and ambience are outstanding and these will tend to be expensive. Others have been selected because they are reasonably priced for Rome and offer good value. The restaurants at the budget end tend to be disproportionately pizza places, but when in Rome go where the Romans go!

❑ **Alberto Ciarla:** *Piazza San Cosimato 40, Tel. 5818668. Reservations required. Closed Sunday, two weeks in August & January.* Considered the best restaurant in Rome by some critics. Especially noted for its fish dishes, it provides attentive, friendly service and modern decor. The sea bass with almonds has received awards and the salmon Marcel Trompier with lobster sauce receives raves. Expensive.

❑ **Al Moro:** *Vocolo della Bollette 13, Tel. 6783495. Reservations required. Closed Sunday and August.* Generally noisy and crowded, and with a wait staff that is noted for being aloof, nonetheless Al Moro serves some of the best food in Rome, so patrons continue to dine here. Expensive.

❑ **El Toula:** *Via della Lupa 29B, Tel. 6873750. Reservations required. Closed Sunday, Saturday lunch, and August.* Near the Spanish Steps, El Toula is a favorite of the rich and famous. Its superb cuisine, attentive staff, and elegant decor with vaulted ceilings and large archways make it a favorite of many Romans. Many think it is the best restaurant in the city. The menu changes monthly and one section of the menu offers Venetian specialties. Try their fresh fruit sherbets. Expensive.

❑ **Relais Le Jardin:** *Via G. Notaris 5, (in the Hotel Lord Byron) Tel. 3224541. Reservations suggested. Closed Sunday and August.* Elegant ambience in cheerful pastel colors, superlative cuisine and an attentive staff rates this restaurant 2 coveted Michelin stars. Expensive.

❑ **San Souci:** *Via Sicilia 20, Tel. 493504. Reservations suggested. Dinner only. Closed Monday and most of August.* Off Via Veneto, San Souci offers discriminating diners luxurious decor, impeccable service, and fine food in an intimate setting amid guitar music and the strains of Italian love songs. Ranked among Rome's top four restaurants with a wine list that appeals to discriminating palates. Expensive.

❑ **Les Etoiles:** *Via Vitelleschi 34, (in the Hotel Atlante Star) Tel. 6893434.* Reservations required. In addition to outstanding cuisine and attentive service, patrons are treated to a spectacular view of Rome—a 360° view of the city including the floodlit dome of St. Peter's. Many regional dishes and a superb wine list are features of Les Etoiles. A definite pick if both outstanding food and a fine view are uppermost criteria. Expensive.

❑ **Roof Restaurant:** *Piazza Trinita dei Monti 6, (in the Hotel Hassler) Tel. 6782651.* This rooftop restaurant on the top floor of the Hotel Hassler set above the Spanish Steps offers one of the finest views of the city including the Spanish Steps and St. Peter's. The service is first rate and the menu depends heavily on what is fresh and in season. The Sunday buffet brunch is both a gastronomic and visual treat. Expensive.

❑ **Orso '80:** *Via dell 'Orso 33, Tel. 6864904.* A bright, busy trattoria in the heart of Rome. Their antipasti table is one of the best. Homemade pastas, meat and fish courses are all excellent. Wood fired pizza is available in the evenings. Moderate to expensive.

- **Da Nerone:** *Via delle Terme di Tito 96, Tel. 4745207. Closed Sunday.* Near the Colosseum this small restaurant with its friendly atmosphere serves a very good antipasti buffet as well as good homemade Tuscan wine. Good value. Moderate.

- **Il Corallo:** *Via del Corallo 10, Tel. 68307703. Closed Monday.* This popular pizzeria near the Piazza Navona offers excellent pizzas and desserts. Although the overall prices are moderate for Rome, for those accustomed to pizza prices in the U.S., prices may seem high.

- **Piccolo Arancio:** *Vicolo Scanderbeg 112, Tel. 6786139. Reservations suggested for dinner. Closed Monday and August.* Located near the Trevi Fountain Piccolo Aramcio is busy with locals and tourists alike. Fettuccine and pasta dishes as well as fish are good bets. Moderate.

- **Baffetto:** *Via Governo Vecchio 114. Dinner only.* This well known pizzeria near the Piazza Navona is patronized by locals and tourists alike. Pizza, bruschette, crostini are enjoyed in its friendly atmosphere. You are likely to encounter long lines, but patron turnover keeps things moving. Inexpensive.

- **Ivo's:** *Via di San Francesco a Ripa 157.* A popular pizzeria serving the usual wood fired varieties. It is usually busy but there is a fast turnover. In general, the earlier you arrive the shorter the line. Inexpensive.

- **La Fraschetta:** *Via di San Francesco a Ripa 134.* Located down the street from Ivo's and with a similar reputation for good food and good value. Try this eatery if the line is too long at Ivo's. Good desserts. Inexpensive.

ENJOYING YOUR STAY

Rome is a non-stop city with lots of things to see and do from mid-morning until the wee hours of the morning. While it doesn't offer Italy's greatest opera on the scale of Milan's famous Scala nor attract the international concerts found in Florence's summer festivals, nonetheless, Rome has a great deal to offer in these artistic departments. If you're interested in attending concerts, opera, film, or theater, be sure to pick up the latest issues of *Where Rome*, *Trovaroma*, *Wanted in Rome*, or

Guest in Rome which list current performances. Rome has a good selection of theaters, concert halls, and a popular opera house (Teatro dell' Opera) offering opera and ballet. Its opera season runs from November to May.

BARS

Rome's bar scene includes everything from elegant hotel bars to wine bars, beer halls, and pubs. Most of these places stay open until 1:30am or 2:30am. Some of the most popular bars include:

- **Bar della Pace:** *Via della Pace 3, Tel. 6861216. Open 9pm to 2am daily.* Located near Piazza Navona, this is Rome's most beautiful and famous bar. It's also one of the "in" spots for business people, artists, intellectuals, and wannabes. The place *"to see and be seen in."*

- **Bar della Fico:** *Piazza del Fico 26/28, Tel. 6865205. Open 9am to 2am, Monday to Saturday; 6pm to 2am, Sunday.* Serves breakfast and lunch. Popular "in" spot.

- **Harry's Bar:** *Via Veneto 150, Tel. 4883117. Open 11am to 1am. Closed Sunday.* A delightful bar open for lunch and dinner.

- **Jonathan's Angel:** *Via della Fossa 16, Tel. 6893426. Open 5:30pm to 2am. Closed Monday.* Colorful and loaded with kitsch! A popular institution for drinking and dancing. Don't miss the unique restrooms which are a truly memorable experience.

- **Victoria House:** *Via Gesù e Maria 18, Tel. 3201698. Open 6pm to 1am. Closed Monday.* Located near the Keats and Shelley House and one of Rome's major shopping areas. Good selection of beers. Popular "Happy Hour" on Saturdays (6pm to 9pm) and Sundays (6pm to 8pm).

DISCOS

Discos usually open around 10:30pm and stay open until 3am or 4am. All have cover charges which run 30,000-35,000 lira and include the first drink.

- **Divina:** *Via Romagnosi 11, Tel. 3611348. Open 11pm to 4am. Closed Sunday and Monday. 30,000 lira cover charge.* Includes an intimate bar and lively disco popular with young people and VIPs.

- **Gilda:** *Via Mario de' Fiori 97, Tel. 6784838. Open 11pm to 4am. Closed Monday. 30,000 lira cover charge on Tuesday, Wednesday, and Sunday; 35,000 lira on Thursday; and 40,000 lira on Friday and Saturday.* Popular with actors, singers, artists, politicians, and other VIPs.

- **Jackie O':** *Via Boncompagni 11, Tel. 4885457. Open 9pm to 4am. 20,000-40,000 lira cover charge.* Popular with VIPs who come here for dinner and entertainment.

- **New Open Gate:** *Via San Nicola da Tolentino 4, Tel. 4824464. Open 11pm to 4am. Closed Monday through Wednesday. 30,000 lira cover charge.* Located near Via Veneto, this disco offers some Rome's most avant guard music.

LIVE MUSIC AND NIGHTCLUBS

- **Alpheus:** *Via del Commercio 36-38, Tel. 5747826. Open 10pm to 3am. Closed Monday. 10,000 to 30,000 lira cover charge.* One of Rome's most popular night spots. Offers four different shows each night in its three rooms. Includes Latino, jazz, blues, pop, rock, soul and New Age sounds along with cabarat shows each night.

- **Big Mama:** *Vicolo di San Francesco a Ripa 18, Tel. 581-22551. Open 10pm to 2am. Closed Monday. 10,000 to 35,000 lira cover charge.* Popular blues club that also includes some rock and jazz.

- **Caffè Latino:** *Via del Monte Testaccio 96, Tel. 5744020. Open 10pm to 4am. Closed Monday, August to mid-October. 20,000 lira cover charge.* Specializes in blues, jazz, and hip-hop bands.

- **Palladium:** *Piazza Bartolomeo Romano 11, Tel. 5110203. Open 9pm to 2am. Closed Monday. 20,000 to 35,000 lira cover change.* Located in a old cinema, this is one of Rome's best places for quality international and local entertainment. Includes everything from rock and soul to hip-hop and acid jazz concerts.

- **Saint Louis Music City:** *Via del Cardello 13a, Tel. 4745076. Open 8:30pm to 3am. Closed Sunday. 15,000 lira cover charge.* This popular club offers jazz, rhythm, blues, pop, and rock music. Also serves dinner.

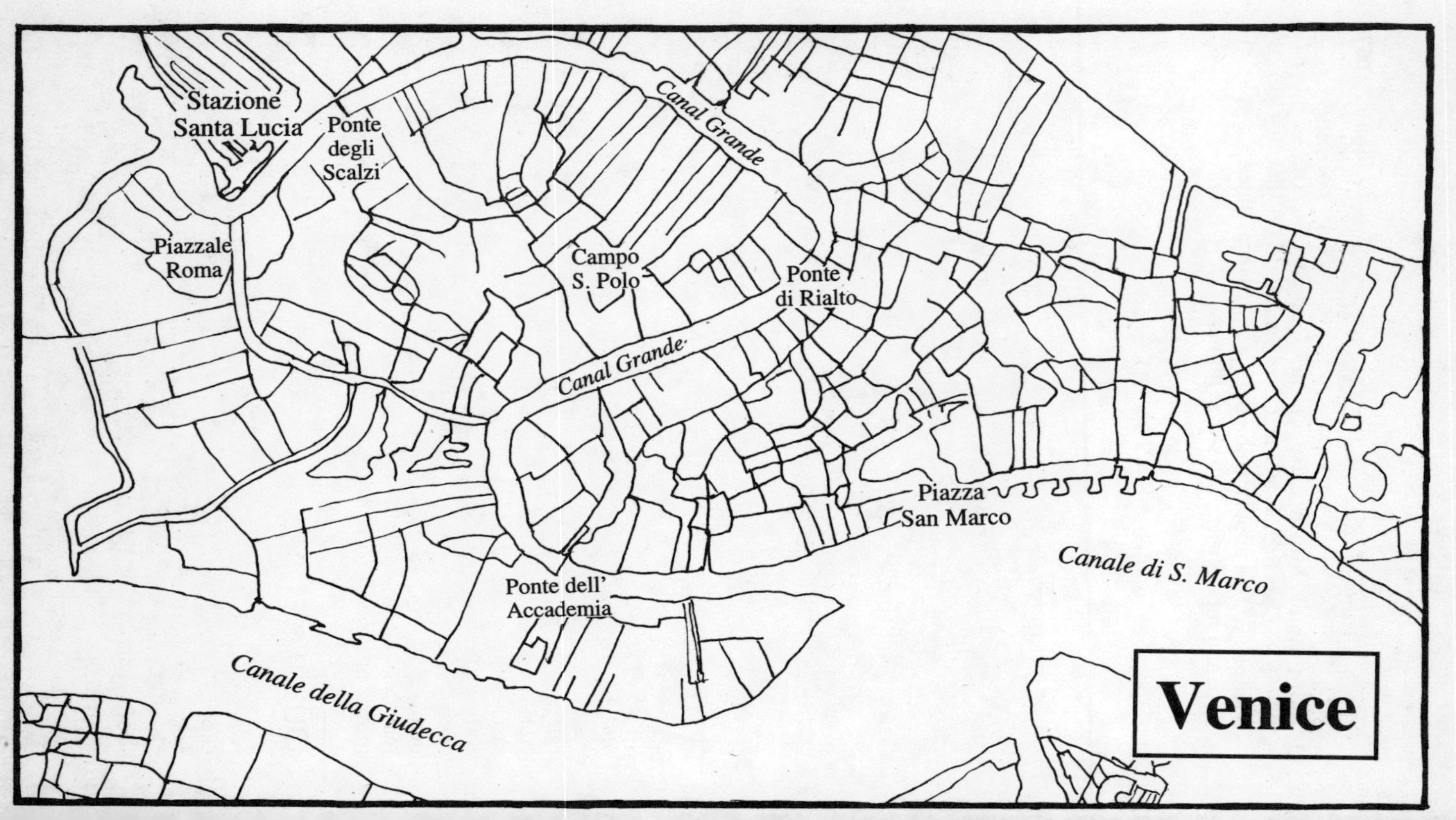
Venice
Stazione Santa Lucia
Ponte degli Scalzi
Piazzale Roma
Canal Grande
Campo S. Polo
Ponte di Rialto
Canal Grande
Piazza San Marco
Ponte dell' Accademia
Canale di S. Marco
Canale della Giudecca

7

Venice

Welcome to Disneyland in the water. You're in for an adventure of a lifetime in what many seasoned travelers consider to be the most beautiful, romantic, enchanting, and mystifying city in the world. If you ever wanted to walk on water, this may be the closest you'll ever get to acquiring the talent, especially in the high tide months of October through April when popular parts of Venice become inundated. This fascinating yet damp city literally lives in and on the edge of water. Come here and you'll know you've arrived at a very special place. Venice is truly a unique sensory experience demanding your close attention—and your money. Indeed, you may need lots of money to fully enjoy what has become Italy's most expensive destination.

QUEEN OF THE ADRIATIC

No Italian city has more character and enduring beauty than exotic Venice, the "Queen of the Adriatic." From beautiful Piazza San Marco (St. Mark's Square) and the picturesque Canal Grande (Grand Canal) to the fabulous palaces, churches, shops, factories, hotels, restaurants, bridges, and back streets stands one of the world's most alluring tourist destinations and fascinating masterpieces of urban design. Narrow alleys (*calli*) and canalside walks (*fondamente*) linked by small squares, quaint foot bridges, aging buildings, and lapping canals make this city one of the great adventures in the art of getting lost and found. It's truly a grand and theatrical city—some even say narcissistic—that seems to live its centuries-old history and bask in its own beauty. Yes, it's faded, it's crumbling, it's polluted, and it's so expensive that until recently hundreds of local residents abandoned the city each year for less expensive mainland destinations. But it's also a powerful, mysterious, and exotic city, reflecting much of its origins and development vis-a-vis the maritime Middle East and Orient.

And times are changing. After 300 years of steady decline, the city is finally undergoing restoration, from pollution and flood control to pigeon removal (those bird droppings do corrode) and incentives for restoring buildings. The city has even stopped sinking as factories on the mainland have ceased lowering the city's water table. Stay tuned to the future: Venice may well be on its way to another Renaissance.

One thing has not changed: between April and October tourists continue to flock here in droves. The place is especially crowded during spring and fall; tourism drops off in July and August, two "peak season" months when hotel rooms can still be found in Venice. Many of Europe's rich and famous still maintain residences here. After all, there is only one Venice, and it is prepared to stand for another thousand years—if the sea doesn't reclaim it first—as one of the world's most interesting and fabled cities.

- ❑ **No other Italian city—not even Florence—has more character and enduring beauty than exotic Venice.**
- ❑ **After 300 years of steady decline, the city is finally undergoing restoration, from pollution and flood control to pigeon removal and incentives for restoring buildings.**
- ❑ **Venice is both a small and large city: 79,000 local residents host 25 million visitors a year!**
- ❑ **Day-trippers, who make up the majority of tourists, feed this city from daybreak to dusk.**

A Timeless, Touristed City

There's a certain timeless character about this city. Perhaps it's the art and architecture or maybe the absence of cars and buses or the labyrinth of narrow pathways lined with people, shops, and restaurants. On a sunny and busy day the city sparkles with light and energy. During high season (April through October), it becomes a festive city with crowds of tourists straining to see the major sights. But during the off season (November to

March), you'll experience a much quieter, more sublime, and less expensive Venice. The same is true if you wander off the beaten tourist path as you accidentally discover the many pleasures of Venice's narrow streets (*calli*) and small squares (*campi*). And this is precisely how one should explore the city: take your time, leisurely stroll the pathways, savor the many special moments, and feast your eyes on a uniquely beautiful amphibious urban landscape.

Few places in the world evoke such instant recognition and emotion as Venice. Whether you have been there or not, chances are you will instantly "connect" with Venice. Once there, it's more than what you ever dreamed Venice would be; it can even be overwhelming. It has a certain ancient, radiant, and almost ethereal quality, especially on a foggy winter afternoon. It looks familiar yet feels so unfamiliar. A decidedly romantic city with beautiful old buildings and pricey gondoliers plying its tidal waters with cute tourist boats, the city offers numerous treasures and pleasures even for the most jaded traveler.

This is a city of tourists who come to visit the world's most touristed city. It's both a small and big city. Indeed, 79,000 local residents host over 20 million visitors a year! Without tourists, Venice would indeed sink in more ways than one. Tourism is its lifeblood. Restaurants, hotels, and shops live or die on the tourist dollar and pray the tidal waters will not discourage many visitors from stepping a wet foot into their exotic city. Day-trippers, who make up the majority of tourists, feed this hungry city from daybreak to dusk.

Everyone's Favorite Tourist Trap

Yes, Venice is one big and expensive tourist trap. Even for Italians Venice is different, a seemingly foreign and exotic country in their midst. Like Disneyland, Venice functions primarily for the pleasure of tourists and the profits of merchants and others who operate the massive, somewhat crumbling, but always high-cost tourist infrastructure. But unlike many other tourist traps, most visitors still come to love this place despite its exhorbitant prices; few leave disappointed. While at times the expensive food may not be great, the shopping can be tacky and inconvenient, and the crowds seem overbearing, there is nothing make-believe about this place. After all, this is a city of great substance, boasting a once glorious history that shaped world politics and economics. It has all the attendant evidence (palaces, churches, monuments) of a truly grand city that has seen its time come and pass. It's a romantic city that will charm you with its quaint buildings, bridges, and canals, singing gondoliers, sidewalk cafés, and squares filled with music. It's a festive city with thousands of tourists exploring familiar sights and shopping for Venice's many treasures.

Despite all the tourists and Venice's legendary high prices (the highest in all of Italy), chances are you will join thousands of other visitors who fall in love with this place. There's nothing comparable to this city anywhere in the world (Suzhou, China and Bangkok, Thailand may claim to be Venices of the East, but they stretch the imagination with such comparisons). Venice leaves an indelible impression on visitors who further romanticize about this already romantic city on the sea. There is only one Venice, and you'll know it when you see it.

The Basics

The first fact of life about Venice is that it is a surprisingly small city that seems big because of its layout and confusing transportation arteries. Home to only 79,000 local residents, geographically it's no larger than New York's Central Park. It seems big to many outsiders given its crazy quilt of islands linked together by bridges, canals, boats, narrow streets, and small squares located in the middle of a large lagoon. The city is literally built on wood piles in the water, and unfortunately, it has been gradually succumbing to the corrosive effects of pollution and heavy canal traffic during the past century. Experts claim it is no longer sinking—just the victim of high tides exacerbated by strong southeasterly winds. It's a particularly wet city between October and April when high tides (*acque alte*) inundate major sections of the city, especially the popular Piazza San Marco. Ingenious attempts to create temporary elevated walkways (*passarelle*) has helped somewhat. At times you may think you're standing in the middle of a beautifully constructed swamp. But cope you must until Venice provides more permanent solutions to its inundation problems, supposedly targeted for the year 2000 when 40 new floodgates should regulate the tides affecting the three entrances to the Lagoon of Venice.

No More Barbarians

This has always been an entrepreneurial city, where nothing seems ordinary and many things appear profound. Since its very beginning, this has been a city of many surprises. How, for example, could a city standing in the middle of a lagoon achieve such greatness and world domination for three centuries?

Originally settled on islands in the 5th century as security against mainland barbarian invasions, the island communities came together in 697 to form a political community and select their first leader, the Doge or duke. Under strong leadership of the Doges, Venice subsequently (13th to 15th centuries) became one of the world's great maritime powers controlling much of the east-west trade, especially the lucrative spice trade, for centuries. Its power started to decline in the 16th century with the rise of the Turks and the gradual shift in world markets elsewhere, especially to the Americas. Venice's power symbolically ended in 1797 when the last of the Doges surrendered power to Napolean and then to the Austrians. Venice would never again regain its former power and glory but it would remain, in an arrested state, attractive to millions of travelers who sought to experience the past glories of this once fabled and commercially decadent city. Indeed, Venice, with its gambling and festivals, became Europe's decadent playground in the 17th and 18th centuries. The 19th century saw the Lido become Europe's most fashionable resort.

Exotic Venice was once a city of great wealth as evidenced in its many opulent palaces and churches and the profusion of art and architecture that still encapsules this city and dominates it urban landscape. It's the city of Marco Polo, powerful Doges, popes, major artistic and literary figures, and many other illuminaries who have contributed to its great fame and fortune. With wealth and power came an extravagant mix of art and architecture, from Byzantine to Renaissance, which often bordered on a Venetian form of frivolity, decadence, gaudiness, and tackiness masquerading as luxury and style. It expresses itself well in glass, lace, jewelry, fabric, and home furnishing designs which contrast sharply with the more contemporary designs found in Milan, Florence, and Rome.

Venice reached the peak of its power and perfection during the Renaissance. It's been downhill for nearly 300 years. But how times have changed. Venice now welcomes daily invasions of tourists in search of its many treasures and pleasures. It's a

- ❑ **By the year 2000, 40 new floodgates should regulate the tides affecting the three entrances to the Lagoon of Venice.**
- ❑ **Venice is built on 117 islands with 177 canals which are tied together by nearly 400 bridges.**
- ❑ **You may find a boat to be the most convenient connection between the airport and city.**
- ❑ **If you arrive by car, you'll need to park in one of the garages at Piazzale Roma or nearby Tronchetto.**
- ❑ **Porters are easily recognized by their badges and blue shirts or coats. They come in handy in taking luggage over bridges, down pathways, and to your hotel.**

lively city primarily engaged in what it has always done well—commerce. And it's as entrepreneurial and driven as ever.

LOCATION AND ARRIVAL

Located on Italy's northeastern coast along the Adriatic Sea, Venice is a remarkable engineering and architectural feat. It's built on 117 islands with 177 canals which are tied together by nearly 400 bridges and covered with over 3,000 walkways totalling 125 miles. The largest canal is the Grand Canal which is crossed by the city's three largest and most famous bridges—Rialto, Accademia, and degli Scalzi. A three-mile long auto and train bridge ties the city to the mainland via the Lagoon of Venice and the town of Mestre. Crossing the bridge, most visitors arrive by car, bus, or train and enter the city at the Grand Canal in the northwest corner where the bridge terminates along with the train station (Santa Lucia Station) and the bus terminal and parking garages (Piazzale Roma).

Most visitors to Venice arrive by plane, train, bus, or car and then proceed into the city by boat. If you arrive by **plane**, you will most likely land at the Marco Polo Airport. Serving both international and domestic flights, this airport is located at Tessera, 10 kilometers north of Venice. The airport is connected to the city by bus, taxi, or boat. If you are traveling lightly, you may want to take one of the blue ATVO **buses**. It costs 5,000 lira and drops you at the main entrance to the city, Piazzale Roma. From there you can walk into the city or take a water bus to your next destination within the city. Yellow **taxis** at the airport cost 50,000 lira and also drop you off at Piazzale Roma. However, you may find a **boat** to be the most convenient connection between the airport and city. The Cooperativa San Marco launch costs 20,000 lira per person and takes about 45 minutes to go from the airport to the landing at Piazza San Marco. You also can take the faster and more expensive water taxi from the airport. But it doesn't come cheap. Expect to pay 100,000 lira per person for this convenient ride.

If you arrive by **train**, you will get off at the Santa Lucia Station which is located on the northwest edge of the city, just across the Grand Canal from the main bus and auto stop of Piazzale Roma. From there you can walk or take a water taxi to your next destination within the city. Since all trains do not terminate at the Santa Lucia Station, be sure to check your schedule. Some trains terminate at the Venezia Mestra Station on the mainland. From there you will need to take another train to Santa Lucia Station which takes about 10 minutes.

If you arrive by **bus**, you will get off at the bus terminal at Piazzale Roma which is just off the Grand Canal and near the train station. From here you can walk or take a water taxi into the city. Porters also are available to assist you with your luggage.

If you arrive by **car**, you'll need to park in one of the garages at Piazzale Roma or nearby Tronchetto. These parking facilities charge by the day and by the size of your car. At Piazzale Roma, the city garage (Autorimessa Comunale) costs from 15,000 to 25,000 lira per day (24 hours). The adjacent private garage (Garage San Marco) costs between 30,000 and 45,000 lire per day. Another large private parking facility, Tronchetto, is located before you reach Piazzale Roma (watch for the sign as you leave the bridge) and costs 35,000 lira per day. If you stay at a hotel that is a member of the Venetian Hoteliers Association, you are entitled to a 40 percent discount at this garage (get a voucher at the hotel and present it when you pay for your parking). From Tronchetto you can take a boat (Line 82) to Piazzale Roma and Piazza San Marco.

PORTERS

If you arrive in Venice with lots of luggage, you'll probably need to hire a porter to carry your luggage to your hotel. Porters are easily recognized by their badges and blue shirts or coats, and they can be found at the airport, train station, Piazzale Roma, and major *vaporetto* landings. Most charge 15,000 lira for the first bag and 5,000 lira for each additional bag. You'll find they come in handy in taking luggage over bridges (luggage with wheels doesn't function well on the cement stairs!), down pathways, and on through the maze of walkways and eventually to your hotel which may be difficult to find on your own.

GETTING AROUND

Forget everything you ever learned about the transportation systems in other Italian cities. Such knowledge does not transfer well to Venice. This is water city where canals are the streets and a variety of watercraft function as taxis and buses. As you will quickly discover, Venice has all new rules for an all new transportation game. It centers on getting around a large lagoon filled with an interesting collection of islands, canals, buildings, squares, and foot paths.

Be sure to get a good map that includes street names, water taxi routes, sites, and various nearby islands. Maps are available at newsstands and in major hotels. A quick look at a map will give you a basic orientation to this somewhat bewildering city. In fact, you might want to take your map to the top of the 324-foot bell tower (*campanile*) in the Piazza San Marco to get a good overview of the various sections of the city. First, focus attention on the two and a quarter mile long Grand Canal which snakes through the city and functions as its major water thoroughfare. Lined with some of Venice's most famous palaces, the Grand Canal tends to be the center for most tourist activities. The bridge from the mainland connects in the northwest corner of the city at two major departure points adjacent to the Grand Canal: the Santa Lucia Station (train) and the Piazzale Roma (car, taxi, and bus terminal). Three major bridges cross the Grand Canal, with the central Rialto Bridge being the most popular. The major destination here is the Piazza San Marco at the other end of the Grand Canal. From there you can venture on to various islands in the lagoon.

There are only two ways to get around in Venice—by foot or by boat. If you're not in a hurry and you've already toured a few canals by watercraft, start walking its pathways; you'll discover this is one of Italy's most delightful walking cities. Indeed, we prefer walking as much as possible because the city is a visual feast as it unfolds through narrow walkways, small bridges, squares, and quaint neighborhoods.

While Venice may initially appear big, you can easily walk to most places within 20 minutes. You'll find plenty of bridges that connect various sections of the city. However, it's sometimes frustrating trying to cross the Grand Canal because it only has three bridges (degli Scalzi, Rialto, and Accademia) which are located some distance from each other. In addition, finding streets as well as specific street numbers can be disorienting given the maze of streets and walkways lacing through the city and crossing its many canals. Nonetheless, this is a great walking city. Follow your map as closely as possible and keep an eye open for signs directing you to the major bridges crossing the Grand Canal. You'll discover many interesting buildings, shops, cafés, and people as you get lost and found walking the various districts and neighborhoods. And you won't get lost for long—at worst 15 minutes.

If you're in a hurry or seek transportation convenience, plan to use the water taxi system. This can be disorienting if you are unfamiliar with the water transportation alternatives and various destinations. Venice offers four types of water transportation:

- **Vaporetto:** This is Venice's public water bus. Operating 20 lines that cover the Grand Canal and various islands in the lagoon, the vaporetto makes numerous stops at designated landings, depending on the particular line. Each landing is clearly marked by name and number (but do check on which direction the boat is running so you don't end up going the wrong way!). Two of the most popular lines are #1 and #82. Line 1 transverses the entire length of the Grand Canal, stopping at most landings along the way and completing its run at the Lido. If you take Line 1 from the train station (Ferrovia) to the San Marco landing, expect to spend 45 minutes on the boat to complete this journey (you can walk it in 25 minutes). Line 82 makes fewer stops along the Grand Canal; it starts at the Tronchetto parking facility and stops at Piazzale Roma, the train station, Rialto bridge, and San Marco. During the summer, Line 82 goes on to the Lido. The vaporetto lines charge 3,500 lira. You also can purchase a 24-hour tourist ticket for 14,000 lira or a 3-day tourist ticket for 20,000 lira. These are good deals especially if you are planning to make several stops as well as visit the islands in the lagoon. While you should purchase your tickets at a landing ticket booth (look for the ACTV sign), you also can pay the fare on board; but it costs more paying this way.

- **Motoscafo:** These are express water buses. They cost more than the *vaporetto* and make only a few stops along the canals. You can buy tickets at the ACTV booths. Long journeys can be expensive.

- ❑ **Forget everything you ever learned about the transportation systems in other Italian cities. This is water city where canals are the streets and a variety of watercraft function as taxis and buses.**
- ❑ **There are only two ways to get around in Venice—by foot or by boat.**
- ❑ **You can easily walk to most places within 20 to 30 minutes.**
- ❑ **Getting lost in Venice is both enlightening and fun. You'll seldom remain lost for more than 15 minutes.**
- ❑ **The two most popular water bus (*vaporetto*) lines are #1 and #82.**
- ❑ **You can purchase relatively inexpensive 24-hour or 3-day tourist tickets for riding the vaporetto.**
- ❑ **However touristy and expensive, gondolas are still great fun. When hiring one, be sure to negotiate the price before getting in and heading off into the sunset. Expect to pay about 80,000 lira for 5 people and a 50 minute ride. Musicians and singers are extra.**

- **Taxi Acqueo:** These are very expensive water taxis that will take you anywhere you desire. Your hotel can arrange for this service. Be sure you understand the costs, including extras, before you use one of these boats. The rates are regulated by the city. Don't be shocked if your water taxi bill comes to 100,000 lira or more!

- **Traghetto:** Frustrated in trying to cross the Grand Canal when one of the three bridges is not in sight? Here's an inexpensive and convenient solution. Try these inexpensive two-person gondolas that specialize in ferrying passengers across the Grand Canal. Rides cost 500 lira which you pay as you enter the boat.

- **Gondola:** You've come all this way so you might as well do what many other tourists do: take a gondola (80,000 lira for 5 passengers for 50 minutes), rent a musician and singer to serenade you (costs extra), and sit back and enjoy the scenery and ambience. Be sure to negotiate the price before setting off into the sunset. In fact, it's best to take this ride around sunset when there is less traffic on the waterways (most day-trippers have left town by now). A nice time includes a segment of the Grand Canal as well as some of the smaller canals that take you into the residential neighborhoods. However touristy and expensive, it's still great fun. Late in the evening, when prices go even higher, such a ride can be one of those magical and romantic moments Venice is so well known for and remembered for years to come.

TOURIST INFORMATION

If you need assistance with maps, hotels, sightseeing and special events, stop at one of Venice's two tourist offices. The **Azienda di Promozione Turistica (APT)** has an office in the southwest corner of Piazza San Marco: 71 Calle dell' Ascensione (open Monday to Saturday, 8:30am to 7pm). Its other office, which keeps the same hours, is located in the Santa Lucia train station.

For information on what's going on in Venice, be sure to get a copy of the useful weekly *Un Ospite a Venezia* (*A Guest in Venice*). This multilingual publication includes current information on museums, entertainment, special events, and current costs of water taxis and gondolas. The magazine *Marco Polo*, published in both English and Italian, includes information on special events. It's available at most hotels and newsstands.

GETTING TO KNOW YOU

Venice is a maze of canals, bridges, streets, and pathways that can be both disorienting and bewildering to many visitors. Addresses are confusing and signs seem nonexistent at times.

No cars or buses here; just you, thousands of other visitors, numerous boats, and lots of lapping water.

LOST IN FANTASY LAND

This is both a walking and boating city. The bad news is that you can easily get lost in Venice by boat (going the wrong direction, or where is the stop?) or on foot (where is this place on the map?). The good news is that it's usually fun to get lost in Venice because you'll discover interesting new places. You won't be lost for long, and you'll eventually find your way out of the delightful mazes that characterize much of this city. In fact, you should plan to get lost at least once during your visit!

LOCATING ADDRESSES AND FOLLOWING SIGNS

One might think Venice has institutionalized its mystery as well as encouraged visitors to explore its city by purposefully developing a confusing addressing and sign system. Addresses in Venice are unlike those found in other Italian cities. So don't feel bad if you can't find a particular address. Venetians have the same problem! The problem is not you; it's the system, or lack thereof, for naming and numbering places. The problem is five-fold. First, shops may have two addresses (Frezzeria 2143 and San Marco 2143). The first will be the street address the second a post office address. Second, addresses on a particular street are not necessarily assigned in sequence. A number 439, for example, might come before 321 rather than after it or it may be found around a corner or on a square. Third, the same street names may be used in different districts; consequently, you need to know which district a particular address is found in. Fourth, finding one of the three bridges crossing the Grand Canal can be difficult when you are walking through a maze of pathways. Look for yellow signs pointing in the direction of those bridges, the train station, and Piazza San Marco; they are attached to the sides of buildings. Fifth, Venetian spellings and language tend to differ from

- ❑ **Addresses in Venice are unlike those found in other Italian cities—very confusing.**
- ❑ **Shops may have two addresses—one street, one post office.**
- ❑ **Street numbers may be out of sequence or tucked around corners.**
- ❑ **The same street names may appear in different districts, so know which district your address is assigned to.**
- ❑ **Look for the yellow signs pointing in the direction of the Rialto Bridge, Piazza San Marco, and train station.**
- ❑ **No way around this confusing system. You'll simply have to muddle through with a certain degree of sleuthing on your part until you finally get to where you want to go.**

Italian equivalents. For example, "street" in Italian is *via* or *strada*, but in Venice the 3,000+ narrow streets and walkways are called *calle*. A *palazzo* in Italian is a "palace," but in Venice a former Doge's palace is called a *palazzo*; other less sumptuous palaces are called *ca'* or house (*casa*). A *piazza* in Venice only refers to the Venice's largest square, Piazza San Marco. Except for the two small adjacent squares, which are referred to as *piazzettas* (Piazzetta dei Leoncini and Piazzetta del Molo), all other squares in Venice are referred to as *campo*; *campielli* are small *campi*. The list of language variations goes on and on and can sometimes be confusing to visitors who believe they have a basic working knowledge of Italian to get around.

If you feel lost in Venice, just ask someone which direction you should go for a particular location. Locals tend to think of locations in relationship to squares (*campi*) when giving directions. Most will point you in the general direction, although you'll still have some work to do to find the specific location. Keep looking and asking and you'll probably get to where you want to go within 10 to 20 minutes. Given the nature of the addresses and the labyrinth of narrow walkways and bridges, you'll need to do some quick sleuthing on the way to a particular location. Quite frankly, you'll simply have to muddle through until you finally get to where you want to go, which you eventually will. Good luck!

We include the district or ward in most of our addresses, often in parentheses, to identify where a particular address is likely to be found amongst the six districts or wards (*sestieri*).

A Small and Expensive City

Venice is both a small and big city. It's small in terms of the size of its local population: 79,000 permanent residents, and still declining. But it's often a big city as thousands of tourists descend on this place each day. Each year those thousands of daily tourists amount to over 20 million visitors. The day-trippers spend lots of money shopping, dining, and hiring gondoliers. To this the over-nighters pay high hotel tabs and frequent expensive restaurants and bars until late at night.

No question about it. This is a very expensive city. After all, it has a very expensive infrastructure to maintain. Goods must be brought in by hand or boat, and the cost of labor is very high. Consequently, don't expect to find many bargains here. While the glass factories may claim their prices are cheaper than elsewhere—because you're shopping at the "production source"—such claims may not be true. When you come to Venice, it's time to bite the financial bullet. Resign yourself to the fact that you will probably spend a lot of money on its treasures and pleasures. It's best to rationalize Venice's exhorbitant prices by telling yourself that this will probably be the last time you will ever visit this unique city. It just makes you feel better. Chances are you might come back someday and say the same thing again!

THE SIX VENICES

Venice is divided into six districts or wards (*sestieri*): San Marco, Dorsoduro, San Polo, Santa Croce, Cannaregio, and Castello. Most are residential districts. The city's major attractions are found in San Marco district, and more particularly in and around Piazza San Marco. In fact, a good orientation to the city is to take a *vaporetto* (Line 1) from Piazzale Roma or Ferroviaria (train station) early in the morning (before 8am) and leisurely travel the length of the Grand Canal to the San Marco landing. Taking about 45 minutes, this journey will give you a good overview of the city's main thoroughfare, a sense of how the city is laid out, and a view of several palaces, hotels, and restaurants along the way.

- ❑ **San Marco District** is Venice's most popular destination. Indeed, the heart of Venice is the Piazza San Marco (St. Mark's Square). This huge marble square and its adjacent attractions is a magnet for most visitors to Venice, many of whom literally begin and end their Venetian adventure here. Crowded with people, pigeons, and players during high season, and occasionally inundated with high tides, this is where the action is from dawn until dusk. For many visitors, this is considered the most beautiful square in the world. The square is bordered by the Piazzetta San Marco (the little piazza alongside the Grand Canal with its Palazzo Ducale), the ornate Basilica of San Marco, and the massive Procuratie Vecchie (old government arcade); accented by the 324-foot red brick bell tower (*campanile*) and a 16th century clock tower; lined with important museums, appealing restaurants, famous outdoor cafés, and attractive shops; and occupied by hundreds of curious visitors and enterprising street vendors. You can literally spend hours—even a couple of days—sightseeing, shopping, dining, and people watching in this area.

- ❑ **Dorsoduro District** is located directly south and east of San Marco District. A residential area for many wealthy and famous individuals, this district is most noted for its art museums, the Accademia, the Peggy Guggenheim Collection, and several good restaurants.

- **San Polo District** is located north of Dorsoduro District and northwest of San Marco District. It is easily reached from San Marco District via the Rialto Bridge. This area is most famous for its art and architecture, wine shops, food markets, tourist market (just west of the Rialto Bridge), and the beautiful Campo San Polo (Venice's second largest square).

- **Santa Croce District** is located immediately north of both San Polo and Dorsoduro districts and is essentially a residential area. You can't avoid this district since it is the major gateway to the city for individuals arriving by car, taxi, or bus. The road from the mainland ends at Piazzale Roma which functions as a bus terminal, taxi stand, parking garage, and departure point for boats. It's also where lots of souvenir vendors and shops congregate to feed off the tourist trade. Includes interesting neighborhoods separated by numerous canals.

- **Cannaregio District** is located on the north side of the Grand Canal opposite Santa Croce and San Polo districts and facing the lagoon. A very old residential area that is not of much interest to visitors other than the Strada Nova (main street), Marco Polo's home, and traces of Europe's first Jewish Ghetto. The train station is located in this district as are the launches for the islands of Murano and Burano. Looking over the lagoon on a clear day from this district, you may be rewarded with one of the best sunsets in Italy.

- **Castello District** is located directly east of San Marco District. It's most famous for the Arsenale, a huge compound used during the 12th to 16th centuries for maritime activity, neighborhood shops and restaurants, noted palazzi and monuments, churches, and three beautiful squares (San Zaccaria, Santi Giovanni e Paolo, and Santa Maria Formosa). Not many tourists venture much further east than the famous Hotel Danieli near Piazza San Marco. Nonetheless, this is a rewarding area for many who explore this district.

THE ISLANDS

If time permits, you may want to visit a few nearby islands. Most can be conveniently reached by regular *vaporetto* service. Some, like Murano and Burano, are artisan islands world famous for their products; they offer varied shopping opportunities. Others, such as San Giorgio Maggiore, San Francesco del Deserto, and Torcello, are noted for their churches and monasteries. And still others, such as the Lido and Giudecca, are primarily resort communities catering to the leisure activities of Venice's more upscale tourists. The most popular islands include:

- ❑ **Giudecca:** Located only 1000 feet south of Dorsoduro District, just across the Giudecca Canal, this island is home for Venice's top hotel—the Cipriani—as well as three fine restaurants—Ristorante Altanella, Trattoria Do Mori, and Harry's Dolci. A real class act, the Cipriani also is one of the world's top hotels and the only hotel in Venice with a swimming pool. If you want to experience a wonderful buffet lunch during the summer, be sure to reserve a table at the Cipriani. Better still, you may want to splurge and stay at the Cipriani. It operates a free motorboat schuttle service for guests to and from Piazza San Marco. Regular *vaporetto* service connects the island with Dorsoduro and San Marco. Some of the best views of the city are from this island.

- ❑ **Murano:** Located less than one mile north of the city, this is Venice's famous island for glass factories. Many visitors go here to see the artisans at work and purchase glass directly from the factory shops. The quality here is mixed—from mediocre to the very best products Venetian artists have to offer. However, beware of ostensible shopping "bargains" in Murano. The theory that prices are always cheaper at the production source is sorely challenged in Murano. Indeed, glass prices in Murano can be higher than in the city proper or elsewhere in Italy. Most of the top glass factories have their own shops in San Marco District. Our advice: do window and comparative shopping in downtown Venice before making any purchases at the factories and shops on Murano (try Venini, Pauly, and Cenedese at Piazza San Marco for comparisons). You'll be a wise shopper for having done such pre-shopping. You also may be interested in visiting the Museum of Glass Art (Museo dell'Arte

Vetrario) and the St. Mary and St. Donato Church (Chiesa di Santa Maria e San Donato). The island is regularly serviced by *vaporetto*. We recommend taking Line 5 from Piazzale Roma or the train station. Alternatively, you may want to take a *vaporetto* from St. Mark's Square which passes through the Arsenale before heading north for Murano.

❑ **Burano:** Located nearly 10 miles northeast of Venice and directly east of the airport, this small and quaint island is known as Venice's "Lace Island" because it produces numerous types of lace items. While you can still find handmade lace items (very expensive) in Burano's numerous shops and vendor stalls, amongst the local products you'll find lots of imported machine-made lace items from Asia. Still a charming island with brightly painted houses, small fishing boats, nets, and canals. Enjoy the ambience of this delightful island by strolling down is main street, Via Galuppi, and exploring adjacent canals. It takes about 40 minutes to get from Venice to Burano by *vaporetto*. Take Line 12 from Fondamenta Nuove or Riva degli Schiavoni. You may want to continue on to two small but charming nearby islands (10 to 20 minutes) noted for an ancient monastery and two churches: **San Francesco del Deserto** (Franciscan monastery) and **Torcello** (Torcello Cathedral and Church of Santa Fosca).

❑ **San Giorgio Maggiore:** Directly east and adjacent to Giudecca Island, this island is famous for its Benedict monks and the church of San Giorgio Maggiore which was initially built in the 10th century and reconstructed in 1565 under the architectural guidance of Andrea Palladio. The church includes many impressive works of art by Jacopo Tintoretto, Girolamo Campagna, and Vittore Carpaccio. The very active Fondazione Giorgio Cini (Giorgio Cini Foundation) also operates from this island. It's especially noted for its three libraries and cultural symposia and conferences.

❑ **The Lido:** Located less than a mile directly east of Venice, this nine-mile long and half-mile wide island is Venice's popular beach and resort community. Made famous in the 17th century as a resort for Europe's rich and famous, it still maintains its sense of class and comfort. It also functions as a barrier island protecting

Venice from the open sea. Wide beaches, luxury hotels (Hotel Des Bains and Hotel Excelsior), and close proximity to Venice (just a 10-minute *vaporetto* ride from Piazza San Marco) make this a favorite location for many visitors to Venice. The island also permits cars which can be ferried in via the Tronchetto terminal (alternative parking area near Piazzale Roma) or driven from the mainland via the connecting southern island of Pellestrina and the mainland town of Chioggia.

Like many other Italian cities, Venice boasts numerous other attractions. One of the real pleasures is walking the city's many pathways to discover all kinds of treasures that make this such a delightful place to visit. Amongst its many treasures is shopping.

SHOPPING TREASURES

While Venice is not Milan, Florence, or Rome when it comes to shopping, it has much to offer visitors who love to shop for unique locally-produced items. Shops are generally open from 9am to 12:30 or 1pm and from 3:30 or 4pm to 7:30pm. While most shops close on Sunday and Monday mornings, others stay open seven days a week in the heavily touristed areas. Prices tend to be on the very expensive side, but that's generally true for shopping in Italy. If you've already shopped in Milan, Florence, or Rome, chances are you're well prepared for Venice's high prices.

- ❑ **Since this is a very expensive city, don't expect many bargains here. When you come to Venice, it's best to resign yourself to the fact that you will probably spend a lot of money on its treasures and pleasures—moreso than in most other Italian cities.**
- ❑ **When you see something you really love in Venice, buy it. Chances are it won't be cheaper elsewhere, it may be gone if you return later, and you may not be able to find your way back to the shop!**
- ❑ **Merchants in Venice seem more willing to pack and ship than merchants elsewhere in Italy.**
- ❑ **Don't be afraid to nicely ask for a discount (*"Is it possible to do better on the price?"*) when making a substantial purchase.**

SHOPPING RULES AND ETIQUETTE

Shopping in Venice is different from shopping elsewhere in Italy. First, given the confusing addresses and difficulty of getting around the city, the old rule that you should *"buy it when you first see it"* is especially applicable in Venice. If you see something you really love and think you can find it cheaper elsewhere or want to think about it, chances are it may be gone if you return, prices elsewhere will be no better, and you may have difficulty even finding the particular shop again.

Second, Venetian merchants seem more willing to pack and ship than merchants in most other Italian cities. They know tourists are reluctant to buy something if they will encounter difficulty taking it with them. Don't be afraid to ask *"can you pack it well, send it to my hotel, or ship it to my home address?"* Venetian merchants are very enterprising, knowing full well they will lose the sale if they can't accommodate your packing and shipping needs.

Third, while northern Italian merchants normally don't like to bargain or discount (*sconto*), many Venetian merchants are not above haggling. You can always ask for a discount and see what happens. We always like to use this polite and suggestive line: *"Is it possible to do better on the price?"* or *"Can you offer a discount?"* After all, if your timing is right and you've come across an accommodating merchant, anything is possible. The worst thing that can happen is to be turned down and then pay the full price. Unless you have an ego problem and don't handle rejections well, go for it. We have no such problems and always ask for a discount on substantial purchases. Merchants tend to be most accommodating to such requests during the winter off season when fewer tourists are around and if you are offering cash or traveler's checks. Many merchants accept personal checks.

- **For all the hype about Venetian glass, you may be disappointed in what you encounter. Much of it is borderline kitsch best left in Venice.**
- **The range of glass products runs from truly tacky souvenirs to quality works of art. Prices are generally very high, even for the tacky.**
- **The island of Murano is Venice's center for glass production.**
- **Much of the lace found in Venice is now made in China and Hong Kong. Real Venetian lace is extremely expensive.**
- **The Venetian maskmaking tradition has undergone a renaissance since 1980. Over 100 small shops now specialize in Carnival masks.**
- **Venice's major shopping areas are found in, around, and immediately to the west and north (Mercerie) of Piazza San Marco.**

WHAT TO BUY

Venice is especially noted for several specialty items. While most items can be found elsewhere in Italy, some are especially delightful to shop for in Venice. Anything imported into Venice, which includes most products, will be more expensive in Venice than in other cities. For example, film and clothes are especially expensive in a city best noted for producing unique glassware, lace, and Carnival masks.

GLASSWARE

Venice is most famous throughout the world for its glass products. It's everywhere in large quantities and in different colors and styles, so much so that it may generally turn you off on shopping in Venice. For all the hype about Venetian glass, you may be disappointed in what you encounter, unless you know where to shop. Much of the glass produced in Venice is borderline kitsch (tourist trinkets) which is best left in Venice or purchased by tourists who either have no taste or bad tastes; it definitely is an acquired taste. Nonetheless, you may find some unique pieces, especially exquisite works of art or inexpensive necklaces and glass beads, that might make excellent gifts or nice display pieces in your home. Venice still boasts fine glass art designs. You'll just have to seek out the "best of the best" in glassware shops and factories to find the good stuff.

Any visit to Venice would not be complete without visiting a glass factory or shopping for uniquely designed and colorful Venetian glass. The range of glass products runs from the truly tacky souvenirs to quality works of art. Prices are generally very high, even for the tacky. Despite claims of entertaining and fast talking Venetian factory salespeople, you may be able to buy the same Venetian glass pieces in other Italian cities, or even in New York City, at lower prices than in Venice. After all, Venetian factories and shops largely cater to tourists who may at best purchase a set of drinking glasses or a decorative punch bowl with glasses as a momento of their visit to Venice.

The island of Murano, located about one mile from Venice, remains Venice's glass factory center. A tradition dating from the 10th century, Murano literally developed as the center for glass manufacturing in 1291 when all glass makers where relocated to this island as a security measure against possible factory fires endangering the city. If time permits, you want to visit the museum and a few of the factories on this island as well as browse through its many shops and see its excellent glass museum. If not, you'll find numerous shops and a few factories in Venice specializing in a large range of glass products. If you're in a hurry and don't have time to visit the glass factories on the island of Murano, you might want to visit one of Venice's large and centrally located shops, **Vecchia Murano** (Calle Larga San Marco 4392/a, Tel. 5204144). Frequented by many tour groups, this shop includes a glass blowing demonstration area as well as a large range of glass products displayed in 17 rooms. Be sure to visit the special room which displays quality works of glass art, especially modern Picasso sculptures. The contrast between this glass art work and the more standard utilitarian and souvenir glass products (flutes, tea sets, bowls, vases, decanters, plates, lamps, necklaces) is quite striking.

Some of our favorite shops for top quality glass selections include **Venini** (Piazzetta dei Leoncini 314, San Marco); **Pauly**

(San Marco 73-77); **Cenedese** (Piazza San Marco 40-41); **Galleria all'Ascensione** (San Marco 72/A); **Salviati** (San Marco 78); **Tre Erre** (San Marco, n.79/b); and **Markus Art Gallery** (San Marco 81). Most of these shops are located on or just west of Piazza San Marco. Other excellent glass shops include **Paropàmiso** (Frezzeria 1701); **L'Isola** (Campo San Moisè 1468); and **Vetri d'Arte** (San Marco 140).

These shops, which display the best quality glass production in Venice, may turn you into an avid collector of Venetian glass. You also may quickly become glass art poor! After visiting them, all other Venetian glass may look truly tacky.

- ❑ **Venini:** *Piazzetta dei Leoncini 314, San Marco, Tel. 522-4045. Open 9am to 7pm (summer) or 9am to 12:30pm and 3:30pm to 7:30pm (winter). Closed Monday morning.* One of Venice's most famous names for quality art glass since it started in 1921. Noted for its innovative work in developing new types of glass and introducing new artistic shapes. Offers beautiful vases, bowls, bottles, bibelots, lamps, and lighting fixtures in contemporary designs.

- ❑ **Pauly:** *San Marco 73-77. Open 9:30am to 12:30pm and 3:30 to 7pm. Closed Monday. Tel. 5209899.* This well established (since 1866) and world renowned glassmaker produces top quality glassware in traditional Venetian designs. Look for vases, goblets, lamps, bottles, chandeliers, and statues in a large variety of shapes and sizes. Also known for its reliable shipping.

- ❑ **Cenedese:** *Piazza San Marco 40-41. Open 9am to 1pm and 3 to 7pm. Closed Sunday evenings. Tel. 5225487.* World renowned glassmaker who offers both traditional and contemporary glass designs. Includes beautiful sculptures, wine glasses, jewelry, and decorative pieces.

- ❑ **L'Isola:** *Campo San Moisè 1468, San Marco. Open 9:30am to 7:30pm. Closed Monday morning. Tel. 5231973.* This glittering gallery shop displays the famous contemporary glass works (plates, vases, tumbler sets) of designer Carlo Moretti. Recognized for his signature spiral motif.

- ❑ **Galleria all'Ascensione:** *San Marco 72/A. Closed for lunch. Tel. 5223129.* This small shop, which you can easily miss, offers some of the best quality contemporary glassware in Venice. Beautiful flutes, bowls, and works of art. Tasteful selections for discerning buyers. One of our very favorite shops. If you get burned out on all the glassware in Venice, come here to recharge your batteries. Yes, indeed, Venice produces knock-your-socks-off glassware that you will be thrilled to own and display in your home. But it's not cheap!

LACE AND FABRICS

Venetian lace also remains one of Venice's most famous products. The nearby island of Burano is especially noted for its lace production. When purchasing lace or embroidered linens, keep in mind that much of what you see is now made in China or Taiwan. You still can find real Venetian lace, but the prices are extremely expensive. Some of the best selections are found at **Jesurum** (Piazza San Marco 60-61), one of Venice's major lace making factories housed in a reconstructed 12-century church. Also try **Martinuzzi** (Piazza San Marco 67) for excellent selections and quality. Two other shops around Piazza San Marco also offer good selections: **Fabris** and **Tokatzian**.

Venice still produces some of the world's most beautiful fabrics, a tradition dating from its 13th century trade with Asia. Several shops in Venice offer gorgeous printed velvets, silks, brocades, damasks, satins, and linens in both classic and modern designs. These shops are a decorator's delight. If you're interested in beautiful Fortuny-inspired (Mariano Fortuny, a popular artist of the 1920s and 1930s, who perfected unique pleating techniques) fabrics, brocades, and accessories, be sure to visit **Lorenzo Rubelli** (Campo San Gallo 1089); **Norelene** (Calle de la Chiesa 727); **Venetia Studium** (San Marco 1997 Palazzo Tiepolo); **Trois** (Campo San Maurizio 2666); and **Arianna da Venezia** (Fondamenta del Traghetto 2793). Milan-based **Frette** (Calle Larga XXII Marzo 2070-A) offers an excellent section of table and bed linens.

❑ **Jesurum:** *Piazza San Marco 60-61 (Tel. 5229864) and at Ponte della Canonica 4310, San Marco (Tel. 5206177). Open 9:30am to 12;30pm and 3:30 to 7pm. Closed Monday mornings.* This is Venice's most famous house of lace. Includes tablecloths, napkins, sheets, and handkerchiefs all trimmed in delicate lace, embroidered, or encrusted with appliqués. The Ponte della Cononica branch includes a Lace Museum displaying some of Jesurum's best and oldest pieces.

❑ **Martinuzzi:** *Piazza San Marco 67.* Offers a wide range of tasteful lace, embroidered items, handkerchiefs, bed linens, and clothes. Good place to shop for infants' and children's clothes, including christening gowns, pillowcases, bonnets, and booties.

- **Norelene:** *Calle de la Chiesa 727. Closed Monday morning. Tel. 5237605.* Excellent collection of Fortuny-inspired hand-printed fabrics, including velvets, silks, and cottons, appropriate for both clothes and interior decorating. Incorporates traditional Venetian designs.

- **Venetia Studium:** *San Marco 1997 Palazzo Tiepolo. Open 9am to 7:30 pm (summer) and 9am to 12:30pm and 3:30 to 7:30pm (winter). Closed Monday mornings. Tel. 5229281.* Famous for its beautiful Fortuny-inspired silk fabrics and velvets. Includes clothes, accessories, home furnishings.

MASKS

Venice is rightly famous for its paper, leather, and fabric masks. The masks reflect Venice's colorful Carnival tradition which dates from the 18th century. Carnival was banned for many years until it was officially revived in 1980. As a result, the mask-making tradition has undergone a renaissance in recent years. While many of the masks approximate tourist kitsch, others reflect excellent quality and craftsmanship and are indeed collectors' items. Over 100 small shops now specialize in these masks. Most are made of papier-mâché and leather, although some also come in plastic. Some of the best places to shop for masks are **Mondonova** (Rio Terrà Canal 3126); **Mondo Nuovo** (Campo Santa Margherita 3063, Dorsoduro); **Laboratorio Artigiano Maschere** (Barbaria delle Tole 6657, Castello); **Le Maschiere di Dario Ustino** (Ponte dei Dai 171); **Adriano Miani** (Calle Grimani 289B); **Emilio Massaro** (Calle Vitturi 2934, San Marco); and **Cà Macana** (Calle delle Botteghe, near San Barnaba). Visiting these shops may well turn you into a collector of Venetian Carnival masks!

- **Mondonova:** *Rio Terrà Canal 3126, Dorsoduro. Tel. 523-1607.* This small but world famous shop produces top quality Carnival masks as well as other theatrical papier-mâché items. Its two dedicated owners have an eye for the fine art quality of this newly revived craft tradition.

- **Mondo Nuovo:** *Campo Santa Margherita 3063, Dorsoduro. Open 10am to 12:30pm and 4 to 7:30pm. Closed*

Monday mornings. Tel. 5287344. Offers a wide selection of papier-mâché masks and other items produced by one of Venice's master craftsmen, Gianni Lovato.

- ❑ **Laboratorio Artigiano Maschere:** *Barbaria delle Tole 6657, Castello. Open 9am to 12:30pm and 4 to 7:30pm. Closed Monday. Tel. 5223110.* Responsible for reviving the mask-making tradition (Giorgio Clanetti), this shop offers a wide range of handcrafted papier-mâché and leather masks representing major Carnival characters.

MARBLEIZED PAPER PRODUCTS

Like Florence, Venice has a long tradition in producing unique and colorful paper goods which make nice and relatively inexpensive gifts. Look for books, desk blotters, notebooks, picture frames, address books, wrapping paper, and desk accessories made from Venetian papers. One of the best shops for such products is **Legatoria Piazzesi** (San Marco 2511). Also visit **Paolo Olbi** (Calle della Mandola 3653) for a large selection of paper products and related gift items. Other shops worth visiting include **Alberto Valese** (Salizzada San Samuele 3135, San Marco, and Calle del Teatro 1920, San Marco); **Il Pavone** (Fondamenta Venier 721, Dorsoduro); **Polliero** (Campo dei Frari 2995, San Polo); and the Florence-based **Il Papiro** (Calle del Piovan 2764). Several print shops producing such products can be found on Salizzada San Moisè and the streets leading to Campo Santo Stefano.

- ❑ **Legatoria Piazzesi:** *San Marco 2511. Open 9am to 12:30pm and 4 to 7pm. Closed Monday mornings. Tel. 522-1202.* This long-established bookbinding shop still produces marbleized papers using traditional hand-block and wood-block printing techniques.

- ❑ **Paolo Olbi:** *Calle della Mandola 3653, San Marco. Open 9:30am to 12:30pm and 3:30 to 7pm. Closed Monday mornings. Tel. 5285025.* Terrific gift shop filled with all kinds of marbleized papers, pens, notebooks, leather goods, and desk accessories.

ANTIQUES AND COLLECTIBLES

Venice boasts several shops specializing in Venetian antiques and collectibles. As might be expected, prices for Venetian antiquities are extremely high. Nonetheless, if you enjoy shopping for such items, or just seeing many of the lovely displays, head for the area around San Maurizio and Santa Maria Zobenigo (east of Campo Santo Stefano in San Marco). The best antique shops are found in this area. Some of the best antique shops include **M: Antichità e Oggetti d'Arte** (Frezzeria 1691, San Marco) for antique jewelry and fabrics; **Pietro Scarpa** (San Marco 1464) for old paintings and drawings; **Casellati Antique Shop** (Calle Larga XXII Marzo 2404); and **Zancopé** (San Marco 2674) for antique Venetian glass.

- ❑ **M: Antichità e Oggetti d'Arte:** *Frezzeria 1690, San Marco. Open 10am to 12:30pm and 4 to 7pm. Closed Monday. Tel. 5235666.* This sumptuous and eccentric shop offers high quality antiques and hand-printed velvets in the Mariano Fortuny style. Includes antique jewelry, objects d'art, ornate mirrors, and numerous home decorative items amongst its collection of luxurious fabrics.

- ❑ **Pietro Scarpa:** *San Marco 1464. Open 9:30am to 12:30pm and 4 to 7pm. Closed Monday. Tel. 5222697.* This small shop and gallery is famous for its master paintings and drawings by several of Venice's major artists—Titian, Tiepolos, Canaletto, and their disciples—dating from the Renaissance. True museum quality.

- ❑ **Zancopé:** *San Marco 2674. Open 10am to 12:30pm and 4 to 7pm. Closed Monday mornings. Tel. 5234567.* Specializes in antique Venetian glass dating from the 16th century. Includes collections of old decanters, goblets, and perfume bottles.

- ❑ **Casellati Antique Shop:** *Calle Larga XXII Marzo 2404, San Marco. Closed Monday morning. Tel. 523096.* One of Venice's oldest and most reliable antique shops.

JEWELRY

Most jewelry shops are found in and around Piazza San Marco. For distinctive handcrafted gold jewelry, visit the famous **Missiaglia** (San Marco 125-127); they also carry the popular Hermès product line. Also look for **Codognato** (San Marco 1295); **Must de Cartier** (Campo San Zulian, San Marco); and **Nardi** (Piazza San Marco 69).

❑ **Missiaglia:** *San Marco 125-7. Open 9:30am to 12:30pm and 4 to 7:30pm. Closed Monday mornings. Tel. 5224464.* Operating since 1864, this small but famous shop has produced some of Venice's finest quality jewelry for wealthy Venetians and others. Excellent gold craftsmanship in classic and contemporary designs. The shop also carries the exclusive Hermès line of jewelry and accessories.

❑ **Codognato:** *San Marco 1295. Open 10am to 12:30pm and 4 to 7:30pm. Closed Monday mornings. Tel. 5225042.* Operating since 1864, this is one of Venice's most respected names for antique jewelry. Its five-star international clientele rely on this shop for outstanding quality and selections. Gorgeous stuff for the money-is-no-object crowd.

❑ **Must de Cartier:** *Campo San Zulian, San Marco. Open 9am to 12:30pm and 4 to 7:30pm. Closed Monday. Tel. 5207484.* This is Venice's luxurious Cartier jewelry shop now in a new location. Need we say more? Yes, they offer the usual exquisite drop-dead jewelry that has made this such an exclusive high-end jeweler.

❑ **Nardi:** *Piazza San Marco 69. Open 9:30am to 12:30pm and 4 to 7:30pm. Closed Monday mornings. Tel. 5225733.* Famous Venetian jeweler offering a wide range of top quality jewelry, from pins to watches. Beautiful window displays.

CLOTHES AND ACCESSORIES

Venice is not a world fashion center nor the place to buy Italian fashion clothes produced in Milan or Florence. But every major Italian designer appears to be well represented in the San Marco District where tourists tend to congregate and window shop. Venice will meet your demand for Italian fashion and accessories. As expected, prices are higher here and selections are somewhat limited. Nonetheless, if you feel the need to do this type of shopping in Venice, you'll find numerous clothing stores to meet your needs. Some are exclusive boutiques representing only one designer label; others represent a wide range of clothing designers. Chances are you've seen them all before in other Italian cities. All are located in the San Marco District: **Arnold's Shop** (Calle Mandola 3720b) for classic English menswear; **Laura Biagiotti** (Calle Large XXII Marzo

2400) for women's knits; **Al Duca d'Aosta** (San Marco 4922) for major women's and men's fashion labels; **Elysée Due** (Frezzeria 1693) for the Giorgio Armani line; **Emporio Armani** (Calle dei Fabbri 989) for the sportier Armani line; **Fendi** (Salizzada San Moisè 1474) for furs, clothing, and leather goods; **Gianfranco Ferrè** (Calle Larga San Marco 287) for fashionable men's and women's clothes and accessories; and **Krizia** (San Marco 4948-9), **Max Mara** (Calle dei Mori 268-269), **Missoni** (Calle Vallaresso 1312), **Valentino** (Salizzada San Moisè 1473), and **Versace** (Frezzeria 1722) for popular designer clothes.

Now for something different and uniquely Venetian, beyond the famous designers. Clothing shops in Venice are not all designer shops offering the latest fashions and accessories from Milan and Florence. For innovative, colorful crowd-stopper window—dressing mannequins (models of former Doges) in drag—and very special offerings, be sure to stop at **Fiorella** (Campo Santo Stefano 2806, Tel. 5310636). Operated by the flamboyant Fiorella Mancini, who is a major player in the annual Carnival celebrations and a community development leader, the shop offers its own exclusive line of exotic clothes which at times might be mistaken for Carnival costumes. Also offers an interesting and humorous line of kitsch.

- ❑ **Arnold's Shop:** *Calle Mandola 3720b. Open 9:30am to 12:30pm and 3:15 to 7:30pm. Closed Monday morning. Tel. 5235039.* Specializes in classic and sporty English menswear which includes lots of sweaters and sweater vests, sheepskin jackets, and herringbone and tweed jackets.

- ❑ **Laura Biagiotti:** *Calle Large XXII Marzo 2400. Open 9am to 12:30pm and 3:30 to 7:30pm. Closed Monday mornings. Tel. 5203401.* This exclusive shop offers beautifully tailored women's clothes using quality cashmere and linen fabrics. Very attractive knits. Very expensive.

- ❑ **Al Duca d'Aosta:** *San Marco 4922. Open 9am to 12:30pm and 3:30 to 7:30pm. Tel. 5220733.* Carries an exclusive line of women's and men's fashion clothes and accessories including such labels as Burberry's, Ralph Lauren, Jill Sander, and Prada.

- ❑ **Elysée Due:** *Frezzeria 1693. Open 9am to 12:30pm and 3:30 to 7:30pm. Tel. 5230145.* If you missed out on the exclusive Giorgio Armani line when you passed through Milan, look no further. It's all here and very expensive.

- **Emporio Armani:** *Calle dei Fabbri 989. Open 9am to 12:30pm and 3:30 to 7:30pm. Tel. 5237808.* Here's where you will find the less exclusive, sportier, and more medium-range Armani line for men, women, and children.

- **Fendi:** *Salizzada San Moisè 1474. Open 9am to 12:30pm and 3:30 to 7:30pm. Closed Monday mornings. Tel. 520-5733.* Need a gorgeous fur? Look no further. You'll also find a good selection of Fendi's beautiful signature clothing and leather goods here for women.

- **Gianfranco Ferré:** *Calle Larga San Marco 287. Open 9am to 12:30pm and 3:30 to 7:30pm. Tel. 52225147.* One of Italy's leading designers offers fashionable men's and women's clothes and accessories.

- **Krizia:** *San Marco 4948-9. Open 9am to 12:30pm and 3:30 to 7:30pm. Closed Monday mornings. Tel. 521-2762.* A two-storey boutique offering gorgeous women's clothes and accessories by one of Italy's top designers. Excellent selection of evening wear.

- **Max Mara:** *Calle dei Mori 268-269. Open 9am to 12:30pm and 4 to 7:30pm. Closed Monday mornings. Tel. 5226688.* Trendy women's clothes (coats, knits, linen suits) by one of Italy's leading designers.

- **Missoni:** *Calle Vallaresso 1312. Open 9am to 12:30pm and 4 to 7:30pm. Closed Monday mornings. Tel. 5205733.* A relatively small shop, it offers a good selection of women's and men's clothing, especially the colorful signature Missoni sweaters.

- **Valentino**: *Salizzada San Moisè 1473. Open 9am to 12:30pm and 3:30 to 7:30pm. Closed Monday mornings. Tel. 5205733.* If you've seen Valentino fashions and accessories before (really can't miss them if you're shopping for fashion), you know the exquisite quality and the astronomical prices. The quality is here, the selections are somewhat limited, but the prices are in-your-face as usual. One of Italy's most exciting designers.

- **Versace:** *Frezzeria 1722. Open 9am to 7:30pm. Tel. 523-6369.* Includes a large selection of women's and men's clothing and accessories by one of Italy's most popular and flamboyant designers. You may find the designs to be an acquired taste, much like Venetian glass.

LEATHER GOODS, SHOES, AND ACCESSORIES

Similar to clothes, the leather goods, shoes, and accessories found in Venice are primarily manufactured elsewhere. Within San Marco District you'll find several good quality shops offering a wide variety of such products: **Bottega Veneta** (Calle Vallaresso 1337) for handbags, shoes, and accessories; **Bruno Magli** (San Marco 1302) for classic footwear; **Bussola** (San Marco 4608) for designer label handbags, wallets, belts, and suitcases; **Fratelli Rossetti** (San Marco 1477) for beautiful men's and women's shoes; **Gucci** (Mercerie 259) for distinctive handbags, luggage, and accessories; **Trussardi** (Spadaria 695) for handbags and accessories; and **Vogini** (Calle Seconda dell'Ascension 1257a) for handbags, accessories, and jackets.

- ❑ **Bottega Veneta:** *Calle Vallaresso 1337. Open 10am to 1pm and 3:30 to 8pm. Closed Monday mornings. Tel. 522-8489.* Offers an excellent selection of signature woven leather bags, handbags, accessories, and shoes. Great quality and decent prices.

- ❑ **Bruno Magli:** *San Marco 1302. Open 9am to 12:30pm and 4 to 7:30pm. Closed Monday mornings. Tel. 522721. Also located at San Marco 1583-1585b (Tel. 5223472).* One of the top names in Italian footwear for both women and men. Classic designs and quality leather. Includes both casual and formal footwear.

- ❑ **Bussola:** *San Marco 4608. Open 9am to 12:30pm and 3:30 to 7:30pm. Closed Monday mornings. Tel. 5229846.* Represents several major Italian designers (Armani, Versace, Trussardi). Wonderful selections of designer label handbags, wallets, belts, and luggage.

- ❑ **Fratelli Rossetti:** *San Marco 1477. Open 9am to 1-2:30pm and 3:30 to 7:30pm. Closed Monday mornings. Tel. 5230571. Also located at San Marco 4800, Campo San Salvador.* This long established and famous shop offers an excellent selection of beautiful men's and women's footwear. Top quality and designs.

- ❑ **Gucci:** *Mercerie 259. Open 9:30am to 12:30pm and 3:30 to 7:30pm. Closed Monday mornings.* Italy's top name in leather bags and accessories offers another tempting selection of quality leather goods, from key chains to luggage.

- ❑ **Trussardi**: *Spadaria 695. Open 9am to 12:30pm and 3:30 to 7:30pm. Tel. 5285757.* Offers the signature Trussardi leather goods for men and women, with emphasis on handbags, wallets, totes, and accessories.

- ❑ **Vogini:** *Calle Seconda dell'Ascension 1257a. Open 9am to 12:30pm and 3 to 7:30pm. Closed Monday mornings. Tel. 5222573.* Offers an exciting selection of quality handbags, accessories, and suede jackets. Their attractive window displays are real crowd-stoppers.

OTHER TREASURES

As you'll quickly discover, Venice has lots of shopping choices for the full range of tourists that daily descend on this city. Walk the main streets and you'll discover other types of shops that make up the crazy quilt of Venetian shopping: art, book, craft, gift, and gourmet. You're certain to find some unique treasure that will bring back wonderful memories of your great Venetian adventure.

MAJOR SHOPPING AREAS

Shopping in Venice can be somewhat disorienting given the canal and pathway structure of this city. However, there are a few major shopping areas which are easy to find and explore, especially in, around, and immediately to the west and north (Merçerie) of Piazza San Marco. Best of all, they are located near several major sightseeing attractions.

PIAZZA SAN MARCO

Piazza San Marco is where most of Venice's shopping action is concentrated. Row after row of shops in the arcades surrounds this popular piazza. Here you'll find just about everything Venice is famous for—glassware, masks, lace, paper goods, souvenirs, jewelry, clothes, and accessories. In addition to exploring the arcades facing the piazza, be sure to browse through the many shops located to the north and west of the piazza. Shops to the north tend to disproportionately cater to tourists in search of souvenirs.

Some of Venice's best shopping is found in shops to the west of the piazza, especially along Calle Vallaresso, Salizzada San Moisè, Calle Larga XXII Marzo, and Frezzeria, Shops in this area offer some of Venice's top quality glassware, antiques, jewelry, clothes, and accessories. Be sure to look for **Pauly** (San Marco 72-77), **Venini** (Piazzetta Leoncini 314), and **Galleria all'Ascensione** (San Marco 72/A) for excellent glassware; **Missiaglia** (Piazza San Marco 125) for exquisite gold jewelry; **Missoni** (Cale Vallaresso 1312-B), **La Bottega Veneta** (Calle Vallaresso 1337), **Valentino** (Salizzada San Moisè), and **Camiceria San Marco** (Calle Valaresso 1340) for quality clothes and accessories; **M** (Frezzeria 1690), **Osvaldo Böhm** (Salizzada San Moisè 1349-50) and **Casellati Antique Shop** (Calle Larga XXII Marzo 2404) for antiques; **Il Prato** (Frezzeria 1770) for quality handicrafts; **Jesurum** (Ponte Canonica 4310) for lace; and **Venetia Studium** (Calle Larga XXII Marzo 2403) for hand-printed fabrics, lamps, scarves, and clothes.

RIALTO BRIDGE

No, this is not the Ponte Vecchio in Florence offering quality shopping with a unique ambience. Best viewed from the water for its architectural beauty and symmetry, the Rialto Bridge is home to numerous vendors who offer a wide range of souvenirs and typical open-air market products. Don't expect to find many quality items here nor many particularly distinctive shops. If you enjoy exploring outdoor markets for clothes and souvenirs and prowling through neighborhood shops for food items, this area just may be your cup of tea. While numerous vendors operate stalls on the bridge, you'll find many street shops and vendor stalls on both sides of the bridge offering everything from clothes to fresh fruits and vegetables.

Nonetheless, you may have some luck here. Look for **Rialta** (Ruga degli Orefici 56, a small shop located under the Rialto arcade) for unique and good quality jewelry, Carnival masks, dolls, hats, purses, and antique glass beads. Many people love visiting the open-air fish (**Pescheria**) and produce (**Erberia**) markets (the "Rialto Markets") first thing in the morning (open Tuesday to Saturday, 8am to 1pm). Chances are, if you explore the city on foot, you will at sometime cross this bridge.

MERCERIA

This is the busy main street that connects Piazza San Marco with the Rialto Bridge in five different sections (Merceria dell'Orologio, di San Zulian, del Capitello, di San Salvador, and 2 Aprile). From the north side of Piazza San Marco you enter this street under the famous clock tower. Merceria and its adjacent streets are filled with small shops offering a wide range of products. Look for **Al Duca D'Aosta** (Merceria dell'Orologio 4922 and 4946) for women's and men's clothing, and **Eredi Giovanni Pagnacco** (Merceria dell'Orologio 231) for fine quality glassware and ceramics.

THE ISLANDS

As noted earlier, two major islands offer special shopping opportunities. The **island of Murano** is famous for its glass factories and shops. While many of factories have shops in Venice proper, in and around Piazza San Marco, you may want to visit the actual factories that produce the many products on display. Some of the major ones include **Colleoni Veteria Artistica** (call for free transportation, Tel. 736355), **Barovier & Toso, Venini, Murano Venezia Glass, La Filigrana**, and **Sent**.

The **island of Burano** is famous for its lace production. Primarily a small fishing village, it continues to produce and sell famous Venetian lace. Once you leave the boat and proceed to the main square, Piazza Galuppi, you'll pass numerous vendor stalls offering lace products. Again, go to Burano if you wish to view the actual production process. Keep in mind that prices on the islands are often no better than prices in the Venetian shops.

THE MARKETS

Where does all the food come from to service the thousands of people who crowd this city each day? Much of it initially comes into what is collectively called the "Rialto Markets," Venice's two major produce and fish markets that attract a colorful mix of housewives, chefs, singing vendors, and tourists near the Rialto Bridge. Depending on how you like to see your food (in the state of nature or prepared for consumption), these two markets can be great fun to visit first thing in the morning (8am) before all the tourists crowd the pathways and major sites:

- ❑ **The Erberia:** *Open Monday through Saturday, 8am to 1pm.* Located at the large square near the Church of San Giacomino, this market sells everything except fish:

vegetables, fruits, wines, cheeses, chicken, and spices. Watching the colorful and expressive vendors haggling and singing makes the visit here well worth while.

- **The Pescheria:** *Open Tuesday through Saturday, 8am to 1pm.* Now this is a real show, one of the best fish markets in all of Europe. View the large variety of fresh fish, many still alive, on display for the regular traffic of daily buyers: shrimp, prawns, lobster, squid, cuttlefish sea bass, red mullet, soft-shelled crabs, eels, octopus, and turtles. Chances are you'll see these critters again at dinner. In fact, you might prefer seeing your fish prepared on your plate rather than displayed dead or alive in this market.

Other Areas

You'll find numerous shops throughout Venice, especially near the major transportation hubs and tourist sites. The area near the train station (Stazione di San Lucia), for example, has numerous souvenir shops offering a wide range of Venetian and imported goods; focus your attention along the main street here, Lista di Spagna. Prices on glassware in these shops seem to be better than in the Piazza San Marco area, although you won't find the same high quality shops that tend to be concentrated in the area west of Piazza San Marco. The bus terminal at Piazzale Roma also has several vendors offering postcards, guidebooks, and typical tacky tourist souvenirs (do you really need a plastic gondola for your suitcase?). The area east of the Galleria dell' Accademia has a few shops worth visiting: **Cenedese** (Campo San Gregorio 175) for excellent quality Murano glass; **Marangon da Soaze** (Campiello Barbaro 364) for furniture and wood products; and **Paola Carraro** (Calle Nuova Sant'Agnese 869) for unique sweaters woven with modern artistic designs. The area northwest of the Accademia also has a few interesting shops: **Libreria Alla Toletta** (Sacca della Toletta 1214) for an excellent selection of books; **Arianna da Venezia** (Fondamenta del Traghetto 2793) for a wonderful selection of hand-printed velvet products (bed covers, clothes, carnival masks, wall coverings, book covers, and curtains); **Mondonova** (Rio Terrà Canal 3126), a world famous workshop for producing quality carnival masks and papier-mâché products. The area north of the Accademia (San Samuele water bus stop at Palazzo Grassi) has several artisan shops and galleries worth exploring especially if you are already in this area visiting the Palazzo Grassi, Venice's second most popular palace. Look for **Livio De Marchi** (Salizzada San Samuele 3157-A) and the **Venice Design Art Gallery** (Salizzada San Samuele 3146) for unique works of art.

MAJOR ATTRACTIONS

In addition to cruising the canals and islands and shopping for Venetian treasures, Venice offers a wonderful selection of sightseeing pleasures to occupy at least two days of your time. You definitely should cruise the two mile long **Canal Grande** which is lined with some 200 marble palaces constructed since the 12th century and exhibit some of Venice's finest architectural achievements. Venice's sights include the usual selection of excellent squares, churches, palaces, and museums that Italy is so well known for and which Venice built with its great wealth in the 12th to 18th centuries.

PIAZZAS

- ❑ **Piazza San Marco (St. Mark's Square):** *Vap 1, 2, 34 San Marco or 5 San Zaccaria.* This is the heart of Venice, where much of Venetian history is centered and where most tourists clamor in their effort to experience the "real" Venice. All other squares in Venice pale in comparison to San Marco. In fact, this is the only square in Venice called a *piazza*; all other squares are referred to as *campi* (fields) because they were once unpaved. Most visitors to Venice spend much of their time visiting the various historical sites, shops, and restaurants or just doing nothing but enjoying the ambience in and around this popular square. Many visitors consider this to be the most beautiful square in the world. It's a huge square filled with pigeons, vendors, and tourists. It also occasionally floods during high tide: you either wade through the water or walk along a network of elevated wooden planks which the city provides for this occasional inconvenience. Standing at the center of this square and facing east, you'll see the 9th century Basilica di San Marco, the Palazzo Ducale (Doges' Palace), the 16th century San Marco Clocktower; the 325-foot 9th century bell tower (Campanile di San Marco), the tallest structure in Venice (you can take an elevator to the top for a panoramic view of the city); administrative offices; and the old library (now an archaeological museum). Arcades filled with restaurants, outdoor cafés (Caffè Florian being the most famous), shops, and music surround three sides of this attractive and vibrant square. The south side of this square becomes Piazzetta San Marco, or the little piazza, which borders the lagoon.

- ❑ **Campo San Polo:** *Vap 1, 34 San Tomà or 1 San Silvestro.* Located in the San Polo district, directly west of the Rialto Bridge, this is Venice's second largest square. A popular meeting place for local residents, this square is used for outdoor movies during the summer. A good place to see and meet the locals and enjoy a free movie on a hot summer evening.

CHURCHES

- ❑ **Basilica di San Marco (St. Mark's Basilica):** *Piazza San Marco. Vap 1, 2, 34 San Marco or 5 San Zaccaria. Basilica open daily 9:45am to 5:45pm; museum open daily 9:45am to 5:30pm. Tel. 5225205.* Originally built in the 9th century to house the bones of St. Mark (smuggled from Alexandria), this is one of the true masterpieces of Byzantine architecture. It's a powerful statement of Venetian architecture, art, religion, and wealth all rolled into one awesome, ancient, and crumbling package. Constructed with massive pillars, huge domes, and ambitious mosaics, this is one of Italy's great churches. Viewed from the square, the basilica is a beautiful statement of well-preserved Byzantine/Venetian architecture. Viewed from the interior, it dazzles visitors with its massive scale, remarkable mosaics, and precious art and artifacts. You can easily spend a few hours looking at all the details that make up the basilica.

- ❑ **Santi Giovanni e Paolo (San Zanipolo):** *Compo Santi Giovanni e Paolo, Vap 1, 2, 34 Rialto.* Operated by the Dominican Friars, this large church is known as the Pantheon of Venice for its role as the center for funerals and burials of the doges. Includes several tombs, chapels, and monuments reflecting important periods in Venice's history.

- ❑ **Chiesa di Santa Maria Gloriosa dei Frari (St. Mary's Church):** *Campo dei Frari, San Polo. Vap San Tomà. Open Monday to Saturday, 9am to noon and 2:30 to 6pm, and Sundays and holidays from 3 to 5pm. Admission charge. Tel. 5222637.* Considered by many to be Venice's most beautiful church after the Basilica of San Marco, this Gothic Franciscan church includes several major works of art including Titian's *Assumption* and the *Madonna of Ca'Pesaro*.

❑ **Chiesa di Santa Maria della Salute (Church of St. Mary of Good Health):** *Compo della Salute, Dorsoduro. Vap Salute. Open daily from 8:30am to noon and 3 to 5pm.* Located across the canal from Piazza San Marco and standing majestically at the entrance of the Grand Canal, this beautiful octagonal-shaped 17th-century baroque church with its distinctive white dome (made from white Istrian limestone), appears in many paintings and photos of Venice. Designed by Longhena and considered to be one of Europe's major architectural achievements, it was built in honor of the Virgin of Good Health for delivering the city from the plague. Includes paintings by Titian and Tintoretto.

PALACES

❑ **Palazzo Ducale (Doge's Palace):** *Piazzetta San Marco (vaporetto stop San Marco). Open daily from 8:30am to 7pm (summer) or 9am to 4pm (winter). Admission charge.* Dating from the 9th century but reconstructed in the 15th century and beyond in Gothic-Renaissance style and with pink and white marble, here's where lots of Venetian history can be found. Venice's most famous palace was once the doge's residence (apartments) as well as the government center. It remains an architectural masterpiece. Visitors to this palace are treated to a tour of the huge Grand Council Chamber with its remarkable ceiling and paintings by Veronese and Tintoretto, a connecting prison and torture chamber with its secret corridor (Ponte dei Sispiri), and several rooms that served as functional government and residential rooms. Huge underground cisterns are found at the palace entrance.

❑ **Palazzo Grassi:** *San Samuele 3231 (Vap 2, San Samuele). Only open during exhibitions. Admission charge.* This is Venice's second most popular palace. Originally built in the 18th century, it was acquired in the 1980s by Fiat who subsequently had it restored to be used as an international art exhibition center. The remodeled interior alone is worth seeing. The designer of Paris' fabulous Musée d'Orsay was one of the major architects involved in this project, and it shows. The palace offers an excellent view of the Grand Canal. The exhibitions are well worth seeing.

MUSEUMS

- ❑ **Galleria dell'Accademia (Gallery of Fine Arts):** *Campo della Carità. Vap Accademia. Open daily 9am to 7pm from April to October; open Monday to Saturday 9am to 1:30pm and Sunday 9am to 12:30pm, November to March. Admission charge. Tel. 5222247.* A wonderful collection of 14th to 18th century Venetian art housed in the 15th century convent of Santa Maria della Carità. Includes 24 rooms of impressive art including such popular works as Veronese's *Supper in the House of Levi*, Titian's *Presentation of the Virgin*, and Giorgione's *Tempesta*. You are well advised to arrive here early morning or late afternoon since the lines tend to be long during the day.

- ❑ **Museo del Settecento Veneziano (Museum of Eighteen Century Venice):** *Fondamenta Ca'Rezzonico 3136, Dorsoduro. Vap 1 Ca'Rezzonico. Open daily 9am to 7pm during the summer. Open Monday to Thursday and Saturday and Sunday from 9am to 4pm in winter. Admission charge. Tel. 5224543.* Housed along the Canal Grande in the 17th century Ca' Rezzonico Palace, this museum is home to one of finest collections of 18th century Venetian art. It includes paintings, furniture, textiles, and objets d'art.

- ❑ **Museo Correr:** *Piazza San Marco 52 (west end). Vap 1, 2, 34 San Marco. Open Monday and Wednesday to Sunday, 9am to 4pm and until 7pm during April to October. Admission charge. Tel. 5225625.* Consisting of three sections, this museum chronicles the history of Venice through maps, paintings, scale models, and documents.

- ❑ **Museo Archeologico:** *Piazza San Marco 17 (southern end). Vap 1, 2, 34 San Marco or 5 San Zaccaria. Open Monday to Saturday, 9am to 2pm and Sunday 9am to 1pm. Tel. 5225978.* Temporarily housed in the old library building, this museum includes archaeological pieces collected by several of Venice's patrician families between the 17th and 18th centuries. Includes statues, base-reliefs, and coins from the 5th century B.C. on, including several Greek and Roman pieces.

- **Museo d'Arte Moderna Ca'Pesaro:** *Fondamenta Pesaro 2076. Vap 1 San Stae. Open Tuesday to Sunday, 9am to 4pm. Admissions charge. Tel. 721127.* Housed in the impressive Palazzo Pesaro, this is Venice's modern art museum. Includes the works of Europe's major 20th century painters.

- **Collezione Peggy Guggenheim (Peggy Guggenheim Collection):** *Palazzo Venier dei Leoni, 701 Calle Cristoforo, Dorsoduro. Vap Accademia. Open Sunday, Monday, and Wednesday through Friday, 11am to 6pm, and Saturday, 6 to 9pm. Admission charge. Tel. 5206288.* Displays the famous private modern art collection (cubist, surrealist, abstract expressionist) of American millionaire Peggy Guggenheim in this unusual one-storey paisleys. Includes paintings and sculptures of Picasso, Jackson Pollock, Max Ernst, Braque, Henry Moore, Jean Arp, and Alberto Giacometti.

- **Museo Vetrario (Glass Museum):** *Fondamenta Giustinian 8, Island of Murano. Open Thursday to Tuesday, 10am to 5pm, April to October; Thursday to Tuesday, 10am to 4pm, November to March. Admission 5,000 lira.* Located in Paisleys Giustinian, this unique museum is divided into three major sections. It includes an extensive collection of glassware produced in the furnaces of Murano's many glass factories as well as some archeological pieces. You'll find numerous pieces manufactured between the 15th and 19th centuries along with many contemporary pieces. Well worth a visit to better understand the unique art and science of Venetian glass making.

- **Scuola di Merletti di Burano (Lace Museum):** *Piazza Galuppi, Island of Burano. Open Tuesday to Saturday, 9am to 6pm and Sunday, 10am to 4pm. Admission 3,000 lira.* If you're interesting in learning more about the history and techniques of lace production in Burano, be sure to visit this museum. In fact, you may want to stop at this museum before you make any lace purchases in Venice.

ACCOMMODATIONS

Most Venice hotels are located in older buildings—some former palaces—that have been converted into hotels and renovated. Some of these buildings are grand, even palatial; some are simply old. Because so many hotels are located in structures that originally served other purposes, the rooms lack the standardization found in most establishments built as hotels. Thus, within a hotel, rooms will vary greatly.

Hotel prices are generally very high in Venice during peak season. Expect to pay US$400 to $700 per night for a double at a five-star hotel. If you select a four or five-star hotel, you will find prices can range considerably for various rooms within the hotel—as much as 50 percent depending on the size and location of the room. In two and three-star hotels, you may be charged an extra 10 percent for air conditioning. If you don't ask about this charge when you check in, it may be automatically added to your bill. You'll pay a premium for a room overlooking the Grand Canal. Breakfast, consisting of a croissant, jam, and coffee, is usually included in the room rate which can be US$20-$35 of the bill. If you don't want breakfast (the same breakfast is available in a café for US$6-12) or did not eat breakfast, inform the hotel when you check in or out; the breakfast charge will be deducted from your bill (it's the law).

The canals that symbolize the romance of Venice for most tourists, have also limited the expansion of many older buildings. Fears that the city is slowly sinking has also placed limitations on the amount and height of new construction. The result is that hotel space is limited, there are lots of tourists who want to see and experience Venice, and the prices reflect the supply/demand ratio.

Because hotel space in Venice is expensive, many tourists—especially tour groups—stay outside the city and become day trippers who clog its walkways by day and commute by train back to their lodgings outside the city by night. Even with many visitors staying outside the city, except for July, August, and the winter months, there are simply not enough rooms to accommodate everyone. The busiest seasons in Venice are spring and fall; December 20th to January 2nd; and the two week period prior to Ash Wednesday.

The hotels which we list are for the most part the best in Venice and offer luxurious old world charm, deluxe amenities, a tradition of service, and a good location in the city. Views of Venice will vary greatly with different rooms within each hotel and those with a great view will be priced higher than other similar rooms in the same establishment. For those who prefer to spend their cash on things they can carry home and stay in less luxurious surroundings, yet desire establishments that offer charm and good value, we have included a few three-star hotels that have received accolades from their guests and satisfied clients who return again and again. They are not cheap, but offer good value and are less expensive than their four and five star brethren. Some three star hotels may charge additional for air conditioning and some do not have elevators. If an elevator is essential, do ask when you book the hotel.

Wherever you chose to stay, reserve well in advance. This is perhaps even more important at the less expensive hotels that offer charm and great value than at the deluxe top-end, because the good value three-star and fewer hotels tend to have fewer rooms and lots of repeat guests. Once a tourist finds a great value, he tends to return again and again. Whatever you select, keep in mind that you only pay the hotel bill once, but your memories will last a lifetime.

Some of Venice's best hotels include the following establishments:

- ❑ **Bauer Grünwald:** *Campo San Moisè 1459 (San Marco), Tel. 41/520-7022, Fax 41/5207557.* Great location on the Grand Canal, and one of the best hotels in Venice, the Bauer Grünwald is situated in a 15th century cloister. All rooms have been renovated and have marble baths and antique furnishings. Some rooms have a view of the canal. Efficient, friendly service. (★★★★★L)

- ❑ **Cipriani:** *Giudecca 10 (Giudecca), Tel. 41/5207744, Fax 41/520-3930.* On the island of Giudecca, across the canal from the Piazza San Marco, sits the Cipriani—one of the top hotels in Venice. The area is less crowded than on the opposite side of the canal and the view of the famous landmarks surrounding Piazza San Marco is stunning. Rooms are furnished with both antiques and contemporary pieces and in either case the rooms are artfully decorated. Many of the marble bathrooms have Jacuzzis and several suites have private shaded terraces. The hotel launch ferries guests back and forth to San Marco at any hour. This separation from mainstream Venice is both a blessing and a curse—you can get away from it all and bask in the peace and serenity of Guidecca, but if you prefer being in the midst of the "action" this location may feel too secluded. (★★★★★L)

- ❑ **Danieli:** *Riva degli Schiavoni 4196 (Castello), Tel. 41/5226480, Fax 41/5200208.* Located next to the Bridge of Sighs, a few steps from Piazza San Marco and across the canal from the island of San Giorgio, this top hotel continues to please discriminating travelers. The four story lobby of this 15th century paisleys is filled with marble columns, and Murano glass fixtures add to the Venetian decor. The rooms are well appointed. The rooms in the most recent addition are thought to be less charming than those in the main building, though they are perfectly comfortable. The best rooms have magnificent views! From the Danieli Terrace there is a superb view of the lagoon and you may wish to dine here even if you are staying elsewhere. However, the view may outclass the food. Some may feel the service is a bit haughty; others may thrive on it. (★★★★★L)

- ❑ **Gritti Palace:** *Campo Santa Maria del Giglio 2467 (San Marco), Tel. 41/794611, Fax 41/5200942.* One of Venice's stellar hotels and home away from home to notables from Winston Churchill to Queen Elizabeth. From its stunning location on the Grand Canal an aristocratic atmosphere pervades this legendary hotel. Rooms are lavishly decorated with Fortuny fabrics and a collection of museum-quality pieces adorn various parts of the hotel. Attentive, unobtrusive service. The dining terrace on the Grand Canal becomes quieter in the evening when there is less boat traffic. (★★★★★L)

- ❑ **Europa e Regina:** *Calle Larga XXII Marzo 2159 (San Marco), Tel. 41/5200477, Fax 41/5231533.* Located near the Piazza San Marco, this CIGA hotel has been recently renovated. The lobby and public areas are decorated with 18th century antiques. Rooms are updated and furnished with copies of period furnishings. In winter, dine in the glassed-in Tiepolo restaurant with its view of the Grand Canal. In the summer the view is still great as diners move out onto the terrace. (★★★★★L)

- ❑ **Londra Palace:** *Riva degli Schiavoni 4171 (Castello), Tel. 41/520-0533, Fax 41/5225032.* Well located a few hundred yards from the Piazza San Marco, the Londra Palace has been renovated to take advantage of its location overlooking St. Mark's Basin and its heritage. Rooms sport antique and reproduction Venetian furniture and dark paisley prints; baths are wood-paneled and have brightly lit make-up vanities. The rooftop suite is romantic. A solarium on the 6th floor and a private beach are special features. Deux Lions restaurant offers fine Venetian and French cuisine. Ask about their complimentary Mercedes for one-day excursions. (★★★★★)

❑ **Monaco & Grand Canal:** *Calle Vallaresso 1325 (San Marco), Tel. 41/5200211, Fax 41/5200501.* Three connected 18th century palaces along the Grand Canal form this hotel less than 100 yards from St. Mark's Square. This luxurious hotel has many rooms with magnificent views. Room are not large, but are well designed and well furnished. The hotel bar features a large picture window with a wide vista of the canal. (★★★★★)

❑ **Saturnia Internazionale:** *Calle Larga XXII Marzo 2398 (San Marco), Tel. 41/5208377, Fax 41/5207131.* Located near the Piazza San Marco, this converted 14th century palace displays ornate coffered ceilings, damask applied to the walls and Venetian furnishings in the main salon. Many rooms have been recently redecorated and baths also given a facelift. Many rooms overlook the garden; others overlook the city rooftops. (★★★★)

❑ **Pensione Accademia:** *Dorsoduro 1058 (Dorsoduro), Tel. 41/521-0188, Fax 41/5239152.* Just off the Grand Canal and near the Accademia museum, this 17th century villa is one of the prettiest small hotels (27 rooms) in Venice. The surrounding gardens filled with flowering plants, give a sense of privacy and peace. The public rooms feel warm and friendly and are decorated with Murano chandeliers and Venetian furnishings. Guest rooms are well kept and have canal or garden views. The bar has a wood-burning fireplace that adds warmth during the cold months. Breakfast is served in the garden in warm weather. (★★★)

❑ **Hotel Kette:** *Piscine San Moise 2053 (San Marco), Tel. 41/5207766, Fax 41/5228964.* Located between La Fenice and Piazza San Marco, and on a canal, one can approach the hotel by gondola or from the street. The lobby is comfortable and magazines and newspapers invite one to sit and browse between forays to shop and sightsee. Rooms vary in size and decor and are furnished with period reproductions as well as more modern pieces that fit well together. Friendly staff. (★★★)

Venice also has a few desirable two-star hotels that offer good value:

❑ **Albergo Paganelli:** Campo S. Zaccaria 4687, Tel. 41/5224324 or Fax 41/5239267.

- **Albergo San Zulian:** Calle San Zulian 534, Tel. 41/522-587 or Fax 41/5232265.

- **Hotel Fontana:** Campo S. Provolo 4701, Tel. 41/523-0533 or Fax 41/5231040.

- **Hotel Mignon:** SS. Apostoli 4532, Tel. 41/5237388 or Fax 41/5208658.

- **Hotel Tivoli:** Ca' Foscari 3838, Tel. 41/5237752 or Fax 41/22656.

- **La Residenza:** Campo Bandiera e Moro 3608, Tel. 41/5285315 or Fax 41/5238859.

- **Pensione Segusa:** Zattere al Gesuati 779, Tel. 41/522-2340 or Fax 41/5222340.

RESTAURANTS

What kind of food do you expect to find in a city of 79,000 residents hosting over 20 million visitors a year? Gourmet? Inexpensive? Forget it. You can find some good restaurants in Venice, but don't expect a great display of culinary arts outside the five-star hotels that cater to discerning travelers. The best restaurants tend to be in the top hotels or off the beaten tourist path—where the locals dine. Like so many other things in Venice, restaurant prices tend to be extremely high—the highest in Italy. After all, this is Venice and it's probably the first and last time you will visit this romantic city. So welcome to the city of expensive okay restaurants. The good news is that you won't go hungry. The bad news is that restaurants are likely to be very crowded and you will probably pay high prices at some truly forgettable Italian restaurants.

Since Venice is located in a lagoon and near the sea, restaurants serve lots of fresh seafood not found in many other parts of Italy. Antipastos and risottos tend to be uniquely Venetian. Look for soft-shell crabs (*moleche*), spider crabs (*granseole*), whitebait (*gô*), squid (*seppie in nero*), scallops (*capesante*), and cuttlefish (*seppiloine*). Pasta dishes tend to include seafood (*pasticcio di pesce*) rather than tomato sauces (avoid ordering spaghetti in Venice except at Arcimboldo). Other Venetian specialties include liver with onions (*fegato alla veneziana*), rice and pea soup (*risi e bisi*), stewed cuttlefish (*seppie alla veneziana*), and the wonder dessert *tiramisù* (a delicious mixture of creamy mascarpone cheese, expresso, chocolate, and ladyfingers with a liqueur or rum-soaked cake) and *baicoli* (Venetian cookies).

Dining hours in Venice are between 12:30 or 1pm and 2:30 or 3pm for lunch and from 8pm to 11pm or midnight for dinner. It's always a good idea to make reservations, especially during high season, since many restaurants are very crowded.

Some of Venice's best restaurants include the following establishments:

❑ **Cipriani:** *Hotel Cipriani, Giudecca 10 (Giudecca). Open for lunch and dinner, April to mid-November; closed mid-November through March. Reservations required.* This exceptional restaurant in one of Italy's exceptional hotels is the favorite of Venice's top diners. Very expensive.

❑ **La Caravella:** *Calle Larga XXII Marzo 2397 (San Marco), Tel. 5208901. Closed on Wednesday during winter. Reservations required.* Offers an extensive menu which includes many Venetian specialties such as stuffed squid, whole-wheat pasta (bigola) with anchovies, pasta with crab sauce (*taglierini alla granseola)*, and fillets of sea bass and sole. Excellent wine list. Very expensive.

❑ **Grand Canal:** *Hotel Monaco and Grand Canal, Calle Vallaresso 1325 (San Marco), Tel. 5200211. Closed Tuesday. Reservations and jacket required.* Tough to beat the view. Sit outside in the summer on the delightful canal-side terrace which overlooks the mouth of the Grand Canal. Excellent local specialties such as scampi Ca' d'Oro, calf's liver alla veneta, and tigliolini tossed with fresh scampi. Also serves a good Chateaubriand. Very expensive.

❑ **Club del Doge:** *Hotel Gritti Palace, Campo Santa Maria del Giglio 2467 (San Marco), Tel. 794611. Open daily. Reservations required.* Beautiful hotel setting overlooking the Grand Canal, excellent service, and fine regional dishes distinguish this restaurant as one of Venice's very best. Wonderful fresh fish dishes. Try the raviolini stuffed with fish, saffron risotto with chicken livers, and breast of guinea hen. Very expensive.

❑ **Antico Martini:** *Campo San Fantin 1983 (San Marco), Tel. 5224121. Open Wednesday to Monday for dinner. Closed December 1 to March 20.* Popular with the theater crowd, this restaurant offers a combination of international and local fare. The local dishes are particularly enticing: calf's liver alla veneziana, radicchio braised with beef marrow and Parmesan cheese, and a variety of fresh fish dishes. Moderate to expensive.

- **Metropole Buffet:** *Hotel Metropole. Riva degli Schiavoni 4149 (Castello), Tel. 5205044. Reservations advised for both lunch and dinner.* Overlooking the lagoon, this pleasant buffet-style restaurant offers a good selection of appetizers, soups, pastas, main dishes, and desserts at an affordable and fixed price (50,000 lira). No need to look at a confusing menu here! Moderate.

- **Antica Besseta:** *Santa Croce 1395 (Santa Croce), Tel. 721687. Closed Tuesday, Wednesday, and July. No credit cards. Reservations advised.* Offers a good selection of fresh fish dishes and excellent bigoli (whole-wheat spaghetti). Moderate to expensive.

- **Da Fiore:** *Calle del Scaleter 2202 (San Polo), Tel. 721308. Closed Sunday, August, and December 25 to January 15. Reservations required for both lunch and dinner.* Especially popular with locals, this charming restaurant is well noted for its outstanding seafood dishes. Try the noodles with crayfish and baby squash (tagliolini con scampi e zucchine). Excellent desserts. Moderate to expensive.

- **Quadri:** *Piazza San Marco 120 (San Marco), Tel. 528-9299. Closed Monday and January. Reservations required.* Opulent setting for this famous two-storey restaurant. Considered to be Venice's most beautiful restaurant, its kitchen turns out respectible dishes worthy of its decor: fennel soup with Pernod, turbot with almonds, sea bass, and pasta stuffed with lobster. Very expensive.

- **Do Leoni:** *Hotel Londra Palace, Riva degli Schiavoni 4171 (Castello), Tel. 5200533. Open daily.* Excellent French and Italian cuisine in an elegant setting. Try several of the local dishes: risottos, baked cuttlefish, and duck in a pepper sauce. Try the Black Forest cake for desert. Expensive.

- **Arcimboldo:** *Calle dei Furlani 3219 (Castello), Tel. 5286569. Dinner only. Closed Tuesday, August, and 10 days before or after Carnival.* Off the beaten tourist path (near the Arsenale) and popular with locals. Try the local dishes: whole-wheat bigoli spaghetti with anchovies, shellfish soup in a pastry crust, and breast of capon. Moderate to expensive.

- **Alla Madonna:** *Calle della Madonna 594 (San Polo), Tel. 5223824. Open Thursday to Tuesday for lunch (noon to 3pm) and dinner (7 to 9:30pm). Reservations essential.* Conveniently located near the Rialto Bridge, this popular trattoria is noted for its fine fresh seafood dishes. Specialties include spaghetti with black squid, fried cuttlefish, and grilled sole.

If the quality of food and high prices are not objectionable, you may want to stop at one of these popular places for people-watching. They have become institutions in Venice:

- **Harry's Bar:** *Calle Vallaresso 1323, Tel. 5286931. Closed Monday.* Many noted writers, movie stars, models, and other famous people have passed through this popular watering hole during the past 50 years which was especially made famous by Ernest Hemingway. Heavily patronized by tourists who come to see the place. Serves lots of drinks and many respectable dishes. Watch your wallet. This is an extremely expensive place.

- **Caffè Florian:** *Piazza San Marco 56 (San Marco), Tel. 5853338. Open 7:30am to midnight. Closed Wednesday.* Operating since 1720, this always popular café is located in Piazza San Marco's arcades. It offers location and ambience along with snacks, ice cream, and drinks. Its outdoor terrace spills onto the Piazza where patronage enjoy the views of the piazza. Small orchestra plays in the evening. Very expensive.

While most of the above restaurants are both excellent and expensive, you can dine at a few restaurants that offer good food and relatively good value:

- **Ai Promessi Sposi:** *Calle dell'Oca 4337 (Cannaregio), Tel. 5228609. Open Thursday to Tuesday for lunch and dinner.* Large portions at excellent prices. Try the three-course set menu at 14,000 lira or the salad and pasta special for 10,000 lira. Inexpensive to moderate.

- **Al Covo:** *Campiello della Pascaria 3968 (Castello), Tel. 5223812. Open Friday to Tuesday for lunch and dinner. Reservations essential for dinner (7:30 to 10:15pm).* Serves excellent pastas and seafood dishes. Try the assorted seafood appetizer for two and one of the delicious desserts. The fettuccine with tomato and basil and Aberdeen steak are excellent, in addition to the seafood dishes. Moderate to expensive.

- **Sempione:** *Ponte Baretteri 578 (San Marco). Open Wednesday to Monday for lunch (11:30am to 3pm) and dinner (6:30 to 10pm). Dinner reservations advised.* Situated alongside a canal in the midst of the central shopping area, this well located restaurant serves a wide range of Venetian specialties, especially seafood. Moderate to expensive.

- **Ignazio**: *Calle dei Saoneri 2749 (San Polo), Tel. 5234852. Open Sunday to Friday for lunch (noon to 3pm) and dinner (7 to 10pm). Reservations essential.* Good food and service in an attractive setting and at reasonable prices. Try the local specialties—eggplant pasta, sole, liver and onions, and grilled filet mignon. Moderate to expensive.

- **Il Doge Gelateria:** *Campo Santa Margherita 3058A (Dorsoduro). Open daily 9am to 1am in summer; open Tuesday to Sunday 10am to 8pm in winter.* Maybe the best place in Venice for ice cream, although Paolin at Campo San Stefano 2962 (San Marco) comes close. Operated by the Giovanni Grazziella family. Includes nearly 50 flavors. For a real treat, try the *panna cotta del Doge*.

ENJOYING YOUR STAY

There's not much nightlife in Venice since most people tend to go to bed early after all the day-trippers leave by early evening. But you will find things to do at night in Venice, be it festivals, concerts, opera, theater, nightclubs, or outdoor activities. However, being a relatively small city (79,000 local residents), there's much less going on at night in Venice than in Milan, Florence, or Rome. At night, many visitors return to **Piazza San Marco** to enjoy the cafés and ambience of the square or just stroll around the city which is especially romantic at night.

If you are interested in attending **concerts**, contact the APT office for information. Many concerts are held in churches, especially at Pietà and San Stae. Some are free whereas others have admission fees. Concert tickets are available through **Kele e Teo Agency** (San Marco 4930, Tel. 5208722) and **Box Office** (Calle Loredan 4127, Tel. 988369).

Theatrical performances (opera and ballet) are primarily held at the **Teatro La Fenice** (Campo San Fantin), one of Italy's oldest and most revered opera houses. The opera season runs all year long except for the month of August. You can purchase tickets at the box office Monday through Saturday, 9:30am to 12:30pm and 4 to 6pm, beginning one month before a performance. However, you may want to write ahead for program information and tickets: Biglietteria, Teatro La Fenice, Campo San Fantin, 30121 Venice, Tel. 041/5210171 or Fax 041/5221768.

Venice also has a few bars, discos, and nightclubs for those in search of such nocturnal pleasures. However, they pale in comparison to those in other major Italian cities. If you're looking for major entertainment, head for the discos and clubs in the mainland city of Mestre. Some of Venice's most popular bars include: **Al Muro** (Calle Sant' Antonio 4118, San Marco, Tel. 5205205); **Le Bistrot de Venise** (Calle dei Fabbri 4685, San Marco, Tel. 5236651); **Ai Canottieri** (Fondamenta San Giobbe 690, Cannaregio, Tel. 715408); **Bar Salus** (Rio Terà Canal 3112, Dorsoduro, Tel. 5285279); **Linea d'Ombra** (Punta della Dogana 19, Dorsoduro, Tel. 5285259); **Devil's Forest Pub** (Calle del Stagneri 5185, off Campo San Bartolomeo, Tel. 5200623); and **Paradiso Perduto** (Fondamenta Misericordia 2540, Cannaregio, Tel. 5220581). If you're looking for a disco, **Club El Souk** (Accademia 1056a, Tel. 5200371) would be a good choice, but you need to know a member to get in. Venice's best nightclub is **Martini Scala Club** (Compo San Fantin 1983, San Marco, Tel. 5224121).

Venice also has two public gambling **casinos** (Il Casinò Municipale di Venezia) which operates in the summer (May to September) on Lido (Lungomare Marconi 4, Tel. 5297111) and in the winter (October to April) in the beautiful Paisleys Vendramin-Calergi (Ca'Vendramin-Calergi, Cannaregio 2040, Tel. 5297111) which overlooks the Grand Canal. The casinos offer a full range of gaming activities, from roulette and craps to blackjack and slot machines. Open daily, 3pm to 4:30am.

Given these late night choices and demanding day-time activities, you might want to settle for a late dinner, a nice stroll around Piazza San Marco or along a canal, and return to your hotel. Get up early to ride the Grand Canal or visit the markets at the Rialto Bridge. You'll find an interesting Venice at 8am, before all the shops and touristed sites come alive.

Index

More Treasures and Pleasures

The following "Impact Guides" can be ordered directly from the publisher. Complete the following form (or list the titles), include your name and address, enclose payment, and send your order to:

IMPACT PUBLICATIONS
9104-N Manassas Drive
Manassas Park, VA 20111-2366 (USA)
Tel. 703/361-7300 or Fax 703/335-9486
E-mail: impactp@impactpublications.com

All prices are in U.S. dollars. Orders from individuals should be prepaid by check, moneyorder, or Visa, MasterCard, or American Express number. If your order must be shipped outside the U.S., please include an additional US$1.50 per title for surface mail or the appropriate air mail rate for books weighting 24 ounces each. We accept telephone orders (credit cards). Orders are shipped within 48 hours. For information on the authors and on our travel resources, visit our site on the Internet's World Wide Web: **http://www.impactpublications.com.**

Qty.	TITLES	Price	TOTAL
___	Treasures and Pleasures of Australia	$15.95	______
___	Treasures and Pleasures of the Caribbean	$16.95	______
___	Treasures and Pleasures of China	$15.95	______
___	Treasures and Pleasures of Hong Kong	$14.95	______
___	Treasures and Pleasures of Indonesia	$14.95	______
___	Treasures and Pleasures of Italy	$14.95	______
___	Treasures and Pleasures of Paris and the French Riviera	$14.95	______

__ Treasures and Pleasures of Singapore and Malaysia $14.95 ______
__ Treasures and Pleasures of Thailand $14.95 ______

Coming in 1998

__ Treasures and Pleasures of India $14.95 ______
__ Treasures and Pleasures of Morocco $14.95 ______
__ Treasures and Pleasures of the Philippines $14.95 ______
__ Treasures and Pleasures of Spain $14.95 ______
__ Treasures and Pleasures of Turkey $14.95 ______

SUBTOTAL $ ______

- Virginia residents add 4.5% sales tax $ ______
- Shipping/handling ($4.00 for the first title and $1.00 for each additional book) $ ______
- Additional amount if shipping outside U.S. $ ______

TOTAL ENCLOSED------------ $ ______

SHIP TO:

Name ______

Address ______

______

______

PAYMENT METHOD:

❑ I enclose check/moneyorder for $ ______ made payable to IMPACT PUBLICATIONS.

❑ Please charge $ ______ to my credit card:

❑ Visa ❑ MasterCard ❑ American Express

Card # ______

Expiration date: ____/____

Signature ______